TEARING DOWN THE ORANGE CURTAIN

======= HOW =======

PUNK ROCK

BROUGHT ORANGE COUNTY
TO THE WORLD

By
NATE JACKSON and DANIEL KOHN

DA CAPO

Da Capo Press
Hachette Book Group
1290 Avenue of the Americas, New York, NY 10104
grandcentralpublishing.com
@grandcentralpub

First Edition: May 2025

Da Capo Press is an imprint of Grand Central Publishing. The Da Capo Press name and logo are registered trademarks of Hachette Book Group, Inc.

The publisher is not responsible for websites (or their content) that are not owned by the publisher.

The Hachette Speakers Bureau provides a wide range of authors for speaking events. To find out more, go to hachettespeakersbureau.com or email HachetteSpeakers@hbgusa.com.

Da Capo Press books may be purchased in bulk for business, educational, or promotional use. For information, please contact your local bookseller or the Hachette Book Group Special Markets Department at special.markets@hbgusa.com.

Print book interior design by Jeff Stiefel

Library of Congress Cataloging-in-Publication Data

Names: Jackson, Nate (Journalist) author. | Kohn, Daniel, author.
Title: Tearing down the Orange curtain : how punk rock brought Orange County to the world / by Nate Jackson and Daniel Kohn.
Description: First edition. | New York : Grand Central Publishing, 2025. | Includes bibliographical references and index.
Identifiers: LCCN 2024056026 | ISBN 9780306832963 (hardcover) | ISBN 9780306832970 (ebook)
Subjects: LCSH: Punk rock music—California—Orange County—History and criticism. | Punk rock musicians—California—Orange County.
Classification: LCC ML3534.3 .J33 2025 | DDC 781.6609794/96—dc23/eng/20241122
LC record available at https://lccn.loc.gov/2024056026

ISBNs: 9780306832963 (hardcover), 9780306832970 (ebook)

Printed in the United States of America

LSC-C

Printing 1, 2025

To everyone who came before us,
and everyone who will keep the music alive after,
this is for you.

I got into punk rock because I like to cause trouble.
That was it.

—*Jack Grisham*

CONTENTS

CONTENTS

FOREWORD

By MIKE NESS

et us not ask what the city can do for us but what we can do for the city. That was not my mentality back then on the streets of Fullerton. Forty years ago, they might have wanted to lock me up and throw away the key. But things change. And now I got a key, a key to the city I grew up in.

I have nothing but fond memories of growing up in Fullerton. My parents moved us here in 1963 to a little house on Malvern Avenue, the east side. We rented the back house from an older woman who was also our babysitter. I was five years old and spent a lot of time alone at the babysitter's house. Her bedroom had a radio and religious art on the wall. The angels were naked, so it was a shrine to eroticism and rock and roll. I already knew that music is what I wanted to do. Music did something for me.

By sixth or seventh grade I'd started to embrace counterculture. We grew up across the street from the park that had Little League and Pop Warner football, but my parents weren't very encouraging about sports. Instead of playing ball there, after seeing *Easy Rider*, I built a chopper bike, cruised the park, and sat on it while I watched the games. I knew that was cool. So it didn't matter that I wasn't playing ball.

My two uncles were part of the counterculture. One was gay and the other wasn't. The one who wasn't was super tough, and the gay uncle was so cool, and they were both very influential role models. The gay one had friends in Hollywood and we'd go to Palm Springs, and my other uncle would have friends over to his house who had lowriders, while the women sported beehives and cat-eye glasses and wore garter belts and fishnet stockings.

For a young kid, it was a crazy world.

When I got into punk, I finally found my voice and my place in the world. Soon I realized I was going to have to fight—physically fight—to keep it. The reaction to punk wasn't friendly. But I wasn't going back.

In spite of these things, overall my life was not that good. Music provided me with something to keep my mind focused in pursuit of a dream, and Fullerton itself enabled that. When I became a punk, it was dangerous to roam the streets of Orange County looking the way we did. Ninety-nine percent of society saw it as a provocation. My personality dictates that telling me I can't do something is about the worst thing you could do because not only am I going to succeed at it, I'm going to enjoy proving you wrong. Then I'll say, "How do you like me now?"

I wasn't going to back down and I wasn't going to change. We were just jamming in my friend's mom's living room, and we had no idea where it was going to go. We were in the moment, trying to put pieces of a puzzle together, and not seeing the big picture at all. But on a local level, we saw other people doing it, and if they could do it, we knew we could too.

Fortunately, at the time, we had a manager who was tied in with Goldenvoice, and he made sure that whenever a big band came to Los Angeles, Social Distortion was the opening act. We went from playing in front of fifty people in Fullerton to playing in front of five hundred in LA. It helped immensely.

Decades later on April 3, 2024, getting the key to the city I grew up in—on my sixty-second birthday no less!—was an emotional moment. It felt good to have someone acknowledge our accomplishments. When we started the band, official recognition wasn't something we were after. We didn't know that our music would have a positive impact. You hoped that it might, but you don't know.

Dennis Danell, our guitarist, was my partner in crime back in the day. He wasn't committing crimes with me, but he was, figuratively, my partner in crime. We would drive to Hollywood on a Tuesday night, see some bands play, and go to school the next day and tell everyone about it.

This stuff doesn't happen. It's not supposed to happen. But like I said, things change.

What a ride it's been.

For lack of a better metaphor, it's almost like you're a pinball. You get shot out, and then it's all the bumps, specials, bonus points, and penalties. It's a funny analogy that you're the ball, but you're not the one in control. And, ultimately, you're only as good as the player.

—*Mike Ness*

THE NEST

In 1979, a small place in Costa Mesa called the Cuckoo's Nest had made itself the epicenter of Orange County punk. Every scene needs a club, and if you were punk in the late '70s and early '80s, the Nest was your place to rage. In the surroundings of a seemingly placid suburban utopia with its patchwork of manicured lawns and cookie-cutter houses with crystal blue backyard pools and straitlaced parents in their corporate jobs, the children of these model citizens were looking for life outside of the American dream—they wanted to make their own dreams, or in some cases their own nightmares. Flying under the cloak of polite, middle-class society, punks throughout OC congregated at underground hotspots in their home cities. In Costa Mesa, the Cuckoo's Nest, or the Nest as it was often called, offered a magnetic pull that started with headlining sets from the likes of Iggy Pop and the Ramones and eventually fostered the homegrown havoc of T.S.O.L., the Vandals, the Adolescents, Agent Orange, Social Distortion, and many others. "And we had all the touring bands and of course, every band that ever never played around OC," Cuckoo's Nest owner Jerry Roach said.

"We were already aggressive, semi-violent kids with nothing much else to do, and then punk rock was a perfect vehicle," T.S.O.L. bassist Mike Roche said in the documentary *Clockwork Orange County*. "If you were an adolescent and angry and malicious and didn't know why, when punk rock came along you're like 'oh yeah that's where I am, I'm a punk rocker.'"

For kids like Casey Royer, punk rock was just in their blood. "It was something that you didn't plan, you didn't apply to be a punk, you just were that kind of person just because of your consciousness," Royer said in *Clockwork Orange County*.

The dawning of punk in OC was sparked during the Ford presidency, gained oxygen during the Carter years, and became a full-blown brushfire under Reagan. But for all the political rhetoric on flyers and in songs damning "the system," OC punks weren't as politically charged as their counterparts in LA, New York, or the UK. "We were from Orange County, we didn't care about politics, or agitators or whatever they were, we didn't care, we just liked the music," said the Vandals' Joe Escalante. "Sure, we liked the Clash and they had some social consciousness, but we didn't take that from them. We took as much as we needed and we were just having fun."

There was no interest in signing with a major label or getting any endorsements; it was all about making noise and venting frustrations while having fun. It all coalesced with the surf and skate lifestyle of the beach towns like Costa Mesa, where the Nest sat on 1714 Placentia Avenue. Surfers and skaters like Duane Peters shaved each other's hair in the bathrooms of the local skate parks.

"It was a real individual thing, it didn't matter what your hair color was, that was what he or she decides to be," Peters said in the *Clockwork Orange County* documentary.

To many early punks, the culture was a hand-me-down from older brothers and sisters who were already dabbling in it. That spark that was ignited by a younger group of kids.

For bands like the Crowd or Shattered Faith who helped jump-start the OC punk scene in the beach towns, the Nest was a slightly more organized alternative to the wild house parties of suburban homes.

In the midst of the wild underground backyard party scene sparking in the mid- to late '70s, a middle-aged man living in Laguna Beach who decided to set up a punk club in the middle of Orange County for a bunch of kids could've never understood at the time that the shows within its walls sowed the seeds of a groundbreaking subculture that would still be talked about to this day. Though this book is the first to chart its beginnings in the late '70s, its near-death experience in the mid-'80s, a rebirth that slingshotted it to peak popularity in the '90s, and into the next millennium. It's a story that's been told but largely undercover, underappreciated, and unwritten, at least in book form—until now.

✕✕✕✕✕✕

On Fourth of July weekend in 1976, as fireworks exploded, spreading smoke and electric tendrils of stardust across the night sky over Huntington Beach, Jerry Roach remembers driving to the seaside hub on Main Street to pass out flyers promoting his fledgling new club. The country at the time was celebrating its 200th anniversary, otherwise known as the "Bicentennial."

Of all the potential punk rock nightclub owners in the world, Roach might've been one of the most unlikely. Before opening the

Nest in 1976, Roach sold real estate to feed his family, a wife and three children. The newly married Roach sold a large restaurant to a client who was in the bar business. The client had heard that in a former life, Roach had been a bar owner himself, and so it seemed only right that he offer him an old, beat-up bar in Costa Mesa as commission for the sale. That day, Roach quit being a Realtor and returned to being a bar owner.

For a few years, Roach ran a rollicking, frat-friendly watering hole called the Bacchus House with his then business partner Larry Bragg. The name was an offshoot of the raging kegger parties at a spot near Orange Coast College dubbed the Bacchus House, named after Bacchus, the Roman god of wine and revelry. Despite having no prior bar experience and "writing a bad check for the first two kegs of beer," Roach said, he and Bragg made the bar a lucrative though short-lived success. "I named the bar the Bacchus House, that place was legendary," Roach recalls. "You were styling if you got to go to a Bacchus party. So I used all that goodwill and the word spread."

"When we first opened it was meant to be one of those meat markets . . . boy-meets-girl, you put a band on that plays all the hits, people dance," Roach said.

When it came time to name the place, Roach surveyed the area around him in OC's bar landscape to come up with one. One of the bars nearby in Costa Mesa was called Jaws after the great white shark horror films. For his part, Roach also turned to the box office to come up with what he hoped would be a solid, memorable name. The 1975 film *One Flew over the Cuckoo's Nest* had become a classic so Roach shortened his new bar's name to the Cuckoo's Nest.

"I just named it after a movie for no particular reason," Roach said. "To me, it was as good of a name as anything else. It didn't matter, it had no bearing on what was to happen, the fact that it turned into a cuckoo's nest."

If the venue was destined to become a punk rock madhouse full of miscreants, Roach was its warden—described as a shrewd businessman by some and a cheap, hard-nosed dick by others.

A lot of people assume the Nest started out as a punk venue—but it didn't. Before the aggressive youth-driven scene caught on in OC, Roach's house bands skewed toward straight rock 'n' roll bands, including one with his good friend and guitarist Terrence "Blondie" Chaplin, a mixed-race kid from South Africa who'd go on to perform with the Beach Boys and the Rolling Stones. Roach also had a band called Elijah that was a ten-piece funk act full of cholos from East LA, including a guy named Edward James Olmos, who went on to be a famous actor, but at the time he was just Eddie.

"I remember the night he [Olmos] quit. I remember saying, 'It's nine o'clock, you gotta go on!'" Roach said. "It's fifteen after and they're having a big powwow, like a bunch of Indians in a big circle. After I stuck my head in there a couple of times saying 'C'mon get onstage!' Eddie walked out. And that was it. That was when he quit the band. I swear it was the smartest thing he ever did."

Roach said the biggest act he ever booked at the club was Bo Diddley for $500. "From then on I was hooked," he said. Even after closing his previous bar, Bacchus, due to tough financial circumstances, Roach decided to give the entertainment business another try with the seemingly ordinary venue arbitrarily named after a hit movie.

The Nest's first house band was a group from Riverside called Squeeze—not to be confused with the more successful UK band with the same name. Though they never really made it, the singer's name, Nikki Sixx, did take on a bigger life when Frank Carlton Serafino

Feranna Jr., the bassist in a band called Mötley Crüe, stole the name and used it himself playing with the lords of '80s hair metal. Eventually Squeeze broke up, leaving Roach with a problem of drawing crowds with new talent the way the former house band did. He tried several times to drum up business, which included booking a reggae festival that was a bust because it "brought a bunch of Black people who didn't drink—reggae people," Roach said. All of a sudden, the Nest went from happening nightclub to a tumbleweed-strewn vessel on the brink of extinction.

"It dried up and there was no way I was gonna make ends meet. I was gonna have to close. So it was desperation," he said.

What he needed was a crowd. What he got was the Crowd.

This scrappy high school band from Huntington Beach was started in 1978 by brothers Jim and Jay Decker. At the time, they were constantly bugging Roach to play gigs. "Go back to high school!" he'd tell them bluntly. But finally, after the situation at the club had gotten bad enough financially, Roach said, "What the hell?" and gave them a shot to perform on Sunday and Monday—these were typically considered off-nights—capitalizing on the band's bookings up in LA on Friday and Sunday. Their first night onstage at the Costa Mesa club, the club was packed with kids coming to see the four-piece band of surf punks, which was rounded out by guitarist Jim Kaa and drummer Dennis Walsh.

Though it helped ignite the California punk rock scene, Roach contends it really didn't happen on purpose. "Punk rock just sorta happened at the Cuckoo's Nest," he said. "It wasn't planned. It was just a set of circumstances where business was off, these kids were bugging me for a gig and I thought 'What the hell, I'll give it a try.' Next thing you know, all hell broke loose. Elvis changed everything, then the Beatles changed everything. This punk rock thing shows up, and at first

I didn't really like it, but after a while I realized 'This is it, pal, you're not supposed to like it. This is their deal, just sit back and watch it go.'"

On the strength of that successful show, Roach pivoted to catering to young fans hankering for this new rebellious sound. That included a jump into the major leagues. He had a booking agent offer him the Ramones, the leather-clad forefathers of New York punk. "I heard of them, so I thought, 'OK, I'll book them.' Then that opened the gates," Roach said. He followed up with shows from the UK's the Damned, which sold out in no time, followed by another packed show from 999.

"The band played, everybody had a good time, and it went real easy, real automatic. No problem. If every night was like that I'd still be there," Roach said.

After Roach and the Nest got its first taste of punk success, it was like blood in water full of thrashing sharks—bands anxious for stage time and young, revved-up crowds looking for some action descended on the place. The Nest became the epicenter of a new sound, a new scene, and a new attitude that by necessity had to blow away the weak, square, and boring rock and pop of the '70s with its dumb blow-dried hair and bell bottoms. It wasn't long before the punks poked their heads in to start asking for gigs. "Let us play, let us play! We'll bring people in!" Roach heard from various bands.

Much like the spontaneous combustion that occurred from the bands who broke all the rules of rock onstage, the magnetic force of the club with its signature backdrop—puffy white clouds against a blue sky—drew young teenage boys and girls alike who would create their own explosions from the bowels of the OC punk scene.

Initially, Roach had put heavy burlap material up on the walls behind the stage for better acoustics. "I didn't want the sound bouncing around," he said. But the fire department came in and told him to get rid of it. "And so then I just got environmental graphics. And that was, you know, one mural that just kept repeating itself. I always liked that idea. You know, using environmental graphics for that thing versus the burlap, so, yeah, thanks to the police! But that's kind of important as far as the legacy is concerned," Roach said.

The outside of the club was just as eye-catching. In a previous incarnation, the venue had been a playhouse, its large marquee still present when Roach bought it. "I had that lit up with all white bulbs, but the sound of the bass would vibrate and the lights would go out because of it. So I kept replacing the lights until I said screw it. But there were like 100 light bulbs on that part of that sign."

It was immediately different than any other venue catering to punk crowds. LA venues like the Hong Kong Café and Madame Wong's, though important, were far less impressive compared to what the Nest had going on.

"Madame Wong's and the Hong Kong Café was the center of punk in LA—it was all slipshod. The real center of punk for Southern California was the Cuckoo's Nest," Roach said.

As bands ripped through their sets, standing well above the crowd onstage but not too high, the place was set up for epic stage diving as the party in the pit raged on at one hundred miles per hour. Luckily, there were several shutterbugs positioned at those early shows to capture all the action, like Ed Colver, Dina Douglass, Alison Braun, and Jenny Lens.

For Colver, the rush of the punk scene pumped him up to start shooting in 1978, first at the Hong Kong Café and then eventually at the Nest. Standing well over six feet tall, wearing all black, and traveling in a hearse, Colver quietly became one of the earliest recognizable figures in the scene. He shot dozens of iconic punk photos and album covers like the Adolescents' *Welcome to Reality* EP, T.S.O.L.'s black-and-white EP (shot from the crowd at the Nest), and China White's *Danger Zone* (a shot he came across while driving by an actual murder scene in Santa Monica after a Fear show). He snapped it in one frame out of his car window with the engine still running.

Not to mention the first cover he ever shot, the Circle Jerks' seminal album *Group Sex*, taken after a joint Circle Jerks/Adolescents performance at the Marina del Rey Skatepark.

"I never really studied art history. I paid attention to the artists who spoke to me, and everything else I didn't give a shit about it. If it spoke to me then I was all over it. And that's the stuff I paid attention to," Colver said. At the time, he lived in Covina and traveled down Azusa Avenue to hang with the bands like T.S.O.L., D.I., and the Adolescents. "Punks didn't look in the phone book for a photographer, I was there—and they liked my work." He'd go on to shoot countless images of the SoCal punk scene. The bands even went so far as to give Colver a nickname.

"It was really strange that they used to have a nickname for me: 'The Viking,'" he said. "And I was like 'What the fuck is this?' and George Belanger, the drummer from the Christian Death, told me, 'Oh, me and Frank Agnew were in the Pleasure Chest and saw that big long black leather suit and thought it would fit you and we're calling it a Viking suit.' I was like 'that's where that came from?' The Vandals even wrote a song 'Viking Suit' about me. Pretty funny."

Like the bands, becoming part of the tribe at the Nest or in LA meant Colver witnessed a self-contained, independent scene blow up. "When I started shooting punk shows there was about two hundred kids in all of LA who were into punk. And half of them were in the bands, you know, and then in 1983, Black Flag played to three thousand kids at the Olympic."

The Olympic was large enough to hold 15,300 people, a massive venue that—while often packed during its brief punk heyday—was often a scary place to go see a show. It didn't have the same vibe and energy as the Nest. At the Costa Mesa club, the stage was high but not so high that bands felt alienated from the crowds they were playing for, and the cloud backdrop added a breath of life to the scene. Most clubs were painted black, but the Nest stood out like a sore thumb. Photos of it denote exactly where you were the minute you saw the stage. It was the kind of platform that was strong enough to showcase rollicking sets by the Ramones or Circle Jerks without crumbling under the weight of their aggression. The venue's stage and PA system made it the ideal moshing ground for bands like Social Distortion, Agent Orange, Black Flag, Descendents, Shattered Faith, Suburban Lawns, U.X.A., and house favorites/criminals in T.S.O.L.

××××××

Featuring vocalist Jack Grisham, drummer Todd Barnes, guitarist Steve Houston, and bassist Laddy Terrell, Vicious Circle was formed in 1978. The Vicious Circle following had a reputation for being real criminally minded headcases with no bones about wreaking havoc and committing senseless acts of violence and vandalism. They were some of the wildest miscreants the punk scene coughed up.

"There was this one Vicious Circle gig in Signal Hill at a place owned by the father of Paul of the Chiefs called Frenchie's Machine Shop," Andy Perrin of the Crewd told Brian Sheklian in a 2020 article on OC punk. "This fight started between two guys but then the Vicious Circle gang guys jumped in and there were way more of them than us. My bandmate Smitty got stabbed and Kevin from Secret Hate was hit by a car. I got off lucky with only a black eye. Jack from Vicious Circle was actually our friend and was trying to stop the fighting that night. Secret Hate wrote a song called 'Frenchie's Machine Shop Massacre' about that incident."

Gangs of longhairs were often on the prowl looking for punk rockers to punch up or throw beer bottles at. One such notorious group of individuals was known as the Cropdusters. When longhairs went sniffing around for trouble with Vicious Circle and their pals, they were barking up the wrong tree.

"These guys who drove around called the Cropdusters . . . they'd beat up anybody with short-cropped hair, like punks," Grisham said. "So one time, they thought, like usual, that they're just gonna roll in and beat up a bunch of punks that are going to scatter and run yelling 'Cropdusters, Cropdusters!' The guys I was hanging out with were real fuckers and they're not running. So one of [the Cropdusters] got thrown off the bridge and I was the one that said chuck him! He ran to the bridge and we caught him on the bridge and I said let's throw the fucker off."

While Grisham fled from Southern California to Alaska—he later said on an episode of *The Blairing Out Show* in 2001 that he was running from "some people who were trying to kill him"—his fellow bandmate, drummer Todd Barnes, had joined bassist Mike Roche, guitarist Ron Emory, and ex-Gestapo vocalist Rick Fritch to form T.S.O.L.

The band's name came to founders Barnes, Roche, and Emory while watching a band performing on a televised evangelical church program. The name of the praise band performing on the screen gave devilish inspiration to the musicians looking for a new moniker. "The band on the church show was called The Sounds of Liberty, and Roche goes, 'Nah, we're the True Sounds of Liberty,'" Grisham told Blair.

As soon as Grisham arrived back in town, he met a girl who told him, "Hey, I met these guys who are just like you. You should meet 'em," Grisham said. That meeting turned out to be with Barnes, and the two kicked off their kinship by stealing a guitar and amp from the girl who introduced them and starting a band. The front man had found his wolf pack and was instantly recruited as the new singer of one of the OC's most intimidating bands. They were also one of the biggest in terms of both popularity and physical stature. Most of the members of T.S.O.L. stood well above six feet tall, and carried a rough, often threatening demeanor both onstage and off.

Despite their "all-American" looks, the band was often a menacing force that stuck together, whether it came to music or committing petty crime. T.S.O.L. took little time usurping the role of Vicious Circle as the beach punk thugs' band of choice.

And unlike other punks, T.S.O.L. were far from outcasts.

"The guys who I first knew that were getting into punk rock were not the cool kids getting into punk rock," Grisham said. "That's why they got mad at us. Because we were accepted. I was already accepted. It's like, I've been causing trouble and fucking up since I was a little kid."

From early on, Grisham caused trouble. Not yet a punk, Grisham was a big, blond-haired surfer type. He was constantly changing schools due to behavioral issues (he says he was first arrested at thirteen). He was, for the most part, well-liked except by jocks, even though he didn't play sports.

Where T.S.O.L. went, violence wasn't far behind.

"Was there violence at those shows? Fuck yeah, there was violence at the shows," Grisham said. "But the violence at the shows was towards the fucking guys coming in to beat us up. They were picking on punks. The thing is, it's like, 'Hey, we're not little and we're in great shape.' I shaved my head so people couldn't grab it in a fight. So you shave your head and put some grease on it. They can't get it."

Their shows at the Nest became legendary. Even with the violence and flair for the theatrical, the musicianship of T.S.O.L. was always solid, from Barnes's powerful drumrolls to the menacingly melodic pairing of Emory's guitar and Roche's bass lines. Grisham's voice and charisma onstage was a mix of poetic sensitivity, brutal violence, and cross-dressing theatrics.

The band's reputation spread quickly. Up in LA, T.S.O.L. was known as much for their behavior as their roaring songs. The LA punks scoffed at Grisham's lyrics, a notion he dismissed as hypocritical considering the lyrics of the early punks up the freeway were just as violence-inciting as theirs.

"I remember when somebody got blamed for something, their lyrics or whatever," Grisham said. "They said, 'Oh, well, these are just lyrics.' It's like what? What are you fucking talking about, man? Words are powerful!"

Grisham and T.S.O.L.'s emergence came at a time when the LA punks were going in an artsier direction than their OC counterparts. It's something that irked them.

"When we started getting into punk rock, a lot of the artsy intellectual guys, they were fucking bummed because they had the market cornered on fucking punk rock pussy," Grisham said. "Then all of a sudden here comes some swinging dicks, all fucking tanned and big—and into punk rock."

The band's debut five-song, self-titled EP was released in spring 1981 by Posh Boy Records, a Hollywood-based label founded by American-born and UK-educated Robbie "Posh Boy" Fields, who took a major interest in the emerging OC punk scene. Featuring an iconic cover shot by Ed Colver at the Cuckoo's Nest, the EP, which clocked in at just over seven and a half minutes, was a statement of intent. It was unapologetically political, featuring tracks such as "Superficial Love," "World War III," and "Abolish Government/Silent Majority."

As punk bands rose in local popularity, the media soon caught on. Though advantageous at the time, Grisham says it was ultimately the first wave of punk's undoing.

The band signed two simultaneous record deals with Posh Boy and Frontier Records. They gave Posh Boy the songs for the first EP, and Frontier got the songs for their 1981 full-length debut album, *Dance with Me*. Though they had totally different sounds, Grisham says both sets of songs were delivered simultaneously. "A lot of people said, 'Oh, you're a political band' after the first, then when *Dance with Me* came out we were suddenly a horror band—they didn't realize we had both sets of songs at the same time."

One particular song on the album that became one of their signatures was "Code Blue," a tune with lyrics about necrophilia. "Some of the girls at the school, they were just trouble," Grisham told Blair. "So it was kind of a joke, like I'd rather be in bed with a dead person than deal with this. But people didn't take it as a joke, they took it seriously."

The EP would go on to influence many bands in Southern California, not just during this time.

"They were a really interesting form of punk," Blink-182 guitarist Tom DeLonge says. "They use these minor chords and these interesting chord progressions with that Bill Stevenson Descendents or Black Flag drumbeat, but yet, he's talking about going out and fucking dead bodies and shit. It's just rad. It's so cool—not so much for the fucking of dead bodies. 'Abolish Government' is just so punk. Jack is like this baby-faced crazy guy that might just snap and kill everybody in the pit, but he was wearing a dress when I saw him. True Sounds of Liberty is probably one of the coolest band names of all time. I wish we were called that."

In time, they'd become the best, most popular, and most feared band in the scene. Grisham said that at one point, T.S.O.L. was the highest-paid and biggest draw in the region.

"T.S.O.L. were the scariest of those bands," Bad Religion guitarist/Epitaph Records founder Brett Gurewitz said. "People think Black Flag were the tough band that everyone was afraid of. Black Flag were afraid of T.S.O.L. They were huge and they were tough. Jack used to wear a dress and play in drag so that somebody would say something to him and he'd have an excuse to beat them up. That was fun for him."

T.S.O.L. added a new layer of dramatic texture to their songs with the addition of keyboardist Greg Kuehn in 1982 and recording *Beneath the Shadows*, which was released through San Francisco–based independent label Alternative Tentacles. The album, produced by Thom Wilson, propelled T.S.O.L. into a radical sonic departure that confused many of their early fans. Critics hailed it as a great album, but for those who were just looking for the sequel to *Dance with Me*, it just did not fit into that mold. Eventually Grisham left T.S.O.L., and the remaining members reformed with a new lineup that wound up creating some confusion and derision among their fans.

∞∞∞∞∞

When bands like T.S.O.L. and the Adolescents asked for more money after selling out the Nest, they were often met with shoulder shrugs, cursing, and doors slammed in their faces.

"I gave those guys as little amount of money as I possibly could," Roach said. "Number one, no one else would let them play there. Number two, I needed the money. I made about $400 a week in cash. So that's like $1,600–$1,700 a month. My rent was $850, my house payment was $850. So what does that leave me? I have three kids, a family of five in Laguna Beach. So I had to make money and those fuckers didn't need it. They all lived at home. So I keep [all the money], fuck you—that was my reputation. And I never gave my side of the story. Bottom line when it came to the money and paying bands—I needed it and they didn't."

Obviously, the bands at the time felt differently . . .

"For a sixteen-year-old who saw a lot of money coming in, we thought we should be making a decent amount of money," Tony Brandenburg of the Adolescents said. "We felt all the way down the line that there were things that were due to us that we weren't receiving, so there was a certain amount of animosity toward the club itself, which was ironic because it was the one place where we could go that offered shelter."

"He was pretty funny because he was a thug," Jack Grisham said. "We used to sell out the Cuckoo's Nest. Sell that motherfucking place out. People are drinking like crazy. Breaking fire codes. And he'd pay us $100. We didn't know! We were fucking kids, man. And he's just like, cha-ching, cha-ching. But it was always a great place to play."

That isn't to say that Grisham and his group didn't start shit at the Nest—sometimes literally.

"People would worm at the Nest," Grisham said, referring to the "worm dance" popularized in the '70s and '80s done by getting on floor and creating a rippling motion through the body, similar to a worm crawling. "So one night, the Nest is packed. I go into the bathroom, and there's a turd floating in the toilet. So I get a beer cup, and I scooped this turd out. And I walk over to the dance floor, and I got the turd in my hand, and I throw this turd on the dance floor. So somebody steps in it, they slip and go down. I start yelling 'worm!' and people start going down on it and don't realize there's shit! So they're rolling in it and I'm in the bathroom and I'm laughing so fucking hard. And this dude goes,

'What's so fucking funny, man?' I go, 'Oh, my God.' I threw a turd on the floor and I look, and he's got shit all over him. And he was big. This motherfucker was big, like some gnarly marine-looking dude."

The chaos may have been inside the club, but the real circus was outside in the parking lot. The club sat toward the back corner of a deep lot across from a liquor store and a laundromat. As punks arrived, their junk-filled rides parading into the lot, the tailgating began.

Groups of friends routinely designated one of the scruffier, older-looking members of the gang to abstain from shaving weeks before a big show so he could slide into the liquor store undetected to buy booze as a minor. The nearby laundromat became a rest stop for bands and fans who ironically probably hadn't washed their own clothes in weeks, chugging beers and chucking the empties into the dryers in case a snooping John Q. Citizen or Costa Mesa PD popped in. Sometimes the parking lot scene surrounding the Nest was so nuts that the show barely mattered. Inside the cars, young punks hurled themselves into a Saturday night spiral of chugging frothy brews and the amphetamine lightning bolt of Black Beauty combination pills, sipping and snorting as they waited for their favorite bands to take the stage.

The sound of dirty sneakers, a mix of Vans and Chuck Taylors, rang through the air as teen boys in ripped shirts and jeans bounded across the aluminum hoods and roofs of cars, scavenging for their next fix and diving into windows with their friends as they plotted the post-show shenanigans. It was the '50s meets the '70s.

The club shared a parking lot with a cowboy bar called Zubie's and a transmission shop.

Everywhere T.S.O.L. went, blood followed . . . in the parking lot as often as the mosh pit. They were an electrifying band, but their audience was trouble.

The legend was that they were more of a gang than a band and got their equipment by showing up to rob a music store, figuring out what to grab, and then suddenly realizing they could play music.

"We truly believed the ethos and the ideal," bassist Mike Roche said in *Clockwork Orange County*. "We absolutely believed it. Therefore we were reckless beyond belief."

The criminal minds of T.S.O.L. and many of the other bands that played were also diametrically opposed to anyone wearing boots and cowboy hats. And a massive group of those people just so happened to cohabitate at Zubie's. The SoCal rednecks, very big, very able, well-fed . . . wanted to indiscriminately punch the living daylights out of anything resembling punk rock. There they were at Zubie's sharing a parking lot with punk rockers.

"It was pretty frightening," the Vandals' Joe Escalante said. "I was only sixteen or seventeen and I didn't want anything to do with it.

"It was like oil and water in that parking lot with all-American families and tipsy hard hat workers and cowboys going to dinner with their families while punks were in the parking lot causing havoc."

Roach remembers one time when six guys in football helmets with baseball bats came to the front of the club ready to beat some punks' asses, until about eighty punks came outside the club and started chasing them. "They dropped their bats and hauled ass, it was great," Roach said.

Aside from being the bedrock of OC punk culture, the Cuckoo's Nest was rumored to have birthed a major physical by-product of the scene—slam dancing.

During any given punk show, a flurry of sweaty limbs and torn T-shirts circled the mosh pit, consuming the heart of the crowd as the music raged and the fans along with it. Born out of the practice of "pogoing," the notably less aggro ancestor of slam dancing, the latter evolved—or devolved, as the case may be—into a violent act that released tension in the room by actually igniting it in sparky combos of fist versus face, elbow versus back of head, flying arm versus neck, and so on. It was a chemical reaction in a punk's blood that fueled the outrage and led to the movements that ended in a release—rinse, wash, repeat for the entirety of a two-hour show.

"The followers of punk acts like 999 don't just dance anymore, they mug each other," the *Los Angeles Times* wrote in June 1980. "It's part of a new 'dance' craze called the Slam, whose popularity, especially with organized gangs of punk youths, has led to numerous incidents of violence at many area clubs. . . . The accounts of senseless violence, vandalism and even mutilation at some area rock clubs read like reports from a war zone."

It was the influence of physical contact that became a necessary element of punk rock. One minute you're standing on the sidelines, then all of a sudden the action starts behind you. You're standing in the same place, but you're in the middle of the floor. So it's either slam your way out, stay slamming with the others, or get knocked down.

The blizzard of limbs colliding in the pit of any punk show around the world could've started anywhere—the UK and New York certainly had their share of violence at shows before Southern California came into the picture. But in the eyes of many a punk rocker who was there to see the difference between pogoing—a communal act of bouncing up and down to the beat of punk music, literally as if jumping on a pogo stick—and the violence of slam dancing, the two were, to quote the Crowd's debut album, a world apart.

The Crowd's front man, Jim Decker, is often credited with inventing slam dancing. In the most literal sense, the dance evolved like a protozoa that morphed into a tadpole that became a bouncing frog. Roach remembers the night it happened. Always an exhibitionist during the early punk days, Decker decided one night at a show to start flopping around on the floor of the club like a cross between a breathless trout on land and a spastic worm. The audience of a couple hundred people immediately turned him into the center of attention as he writhed on the ground spastically until bouncers picked him up and threw him out of the club.

The following week, Decker returned to the Nest, this time with seven or eight of his friends. "And they're in front of the stage, and they're pretending to fight in front of the stage," Roach said. "And so, I told the bouncers to throw them out. So they rounded them up and kicked them out." Of course, that wasn't the end of it. "I'm sure they went back to school and said, 'you know, if we all do it, he can't throw us all out,'" Roach said. "And the next week, they had enough people that it was too many people to throw out. So I just said, just try to contain it. Keep it on the dance floor."

At that point the violence hadn't really started yet, but the rise of jocks discovering punk and the metamorphosis into hardcore changed the dynamics of a fun romp to a bloody brawl. Hardcore music—the faster, louder, and rowdier cousin of punk—created a sub-scene that attracted a different element than what the original punk scene intended. Shaved heads, swastikas, and raging testosterone tainted the fun spirit of the pit.

"It was still fun to play onstage, but when you looked down into the pit, it got very frustrating to see guys just pounding the living crap out of each other when they're supposed to be there to have a good time and see some bands that they liked," Decker said.

"I was always relieved at the end of every show that no one was seriously hurt," Roach said.

The Nest's new status as a hub for punk rock for bands like the Adolescents, T.S.O.L., and the Vandals came with some major foils.

Specifically, the cowboys of the Crystal Saloon—a lesser-remembered but equally punk-bashing establishment—and the rednecks of Zubie's, which shared the central parking lot. The cowboys were on the corner in a separate lot, and Zubie's was next door to the Nest.

But of all the foes of the Cuckoo's Nest, the police and city council were the biggest. The cops and city wanted the venue gone. They saw Roach and his club as a big problem, something that had gotten out of their control. So they did everything possible to crush it under their thumb.

As the hardcore scene raged on, tensions mounted within the local community of Costa Mesa over the raucousness of the Nest. Police began nightly sting operations, stationing themselves outside of the club and cracking down hard on both the punks and the club itself. Inside the club, undercover officers often infiltrated the dance floor or staked out the parking lot waiting for trouble to arise.

Arrests became commonplace in and around the club over small, arbitrary infractions like jaywalking or littering. The heavy police presence caused business to suffer. After a while kids stopped coming, fearing they'd be arrested—like dogs tired of being whipped.

At one point during a city council hearing in 1981, Roach intercepted the cops' plan on how to harass punks or arrest them at shows as economically as possible. Turns out showing up to cuff punks one at a time was just making their job harder. "When they arrest an underage kid, that officer's got to go to the jail and stay there until the parents come," Roach said. "So for everybody they arrest they lose an officer in the field."

To prevent this, the cops devised a way to arrest twelve punks at a time so they could fill up a paddy wagon and take only one officer out of the field. Even Roach spent some time in the back of the rolling jail.

They would arrest punks for frivolous things like not crimping your car wheels to the curb. One guy got taken to jail for not having glasses because his license said he was supposed to wear them.

They even arrested Roach for jaywalking.

He remembers being paraded into the paddy wagon. "That was the night when I got arrested when they brought the city council by to do a little fact finding so they want to come and see what's going on," Roach said. "And they introduced me to the city council and I'm in handcuffs in the back of the paddy wagon. 'Oh, nice to meet you.' Nice first impression."

At one point, Roach decided to get a film crew to film the police arresting punks as proof of the injustices going on at the club. Naturally, the idea came during a dry spell when oddly the arrests had hit a lull, so the film crew started shooting the bands. The footage spliced together by director Paul Young would become the documentary *Urban Struggle: The Battle of the Cuckoo's Nest* in 1981.

Urban Struggle features rare footage of early performances at the Cuckoo's Nest by punk bands like Black Flag and the Vandals.

"The guy who was shooting it was kind of a punk rocker," Roach said. "And he was into the bands and I was into the slam dancing. So we were always arguing about what to film. But when it comes to slam dancing, you'll never see it like that again."

Roach would later use bits of the film in his own documentary, *We Were Feared*, while also incorporating new interviews with musicians from some of the bands such as D.I. and T.S.O.L.

The frustrations among punks in the scene ultimately led to an infamous incident on the night of January 30, 1981, when Pat Brown, a wild regular at the club, attempted to run over two police officers with his car. According to multiple eyewitness accounts, Brown was driving through the parking lot with a group of friends, beer in hand, looking for a place to park. A man dressed as a cowboy who was walking past approached the car, quickly told Brown that he was a cop, and reached inside the car to presumably put it in park. Brown punched the gas and took off with the undercover officer hanging onto the car.

An on-duty officer who had come to back up the other officer was then catapulted over the hood of the car. Some eyewitnesses claim Brown intentionally swerved to hit the officer, who was dragged several hundred feet before letting go and firing three shots into Brown's car, which had several passengers in the back. Tires screeching, Brown peeled out of the parking lot and sped up Placentia Avenue with his headlights off. Though no one was seriously injured, both officers were taken to the hospital.

Brown was pulled over a few blocks away for not having his headlights turned on, after which he was quickly arrested for attempted murder and beaten severely by the police.

Following the incident, the Costa Mesa city council revoked the Nest's entertainment permit, alleging that the club's patrons were unruly and violent. Roach took the matter to court, claiming that the city had violated the constitutional rights of free speech and liberty for both himself and the punks.

In March 1981, an Orange County Superior Court judge ruled in favor of the city and rejected the allegations that it had at any point been unjust in its decision. However, less than a month later, the California Supreme Court overturned the lower court's ruling, and the Nest was allowed to reinstate live music, much to the city's chagrin. Overall, Roach had been fighting the city for nine months to ensure that his own basic freedoms and those of his customers couldn't be trampled, with no help from anyone else.

"They had one session where they talked all about how bad I was and all the people that testified against me," Roach said. "And then it was my turn, but there wasn't enough time. So they said, 'Well, we'll just continue it to next week.'"

The club owner recalls that his attorney at the time also represented the Costa Mesa Police Department, a pretty blatant conflict of interest considering the club had become one of their main stomping grounds—literally.

"Whenever they would ask something I go to my attorney and my attorney said, 'I'm sorry, I can't represent Mr. Roach because there's a conflict of interest because I represent Costa Mesa Police Department.' And so it was like I didn't have an attorney," Roach said. At one point, the club owner lost his cool in court, shouting, "You know this is a kangaroo court. . . . I'm gonna get myself a kangaroo to represent me!" before storming out of the chambers.

"They tried to get rid of me, actually that's why I sort of turned radical. I spent most of my time trying to placate them and make them happy and keep it under control, but once they tried to get rid of me I kind of let it go wild," Roach said. "I really just wanted to shove punk rock right up their ass."

Roach reopened on May 1 with Black Flag, which was over triple capacity, and on May 2 with T.S.O.L., Agent Orange, and the Adolescents. "Once the city wants you, they're gonna get you, so I decided to go down swinging," Roach said.

Not long after the club got rolling again, Roach was blindsided by the city when they took advantage of the fact that the Cuckoo's Nest did not have a dance permit and effectively crippled the club by imposing a ban on dancing, refusing to issue a permit, and having a judge uphold the ban in court.

"They told me I had to have a dancing permit. It used to be when you got your entertainment permit, dancing was part of that," Roach said. "They tried to take my entertainment from it, and the Supreme

Court said no, that's why he got to reopen. Because they reversed their ruling. I had to go all the way to the Supreme Court of the state."

The police started to strengthen their presence and upheld the ban without exception, making countless arrests, and club attendance dwindled drastically by December 1981 from nearly 350 people a night to a few dozen some nights.

The Nest finally closed its doors in 1981 as a result of the dancing ban, as Roach said he did not want to see kids being arrested for simply expressing themselves. Almost all those involved believe this was the city's plan from the beginning—to systematically wear him down since they could not simply shutter him and smother the punk scene. In later years, Roach said that he would have continued to fight the city if he'd had financial backers or more support from the very scene that he was sticking up for.

Then the legislature made a new law to take effect in 1982 that would split dancing and entertainment and make them two licenses. So they couldn't take his entertainment, but they could refuse to give him a dancing license. At that point, Roach was so defeated that he didn't even apply for it. "January 1 is when they went into effect, so I just packed up and left—big mistake." He sighed. "I could have had someone else come in and do it. But I had another club to go to."

In 1982, the building became another music venue called the Concert Factory, which reopened under different ownership, before closing down after a couple of years when attendance lagged. At that new club, Radio City in Anaheim, he would go on to book Mötley Crüe, Guns N' Roses, and even Metallica's first gig.

"I mean, that's much more important, Guns N' Roses compared to Black Flag, but on the other hand, though, punk was forging new territory," Roach said.

The space was then absorbed by former adversary Zubie's and

became a pizzeria named Zubie's Gilded Cage. The former site of the Cuckoo's Nest, along with Zubie's, was bought in 1998 by Hank's Electric Supplies, which demolished both to make way for a warehouse. Roach, who went back to real estate after the club closed, said he was relieved it would be demolished: "I don't have fond memories of losing, of unfairly having my means of making money taken away from me," Roach told the *Los Angeles Times*. "I still think I was railroaded, but that's the breaks. I don't have any nostalgia for it. I'm kind of glad it's getting torn down. I'd rather have it not be there than be a pizza place." Jack Grisham of T.S.O.L. also said, "It was wrecked the day Zubie's got it."

"It was so damned exciting, but it was a monster. It was overwhelming in so many ways, in a way I was relieved when it was over," Roach said. "It was a long, hard road, it burned hot and fast, and it wasn't meant to last."

By the end, one thing Roach knew was that the music that changed the SoCal scene also changed him. He became one of "them"—even though he started out as the adversary of the punk scene, he became the ultimate punk rock parent. He sacrificed, took risks, took beatings, and got arrested for the sake of protecting his kids, even the ones he allegedly ripped off. But what started in this rowdy Costa Mesa club became the cradle of an angry baby that was spared long enough to grow into something far more profound.

SURF CITY OUTLAWS

I t's hard to pinpoint exactly when punk rock bled into Orange County. Many would cite the Cuckoo's Nest in Costa Mesa, of course. But there were pockets of punk history that predated Jerry Roach's famous club, several of which happened about eight miles west in the nearby beach cities and a little further inland. Some count the Runaways putting its stamp on suburbia—on December 31, 1975, at a rock 'n' roll nightclub in nearby Garden Grove called Wild Man Sam's that was owned by Jim Caron (who also played drums in a rock band called Kickfire!)—as a good place to start.

Then there was the Ramones' classic performance at the city's legendary venue the Golden Bear on August 23, 1976. They quickly followed up the show with a local street festival date in Huntington Beach called the Fest-a-Fair.

The jet-black hair, bowl cuts, and black leather jackets instantly stuck out amid the tanned and salt-weathered beach crowd. The four-piece from New York looked like a pack of dirty, scuzzy bikers

with guitars. The count-in on every song was kicked off with a raw electric cadence of "1-2-3-4, 1-2-3-4!" that shot from Dee Dee Ramone's
mouth like a Gatling gun.

At the time, a young, blond skater and HB local, Eric Groff, who
later adopted the name Eric VonArab, was too busy chasing girls and
trying to get loaded to really appreciate the punk history that was
unfolding in front of his stoned, adolescent eyes. "I just kind of looked
at them at the fair and went about my business," he said. It wouldn't
be until later on March 13, 1977, when the band played again at the
Golden West Ballroom in Norwalk with future FM rock gods Van
Halen that the music started to grab his attention. Van Halen was the
unlikely opening band.

Van Halen ended up not playing (the Dogs filled in), but getting a
chance to experience the Ramones was not wasted on him again. The
next time they crashed the stage hard with their "1-2-3-4, 1-2-3-4!"
VonArab stood in awe as he watched their whole set. "The next day I
went out and bought a leather jacket," he said. Even though he rocked
long hair, the look and feel of punk was taking over the suburbs—kids
started shaving their heads, sporting brothel creepers often shortened
to "creepers"—shoes with immensely thick rubber soles that were suede
or leather on top with buckle straps or laces—and paying attention to
high fashion and artsy looks. The style of punk adopted in Huntington
Beach would soon develop thanks to local kids like VonArab who took
inspiration from the Ramones, the Dead Boys, and the Sex Pistols and
merged it with the sun-tanned brutality of surf culture to create a style
all their own.

From 1978 onward, the eight-mile stretch of coastline along Huntington Beach became a haven for an especially rowdy punk rock scene.
Within the chaos of the scene was a self-destructive haze of backyard
keg parties and DIY shows. For many of the city's suburban youth,

punk was an escape from mundane middle-class life. Others were given a license to be creative, or for those with a more primitive psyche, it offered the chance to beat some ass to a hard-charging soundtrack.

✖✖✖✖✖✖

In 1974, Jim Kaa was a freshman at Edison High School in Huntington Beach. From the time he stepped onto campus, his initiation into the punk rock lifestyle had begun.

Edison was already becoming known as the punk rock high school, akin to what was developing with Fullerton kids at Troy High School, only this campus was where the surfer kids roamed, for obvious reasons. There was also a culture of house parties a la *Fast Times at Ridgemont High*—almost every weekend, a consortium of football players, surfers, stoners, cheerleaders, etc. would roll into a house temporarily vacated by the unwitting parents of a nice suburban family who left their kids in charge for the weekend. Almost invariably phones around the neighborhood would start to ring as word spread about whose empty house would serve as the party spot. Anywhere from a handful to one hundred or more kids found their way to the temporary party pads to crack some beers, crank up some music, raid the liquor cabinet, and let loose.

"It was like let's get the party going," T.S.O.L.'s Jack Grisham said. "Let's fucking get the kegs happening. Let's jump off this roof. Let's make a bomb. Let's have a blast!"

It was against this typical weekend backdrop that bands would set up and play punchy, amateur renditions of rock radio hits by KISS, UFO, Led Zeppelin, or Black Sabbath. Among these bands in the mid-'70s was a group called Witchcraft with a young Sandy West on drums. Soon West would go on to join a band called the Runaways, which became a spark plug that ignited an early feminine ferocity across the punk landscape and made stars out of Cherie Currie and Joan Jett. Kaa remembers watching the Runaways perform before Currie had even joined the band at her house party near the corner of Magnolia Street and Indianapolis Avenue.

The Crowd's Jim and Jay Decker and their brother Jeff soon became ringleaders of the Huntington Beach high school party scene, hosting many wild nights at their home in the cul-de-sac of Hilaria Circle when their parents weren't home. "We used to set up right inside the living room, and there'd be a hundred kids here on a Saturday night for a wild punk rock party," Kaa remembers. As for neighborhood complaints—"It was an unwritten rule with the neighbors that if nothing got broken or damaged, nothing was mentioned," Kaa said.

"All that music was coming in because we had the Golden Bear, and this culture of house parties, so I think that culture of bands and live music always existed in the area," Kaa said.

It didn't take long for Kaa to realize that he wanted to be in a band. "I played sports all growing up, but for me by the time I got to high school I was bored with sports and I wanted to try something different." And that led to him and some friends starting a band called the New, which would soon become known as the Crowd and make its debut the way most bands of the era did—at a house party in the summer of 1978.

From the beginning, the Crowd captured the high-octane energy of surf punks to the tune of catchy melodic songs performed at breakneck speed.

While many punks credit the Sex Pistols and the Ramones for exposing people to punk, the Crowd made them think about starting a band themselves in their own garage.

Though the lineup started with Kaa's high school friend Peter Roach as the lead singer, he would soon be swapped out for Jim Decker.

By the time the band really started to jell, Kaa and the Deckers graduated high school but were still asked back by popular demand to perform at a sock hop at Edison. The event quickly turned into a raucous punk show with students reveling in the pit with dyed black, blue, and red hair, which at the time seemed completely alien to school faculty.

"It was shocking at the time even though today it would be nothing more than what you'd see at the mall or at Hot Topic, but at the time it was like a whole different world. It did open a lot of kids' eyes. But the same way the Beatles did in the '60s and the Stones and Led Zeppelin, all those cultural changes are part of music to some degree. But here was the surfing and the skating and the energy of the beach igniting with punk rock to kind of explode during that time," said Kaa.

Praise for the Crowd was almost instant, like a heatwave in the middle of summer. By year's end, the band had already gotten press in the coveted punk periodical *Flipside*.

By that time, the band's house parties had become so legendary that they caught the attention of Posh Boy Records founder Robbie Fields, who showed up to one of them to watch the band play and afterward made them an offer to put out their first record, Kaa says.

Gathering the band in an upstairs bedroom in the back of the house, Fields pulled out a vinyl record from LA band the Simpletones, who were just the second band to sign with the new label. "Do you guys wanna release a proper record?" he asked. That was pretty much all it took to get the Crowd's attention. Before the songs like "Modern Machine," "Suzy Is a Punk Rocker," and "Right Time" would inevitably end up on their 1981 debut *A World Apart*, the songs landed on the iconic *Beach Blvd* compilation next to songs from the Simpletones from Rosemead and West Covina punker Rik L. Rik in 1979.

The Crowd's debut album, *A World Apart*, is still regarded as a sleeper favorite by OC punk fans for its tight, punchy sound, electric energy, and upbeat songs about love, partying, and surviving young adulthood. The band photo on the front cover was shot underneath the old Huntington Beach pier, originally built in 1914 and eventually reconstructed in 1990. On the back cover of the album, the members lined up in goofy poses in front of the Huntington Beach Power Plant, which still looms over the Pacific Coast Highway like a smoke-churning iron monolith—it was classic Huntington Beach.

Still, not everyone was so positively tuned to the more aggressive physical aspects of the Huntington scene. Though bands from the scene were credited with creating and popularizing slam dancing, they were often labeled by people on the LA scene as the thing that single-handedly ruined punk rock once they started making their presence felt outside of their hometown, especially at shows like the Masque in Hollywood when these suburban devils made the trek up north to the City of Angels.

Too young to get into clubs, they were restricted to playing house parties where stuff got broken and sticky-fingered teens pilfered the bedroom drawers.

The Huntington Beach scene was divided into a few different factions. You had guys like the Crowd, often described as the "dayglo" precursors to pop punk. Then there were the T.S.O.L. guys who represented a darker element of the scene. The art-punk sounds of Mnemonic Devices also became popular in the scene at the time, though their sound was more influenced by Roxy Music and Siouxsee and the Banshees instead of the Sex Pistols and the Damned.

For a short time the Crowd's Jim Kaa played guitar for the Devices. The band's violin-playing front woman, Ann De Jarnett, was known for experimenting with androgyny. Her thoughtful, poetic lyrics fueled their dark punk sound that drew a crowd at packed shows in Los Angeles and Orange County. The *Playing on the Dark Keys* EP was one of the early OC goth punk band's best albums. One of the things that made Mnemonic Devices stick out early on was that they had women in the band.

Multi-instrumentalist Linnea Ahms's love affair with music started at age nine in Huntington Beach, when she would practice lip-synching to Monkees songs with her sisters while playing a makeshift drum-kit made of cardboard boxes and Bundt pans. Ahms discovered punk rock while working at famed LA record store Licorice Pizza. Her early influences were Roxy Music, David Bowie, the Stooges, and Captain Beefheart—she was inspired to pick up the saxophone and started playing it with Mnemonic Devices before eventually switching over to bass.

"I fell in love with bass because I can fill that perfect pocket between the melody and rhythm and magically bring them together," Ahms told *OC Weekly*. The talented local musician performed not only with the Devices and the Crowd but also with Babylonian Tiles, the Dead Sea Squirrels, and others.

The Flyboys were also a popular punk band in the early HB scene, though they originally hailed from Arcadia. Flyboys drummer Dennis Walsh would later go on to play drums in the Crowd.

The Crowd would first perform at the Cuckoo's Nest in 1978, though the club was still mostly booking '70s rock bands until they started packing in audiences that came to rage and turn the tide toward punk rock. From there they became regulars in the Southern California club and punk party scene, despite the fact that they never toured nationally like Black Flag or some of their other punk peers. The Crowd were a solid staple in the live music scene until taking a five-year hiatus in 1982 before resurfacing again in 1987. Kaa noted violence in the scene with the birth of hardcore as one of the reasons the band bowed out for a while. Today the Crowd's lineup still features Jim Kaa, Jim Decker, and Dennis Walsh, along with Jeff Milucky from Social Task and Corey Stretz from the Outsiders.

A wave of bands followed the Crowd starting in the fall of 1978, including the Idols, the Slashers, Vicious Circle, and the Outsiders. The Crowd's debut album, *A World Apart*, was mainly comprised of cartoonishly spastic songs with lyrics about relationships and having fun.

The Outsiders, on the other hand, favored black leather jackets and boots as opposed to the playful dayglo colors worn by the Crowd, and they were made up of a more criminal element. Early on, some in the Outsiders' following did not get along with the Crowd's following, and vice versa, though that short-lived animosity was not held by the band members themselves. The Outsiders were originally formed out of a half-rock, half-punk cover band with long hair that featured Corey Stretz, Mike Drake, Frank Ruffino, and Joey Ruffino. Though they often sounded melodic and catchy, the Outsiders' sound was also driven by heavy guiter riffs.

"Our vocalist Donny got us a gig at a state mental hospital by claiming that we were a Beatles cover band," Frank Ruffino, the late guitarist for the Outsiders and China White, told Brian Sheklian in a 2020 article about the Huntington Beach punk rock scene. "We got to play for about 20 minutes before they made us stop. We were too heavy for some of the patients there. One kid got hyper and smashed a radio over another kid's head. Outsiders parties were huge with hundreds of people showing up, often destroying houses and people's dreams. One house going through foreclosure sustained $30,000 in damages. The son threw a party and did not realize what kind of people would show up. They were ruthless back then."

Another HB punk band the Slashers rose out of the same Surf City tract of condos where the Outsiders' Frank Ruffino and Mike Drake grew up. Formed by Butch Livingston and future Adolescents guitarist Rikk Agnew, they came up with the tune "Creatures" before it eventually became part of the Adolescents' self- titled debut, known as the Blue Album.

On the heels of those bands came the Hated, which started in mid-1979 with Steve "Real" on vocals, bassist Joe Wood, guitarist Bob Johnson, guitarist Gary Van Boemel, and drummer Bob Haddad.

✖✖✖✖✖✖

If there was one thing that set Huntington Beach punk apart in the early days, it was the band names. Eric VonArab rattles off a list of ludicrous band names from the region, including bands he played in himself—Arab and the Suburban Turbans and Love Canal. It's like playing a lewd game of Mad Libs with a rotating cast of characters.

The beginning roster of Love Canal, for example, included original Suicidal Tendencies guitarist Mike Ball. "When we started Love Canal, our first singer Mike Ball, who also played in a local band called the Skoundrelz, would just come to rehearsal and sing Suicidal lyrics over our songs," Arab said. Arab would later recruit the Skoundrelz singer Mr. Carey to sing for his band, and thus the band Love Canal was born in the summer of 1983.

And in the scene where these bands came up, shows were often just an excuse for violence. "Parties in Orange County were basically just fights. It was like going into a warzone, it was scary," Arab said. He knows from experience, having gotten his fair share of teeth chipped or knocked out of his head during brawls, even as a bystander.

"One time I was standing on the side of the pit because I didn't want to go in and like with my beer in my hand, and all of a sudden fucking somebody throws a football, like over the pit, and bam. I just looked and I swallowed my tooth," he continued.

Another night when he and his friends were coming out of short-lived HB punk club Safari Sam's after playing a show, they were walking down a busy street when suddenly people started throwing pennies and nickels and dimes at him and his bandmates. "I got hit with a quarter in the tooth and it felt like I got punched, man," he remembers. "So I had like two broken teeth because of music."

If he wasn't sustaining injuries over music, it was due to falling off a skateboard. By the mid-'70s, skate culture in OC went hand in hand with punk rock—it was a match made in suburban hell. Both relied on aggression, tension, release, blood, sweat, and devotion. "We would go skate all day and then go to Cuckoo's Nest. You'd like get beat up on your skateboard all day to get beat up somewhere at night," Arab said. "It actually went together, you skate all day and then everybody met at the skate park, went to the show at night, and you pogoed and then you partied, then you woke up at noon and you skated and you found a show the next night, then you put a band together," Duane Peters said in *Who Cares?*, a documentary about his life as both a skateboard revolutionary and singer for OC punk legends the U.S. Bombs, along with the Exploding Fuck Dolls and the Duane Peters Gunfight. "Skateboarding's great but it'll always be great to me. I don't care about the sport of it. I never called it a sport. I got into skateboarding because it wasn't a sport and you do it on your own. I'm a punk rocker and a skateboarder, period."

In the early '70s, the grip and glide of the urethane wheel carried skaters away from the rough-riding, clay-wheel days of the previous decade, and skateboarding ascended toward a second spike in popularity. Many of this new generation of skateboarders ignored the gymnastic trick book left over from the '60s and instead hit the streets with style and speed born from shortboard surfing. Skateboarding found Peters living in Newport Beach.

By 1980, if you skateboarded, you were hated. Peters took on the idea and the feeling of that time—it was aggressive, it was rebellious, and it was on edge, whereas today it feels more like Little League. Unlike the way skateboarders are perceived today, the skaters of the '70s and '80s were never taken seriously for their courage. They got no love and no sympathy for being banned on the streets and sidewalks of Orange County. Like punk rock bands of the era, it was them against the world, them against their parents, them against every 7-Eleven clerk who tried shooing them away.

Two things skating and punk had in common were that both turned kids into targets for local law enforcement. Similar to the profiling that happened in other parts of OC, cops had taken notice of the growing "punk threat." If you had a punk band name written on your shirt like the Slashers or Outsiders, you were immediately identified by police as members of the "Slashers" or "Outsiders" street gang. Tales of getting detained by the police while they took your picture, called you a "faggot," and threatened you were common.

When the Outsiders decided to call it a day in late 1979, guitarist Frank Ruffino started China White, leaving Mike Drake, Corey Stretz, and Dave Stewart to team with Butch Livingston from the Slashers and Jesse Rodriguez from the Klan to form the Blades. Said lineup would last about a year until Jesse split, leaving Mike Drake to take over on vocals, and with that version they soldiered on until early 1982.

Despite making their mark in the HB party scene, few of the early punk bands from Surf City went on to record any real albums that made noteworthy record sales. Few established music business execs were interested in providing a platform for the "live fast, die young" nihilistic tendencies of the band members.

China White was one of the few groups to emerge from Huntington

Beach, attracting popularity in SoCal thanks to the metal guitar influenced shredding of Frank Ruffino, who'd been doing the same thing with the Outsiders. The band's lineup consisted of sneering vocalist Mark Martin, Joey's brother Frank on drums, and fast-fingered James Rodriguez on bass. They signed a deal with Frontier Records, home of T.S.O.L., for their 1980 album *Dangerzone*. Ultimately they weren't able to fully capitalize on the LP's nationwide distribution.

"Kimm [Gardener] from Channel 3 wanted us to go on tour with them, he had also been talking with Black Flag about the tour as well. Some of the other members didn't want to go," Rodriguez told Sheklian in an article on HB punk. "At that point it was like what have we been working for if we don't go on this tour, it was like closing the door on an opportunity. Mark Martin and I decided to leave at that point, as we were both disappointed with the other members' decision not to tour. I joined the army in late 1982 to get away from Huntington and clear my mind."

The punk bands of Surf City emerged like a fleet of ships full of pirates, many of them floating aimlessly to pillage and plunder in every direction. And like most pirates, these bands' lives were often short-lived. In that regard, perhaps the small venue in downtown Huntington where many of the early bands played was no different. However, its presence did swiftly become an anchor for the scene when it opened its doors.

Safari Sam's was located at 411 Olive Avenue in downtown Huntington Beach and opened as a restaurant in October 1984. The club, owned and operated by Sam Lanni and Gil Fuhrer, garnered a reputation as Orange County's most eclectic and adventurous nightclub for bookings of a wide range of new music, theater, and poetry. It was also virtually the only outlet for hundreds of county bands.

Lanni, Safari Sam's founder, immigrated from Italy. His parents didn't read or write English when they emigrated to Huntington Beach and ran a neighborhood liquor store. By the time he was nineteen, Sam was already married, and he and his first wife were watching all kinds of entertainment from concerts to plays. "I saw a lotta stuff so I fell in love with artists and the whole entertainment industry," he said.

In 1977, Lanni moved to England for a year with his English wife. They moved to Huddersfield, the same town where the Sex Pistols played their final UK show on Christmas Day at Ivanhoe's Nightclub. Lanni wanted to go to the show, which started a huge argument with his then mother-in-law, who was adamant they didn't go—to the point she chased him around with a knife. "That was my introduction to the punk world," Lanni said.

Nine months later, Lanni and his wife moved back to the States, first to Fallbrook and then back to Huntington Beach. He ran a small construction company there that made enough money for him to buy a small restaurant in downtown Huntington Beach called Chilies (no relation to the fast-casual mecca of baby back ribs), which he renamed Safari Sam's. The restaurant would cater to a slightly younger crowd but was not yet considered a music venue. He hired his friend Gil Fuhrer to help him run it. At the time, Fuhrer worked at Lanni's parents' liquor store before the restaurant. Lanni also hired a chef from New York who he says he later found out "had a metal plate in his head." In a matter of months, Lanni said the chef began acting erratically to the point that it was ruining the restaurant's reputation with customers and sinking the business. The chef was fired, and things had to change fast.

After letting go of the chef, Lanni was approached by one of his customers at the restaurant, who asked if his son's band, an early punk outfit called First Glance, could play at the restaurant Christmas week in 1984. Lanni—who was equal parts young, hip, and desperate at the time—said, "Sure, come on down." The result was the single biggest, most chaotic night of business the fledgling restaurant had ever witnessed. "[First Glance] brought two other bands to play, they packed the place, we sold out of beer, we sold out of food, and then the crowd all went outside to have a big fight in the street on Olive," Lanni recalls. As he watched the brawls in the street around the club crawling with kids who were now magnetized to the place, Lanni and Fuhrer stood on the curb in front of the club with folded arms, heads shaking, and mouths grinning. "I think we found what we need to be doing," Lanni told Fuhrer. From then on, Safari Sam's was a music club.

They redesigned the look of Safari Sam's, adding a hut-like stage in the corner of the bar that hosted bands like the Meat Puppets, the Crowd, D.I., and the Minutemen, and even became the site of Jane's Addiction's first gig in front of just twenty-five people. After a run of successful shows, by the summer of 1985 the club became a popular stop for touring and local bands on SST Records. The South Bay label frequently booked Safari Sam's for its acts, including Black Flag bassist Chuck Dukowski's side project SWA.

The small club was garnering an outsized reputation for the sheer amount of noise it was generating. A literal representation of that was wheeled in at one point by Safari Sam's sound guy Dave Rat, who also went on to do live sound for Huntington Beach–based concert promoter Goldenvoice, created by Gary Tovar, which would go on to book some of the biggest punk shows in the world and later massive festivals like the Coachella Music and Arts Festival that singlehandedly changed the face of live music in America. But at the time, it was just a scrappy operation full of young punk rockers who did and made everything by hand. Rat once brought in a prototype of a new PA system he was developing that was capable of churning out sixteen thousand watts—it was almost too big to fit in the club.

In just a handful of shows, Lanni's building went from a struggling restaurant to a popular all-ages venue that catered to the wide spectrum of artists in the city. Most importantly, Fuhrer said, "We were creating more than a bar, we felt like we were creating a community and family and we really had that sense of things going on there."

Huntington Beach's city council and police department wasted little time descending on the club. Squad cars would even roll up to the all-ages club on poetry or theater nights, which were almost as well-known as the punk rock shows. "We were having parents come and grandparents come and the police would show up at least two times a week . . . they were checking everyone's IDs, intimidating the parents," Lanni said. "It was stupid, we never had anything bad happen at the club, inside we didn't have any issues." That included any rowdy behavior from mosh pits that Sam's didn't allow. Sam's booked acts six to seven days a week. "Downtown was a surf punk place and an artistic hub, a lot of artists downtown—it's not like that now, it's mostly very wealthy people. Back then kids there had issues . . . we had a lot of people who would come to my club two to three times a week just to hang out and have a place to go," Lanni said.

One of those musicians was Mike Ness, who, between 1985 and 1986, often frequented the club. Around that time, on two separate occasions, Social Distortion played five nights and used the venue as a rehearsal space for a while. Ness often came to the venue with his guitar and also invited his friends' bands, and those shows were always awesome, chaotic, and full of drama. "We only held 100 people and everybody wanted to get into those shows," Lanni said. One night a guy who was pissed about not getting in shattered three of the club's windows with his fists. "We had to call the ambulance . . . even during that the police didn't break up that show. They never really tried too hard to close us down until they did but they were always around to hassle us."

From the time punk got rolling at Safari Sam's, its days were numbered—not only because of the rowdy nature of the punk scene, but due to the pall cast over the city in the wake of turmoil during a major surf contest on Labor Day in 1986.

The air off the coast of Huntington Beach was thick with tension during the now defunct OP Pro surf competition, with some fifty thousand partiers blanketing the shore of Huntington Beach. Most of them probably had little clue that the world's biggest surf contest was happening in the water; instead, it was the prospect of bikini-clad debauchery that brought them down to the beach. Sadly, that's exactly what they got. As pro surfer Mark Occhilupo paddled out during the '86 final, a group of testy young men created some commotion, hurling sexist comments at women in the crowd.

"Show us your tits!" they yelled at young ladies sitting on the nearby balcony of a restaurant called Duke's. Some women obliged. Some not so much. One woman allegedly had her bikini ripped off as she made her way to the restroom. Clouds of dust were kicked up and blanketed the crowd as more young men rushed over in hopes of a Mardi Gras–style flash fest. A handful of police officers also saw the scene flaring up and went to check on it. They were greeted with a barrage of bottles and sand bombs, leading them to retreat and call in reinforcements.

Soon a team of one hundred police officers in full riot gear showed up swinging billy clubs and kicking off several hours of mayhem—a sleepy beach town turned nightmare with the rioters looting and fighting with cops while everyone else scrambled for safety. At some point, the mob descended on the Huntington Beach lifeguard headquarters. Like a rowdy militia, the group busted through the doors of the building and found flares that they ignited and used to set fire to a string of vehicles, including three cop cars, a lifeguard jeep, an ambulance, and a couple ATVs. As the flames and plumes of ash and smoke rose into the sky, the ill-fated Huntington Beach competition put a shameful black eye on Surf City.

Even though cops ended up arresting only seven people for being drunk in public, the incident made national headlines and caused a ripple effect of strict city measures to clamp down on large youth entertainment gatherings around the city.

In the wake of the OP Pro riots in 1986, Sam's was one of the several venues that were initially denied entertainment permits after two years of being approved with no issues. At the same time, the council approved a $200 million redevelopment of downtown Huntington Beach. Prior to the OP Riots, the Golden Bear, an iconic music venue that had been in Huntington Beach since the 1920s, was shut down in January after the owners filed for protective bankruptcy in 1985. It was demolished shortly after despite an effort by the community to save the building. "What I saw in that was they were going to change the dynamic of Huntington Beach, which they did . . . and they couldn't have us there in the middle of it."

"Within two weeks of [the OP riots], five clubs in Huntington Beach were shut down and we were on that list. It was almost like the police department said enough is enough," Fuhrer said. "We were informed by the police to stop having shows or else we would be arrested. In true fashion at that point we just kept having shows." Lanni and Fuhrer pushed the line for two more days of live shows through the first weekend in September before cops showed up and finally put a stop to it on Sunday.

"The police showed up and told the bands stop setting up, that's it, you don't have music anymore."

Despite loud demonstrations from fans, bands, and the venue's theater department, the city moved ahead with the closure, and by the fall of 1986, the Safari Sam's era was over. Just as with the Cuckoo's Nest, punk culture clashing with the powers that be in OC forced the scene to splinter. Even a second attempt for the club to reopen in Costa Mesa ended in failure, and a version of the club later opened in LA.

"There was nothing like it," Lanni said of the club. "Nobody was doing the amount of punk shows we were doing at the time, even though we were probably only doing a third as many shows as the Cuckoo's Nest. . . . In Orange County after that punk kinda dissipated."

Though it was a short period, one of many that revived the punk scene in Huntington Beach punk scene many times over the years, the short run of Safari Sam's is still part of the area's hidden DNA. Walking past the site now, which became the Huntington Beach International Surf Museum, the little building on Olive Avenue still looms large in OC punk history.

"I feel like within that period of twenty months we were open it felt like we'd made a real club—not just a club where you went to see things but more of a family," Fuhrer said. "You really had that sense every time you walked in there—it was magical."

EARLY FULLERTON

ou'll have to ask the Agnews about that," Social Distortion's Mike Ness said about the origins of what became known as the Orange County sound.

The Agnews, Rikk, Frank, and Alfie, were the sons of a disciplinarian Irish father who worked for SoCal Gas and a Mexican mother. They grew up in La Puente before moving to Fullerton when Rikk, the oldest of the three, was in sixth grade. Richard Francis Agnew was born December 9, 1958, Francis Thomas Agnew followed in 1964, and Alfonso Agnew arrived in January 24, 1969. Despite the ten-year gap between the oldest Agnew and the youngest (with a sister born in between Rikk and Frank), they were all pretty close and bonded through music.

Rikk's musical journey started before he picked up a pencil. At the age of four, he was given his first drum kit. Instantly, he realized that he had a natural sense of rhythm. The Agnews' maternal grandfather was a drummer and had become known in the Latin scene in California for his work with Xavier Cugat and the Latinaires, so rhythm was already in the family's DNA.

Citing the Beatles, the Rolling Stones, the Beach Boys, and Motown as early influences, Rikk would bang his drums while their father strummed along with his acoustic guitar and sometimes improvised songs that Rikk would play along to. Rikk remembers coming home from school and strumming heavy, pissed-off chords on a family guitar. It began a lifelong love of playing music.

"He [Rikk] was obsessed with the Beatles, in the '70s it was prog rock, by the mid-'70s it was Kraftwerk and electro imports from Europe. What was neat about Rikk was that he was always looking for something new, he was always fascinated by new music," Frank said.

Naturally, Frank and Alfie were Rikk's first coconspirators and were also musically inclined. The Agnew boys jammed the instruments that were present around the house.

Frank started playing before he was ten, and just like Rikk, he was musically gifted.

"Immediately, Frank was so fucking good," Rikk said. "He could do Jimmy Page stuff when he was a fifth grader. Alfie was in second grade at that point. And the two of them would go in the garage and rehearse Led Zeppelin songs."

"None of us was a good skateboarder," Frank said. "So we stuck with the instruments."

When the Ramones' debut album came out in April 1976, Rikk was immediately hooked on the raw, aggressive sound, black leather jackets, and tough-guy swagger from the Queens-bred quartet.

"I remember I had gotten birthday money and was planning to buy a Foghat album but Rikk and his friends convinced me to buy the Ramones album, instead," Frank said. Obliging his older brother, Frank used his cash to buy the seminal punk rock vinyl. He and his brothers huddled around the record player and dropped the needle. Frank's reaction was . . . not very positive. "At first I was like 'what the hell's this?' I was used to listening to Sabbath and the prog rock stuff, and at first I didn't like the Ramones, the songs were fast, short, and noisy." But for some reason the tunes got stuck in Frank's head. Listening again and again, he eventually grew to love it, not only for the melodies and the style but because of how accessible it was. The ability to be in a band and play a few chords inspired the Agnews and many other kids growing up in the era of often complicated, overinflated virtuoso rock 'n' roll to feel like they too could be onstage without putting in ten years of lessons.

However, that jolt of youth culture and passion for music didn't translate with their neighbors. They often complained about the noise emanating from the Agnews' garage.

"The lady who lived next door would get all pissed off and come over and threaten to call the cops," Rikk said. "She said 'Stop making that noise' and we kept saying 'It's not noise, it's music!'"

The brothers' intricate blend of influences combined with their natural ability would shape the sound of their bands in the years to come.

"People were calling him [Rikk] the Brian Wilson of punk," future bandmate Steve Soto told *OC Weekly*. "And he was."

"I could hear an 'Orange County sound' starting to identify itself amid the SoCal punk scene," early Social Distortion drummer Derek O'Brien said. "Elements of surf guitar and drums, certainly with Agent Orange but others like the Adolescents, D.I., Channel 3, and the Crowd also. Then you had rough but still actually melodic lead vocals as opposed to just yelling, two-part guitar, two-part melodies where one or both would play the melodies with octaves and the backup vocal harmonies soaring with or around the lead vocal."

Punk roared out of London and New York in 1976 before making its way out west not too long after. First in Los Angeles, by the time the sound trickled past the Orange Curtain, which was the not-so-flattering nickname Angelenos gave to the county directly to the south, it gained its own flavor.

Impressionable young punkers, who came from broken homes that fit outside of the idealistic nature of the Reagan presidency, were influenced by British bands like the Sex Pistols and the Damned. It could be heard in the voices of the emerging singers.

"Your punk band sings in an English accent," the Vandals bassist Joe Escalante said. "That's what we do. You might be able to make your own style, but you start there."

In bands like Huntington Beach's T.S.O.L., Fullerton's Adolescents, and Social Distortion, traces of those British bands can be heard. Escalante points to T.S.O.L.'s "World War III" as the prime example.

"That's our leader in Orange County, Jack Grisham, telling us how to do what we need to do," Escalante continued on a podcast. "We're not going to argue with that."

Looking back at his first time singing, Escalante remembers the Vandals singer Dave Quackenbush telling him that he sounded like a "Republican who sounded like they just got out of a John Birch Society meeting." From there, he went with an English accent himself before incorporating some of his own natural style.

When all of this adds up, it becomes clear that the brand of punk that broke through in the 1990s could be traced back to its origins in Orange County. Many of the early bands' sound had a preciseness to it and a simultaneous lack of pretension.

"I believe that the California punk sound came from Orange County," NOFX front man Fat Mike said. Born Mike Burkett, the singer was first introduced to punk by his camp counselor, who just so happened to be the Vandals' Joe Escalante.

Even in a major city like Seattle, where Guns N' Roses bassist Duff McKagan grew up a thousand miles away, the sound of Southern California punk was echoing into the consciousness of punk social circles. "We were aware of what they were doing—and why," McKagan said. "Even though in Seattle where we didn't have suburbs, we envisioned these punks from sprawling suburbs whose parents were Reagan conservatives and these kids were rebelling against it. We got it. Could we fully identify with it? Not really. But we knew what they were about."

Fullerton had the fortune of being the home of Fender. Leo Fender's factory often discarded guitars that they deemed unusable. For the locals who couldn't afford one of his instruments, dumpster diving to obtain a guitar was frequent and critical. These discarded guitars found a new home, often in the hands of young punks.

It was the literal embodiment of "one person's trash is another's treasure."

In addition to being the home of Fender, Fullerton was also the place where many families moved in search of the ideal, pleasantville life depicted as the American dream. The area was gentrified by tract homes where nuclear families would settle. By the 1970s, that dream vanished for many disaffected youths, and a new scene emerged that many in the community would instantly hate.

4

A FUZZ PEDAL SPARKS A SOUND

orn on April 3, 1962, in Massachusetts before moving to Fullerton later that year, Mike Ness grew up in a "chaotic" household, spending a lot of time with babysitters. From the time he was born, Ness's family life was a whirlwind of uncertainty. His mom did her best to raise him while living a hand-to-mouth existence in 1960s Orange County and occasionally dipping her toe in the surf and psychedelic–bred "counterculture" of the area.

"She could have been a grifter," Ness said. "If she would have got with the right guy, they could have been great grifters."

When he wasn't being looked after by his mom, Ness spent lots of time with one particular babysitter, an elderly religious woman who lived in a house near his and had a spare bedroom where he would sit with a radio for hours. Even as a five-year-old, his eyes darted around the room at the art depicting angels, saints, and playfully nude cherubs as he listened to the twangy guitar of blues and rock songs on the radio. "There was the sex and the rock 'n' roll right there," he recalls. "The

music had done something for me, it gave me an escape from everything . . . my parents were drinking, you know. And so it provided
entertainment, escape." Already as a kid, he'd been touched by music
and wanted to be involved with it in any capacity.

His uncles, who were steeped in '60s counterculture, were the first
ones to reinforce that passion. Being around them, one of whom he
describes as a "gay hippie" and the other a "low rider, greaser kind of
guy," they introduced Ness to the sounds of artists ranging from Sam
and Dave and Otis Redding to Creedence Clearwater Revival and the
Rolling Stones. His earliest heroes were outlaw gangsters like Bonnie
and Clyde and John Dillinger. He also saw the movie *Easy Rider* at a
young age and made a chopper bike, beginning a lifelong fascination
with greaser culture.

Ness didn't fit in at school, which would set the tone for his admiration of outlaws, outcasts, and working-class heroes. Though he grew
up across the street from a Little League/Pop Warner field and says he
could have been a good athlete, he didn't have the support at home to
pursue those activities.

"I would just cruise the Little League field looking at all the guys'
sisters," he remembered.

Instead of hitting home runs or scoring touchdowns, Ness would
be at home "with the stereo and just staring at an album for hours, listening to it over and over."

Despite liking those melodic radio rock bands, which also included
Bad Company and Johnny Winter, hearing the Sex Pistols altered the
course of his life. Whether he knew it or not, the music that caught his
ear was already becoming the soundtrack to his life on the fringes.

"Johnny Rotten sounds like how I feel inside," Ness says of that
tumultuous time. "That's more of an expression of where I'm at than
'Stairway to Heaven' was."

When he was fifteen, Ness was thrown out of his father and step-mother's house due to his out-of-control behavior, so he started living with neighbors and hanging out with older kids. Describing this home environment as "chaotic," Ness was introduced to the black market, in particular drug dealing and burglary. He also started using drugs. The leather-jacket mystique and seething angst in the music of the Ramones, the Dead Boys, and the Sex Pistols was the sound that seemed the most in line with his lifestyle. "Punk kind of just, I wouldn't say supported that [lifestyle], but it all coalesced," he said.

Punkers like Rikk Agnew and Ness were often targets for jocks and rednecks. They were picked on, got into fights, and had beer cans thrown at them.

By 1979, Ness was fully immersed in punk culture. He started hanging out with fellow Troy High School student Dennis Danell, who was a year ahead of him. Until that point, Ness had only known Danell from afar in elementary and junior high because his family lived close to the schools they attended together.

Danell, a senior, was a good-looking surfer type—blond, freshly cropped spiky hair, tall, and lean. His family lived inland at 2009 Sudene Avenue, not too far from Ness. Born prematurely weighing around two and a half pounds on June 24, 1961, Danell was always a fighter.

"His dad described holding him in his hand like a little bird," said Danell's future wife, Christy Danell-Walker. "They really didn't know if he was gonna survive. His dad said when he peed on him, he knew that he was gonna be OK."

Danell wasn't one of the rich kids, but he had the desire and determination to succeed. He had an outlaw way about him at the time, from the way he dressed to the swagger in his step and how his peers treated him. Yet even at an early age he was always present, willing to listen to everyone and make someone feel like the most important person in the room. He loved skating and surfing. Ness knew that this kid was "in the know." They didn't officially meet until they both wandered into the same photo silk-screening class at Troy High School. "I just started talking to him because I loved music and he did too. So we had that in common. And, you know, we just became really good friends," Ness said.

During those early years, Ness and Danell would zoom up to Hollywood, often on school nights, and they'd watch X perform at LA's Hong Kong Café and see the Blasters.

One moment stood out to Ness among all of their punk excursions.

"Dennis and I drove down one night to San Diego because the Clash was playing in San Diego at the university or something and we fucking snuck in," Ness said. "Man, they had a tour bus, they had roadies, and they put on a fucking great show. It was professional. And it was like 'Thank you! That's what I want to do.' Just like that. Their work ethic . . . that's the example."

Before meeting Danell, Ness and his friend and fellow Troy classmate Casey Royer formed a band. They called it Social Distortion.

"There were a couple of bands that had the word 'social' in it already. I didn't really care and decided I am gonna use it," Ness said. "At the time, we had a little distortion box—an MXR distortion box. That was kind of our sound. Little did I know it was saying so much more with that name. But I must have felt that."

"Social Distortion was named for my distortion pedal, which I gave to Mike to play 'cause back then he was no good," Royer said in *American Hardcore*.

The duo would sit at Royer's parents' house on Friday nights and jam, with Ness writing the songs and Royer drumming. They'd be joined by Royer's friend, Cal State Fullerton basketball player Tom

Corvin ("He looked like a cross between Ric Ocasek and Mick Jagger," Ness said), who would handle vocals despite his lack of experience. Ness knew that they weren't a typical rock band. They looked different, and Corvin was a "very theatrical" singer. "He'd do his weird things onstage, like, just curl up in a ball or do something," he says. "I just hoped no one turns a hose on, like some hesher."

From an early age, Ness was fascinated by house parties. His next-door neighbors, on account of having a truck-driver father who wasn't around often, would host keg parties where bands would perform. Ness would sit on an adjacent wall and watch the sets from acts like the Middle Class and the Mechanics.

The Middle Class consisted of the Atta brothers (Mike, Jeff, and Bruce) and bassist Mike Patton. Formed in 1977, the brothers were always arguing and fighting among each other. Sibling squabbles aside, they were one of the first punk bands to emerge from Orange County, and with that, they brought a distinct, edgier sound. Their single "Out of Vogue" was played on KROQ by Rodney Bingenheimer, and they're widely considered the pioneers of hardcore.

When they played live, they were very particular about whom they played with. They opened for the Germs and the Screamers and were one of the few Southern California bands to gain popularity in San Francisco.

Around this time, Ness and Danell would bond over their mutual love of music. Armed with a twelve-pack of beer (which they hid three at a time in the pockets of their black leather jackets), they'd walk an hour down railroad tracks from Danell's house to downtown Fullerton to watch the Mechanics practice at Sherpa Studio on Harbor Boulevard and Commonwealth. Danell met the Mechanics singer Scott Hoogland at church in 1972, and the Mechanics would greatly influence the pair.

"They were these older guys," Ness said. "We looked up to them and they were really cool. They drove VW buses and we wanted to be like them. But that band saved me just as much as the Rolling Stones or the Ramones. They'd come out onstage and say 'We're the Mechanics and we don't play no fucking slow songs!'"

Ness and Danell weren't the only ones influenced by the Mechanics.

When the Agnews moved to Fullerton in 1976, their next-door neighbor happened to be Hoogland. At the time, Hoogland played in Wink, which played David Bowie and Alice Cooper covers, and the impressionable Agnew boys served as the band's roadies.

According to Rikk, Hoogland's presence as a front man was a sight to be seen.

"He had these balloon pants, didn't wear a shirt, and had a brown leather jacket and clap platform shoes," Rikk recalls.

One Wink performance, which took place at a house party with Hoogland at the center, stood out to Rikk.

"I remember maybe they did 'Train Kept A-Rollin',' it was epic," he says. "And they start playing it and he took the cord of the bike and started strangling himself. Then suddenly, he's just singing. Pulls down his fucking balloon pants and stuff and had this huge handful of mayonnaise. These girls were in shock, you know, because they've never seen anything like that. But at the same time, they couldn't take their eyes off him because he was like . . . huge. Most of them had probably never seen a wiener before."

The Mechanics befriended Rikk Agnew around '77–'78, and they hung out and rehearsed at the studio every day. It became a magnet for a lot of the early punkers who hung out late into the night.

"What was fascinating about the Mechanics was that they were the root of the O.C. sound that eventually became the O.C. punk sound. They were more rock, but more raw—and excellent musicians," Frank said.

While Hoogland's theatrics kept the crowd's eyes on him, the band's sound was a powerhouse unlike anything OC produced. The Mechanics melded metal and melodic-based punk a la the Dead Boys, MC5, Iggy Pop's New York Dolls, Johnny Thunders, and a "harder version of the Kinks," all of whom had a major influence on the teens. In fact, in a cruel twist, the members of the band who were friends with Rikk Agnew invited him several times to try out for the band. Each time, it would end up being a cruel joke with him leaving without the role.

At the time they started, the brash four-piece band had few if any contemporaries in Orange County who could match the sound of their energy—a mix of the Stooges, MC5, and the Ramones, albeit a lot less polished and ten times weirder.

Sandy Hancock was a powerfully skillful drummer, and the lead guitarist, Dennis Catron, was a great guitar player—not flashy but very tasteful. Tim Racca was the lead songwriter. "He was the first guy any of us heard that did melodic octaves over chords—we snaked that, we adopted it and adapted it to our own thing," Frank said. Rikk Agnew was fascinated with Tim Racca's ability to come up with songs that had melodic octaves. "The Adolescents were much more punk and so we kinda got that technique and adapted it to our own stuff and it really worked. So Racca's playing was a huge influence on the original OC sound. Then other bands started incorporating it like Social Distortion and Agent Orange."

During their four years, the Mechanics released only one single titled "No Brakes" in 1980, but their influence extended far beyond that.

To many in OC, the Mechanics were the godfathers of Fullerton punk. The Mechanics fused two bands: the L.A. Brats and Head Over Heels. Though the group was short-lived (they broke up in 1981 a few months after a tumultuous gig in Long Beach where Racca left the stage after five songs), they made an indelible mark on Southern

California. Their distinct sound gave them balance and variety and enabled them to share bills with artists such as LA punks Fear and the Runaways. Plus, they liked to play *loud*.

Onstage, the Mechanics leaned heavily into their moniker. The group wore grease-stained gas station attendants' outfits and decked out stages with oil cans and brake drums.

"I remember Dennis [Catron] doing a slide solo using a big wrench," Agent Orange's Mike Palm said to the *Los Angeles Times*. "Tim Racca had such great attention to tone and played jackhammer rhythms. They were like a cross between AC/DC and Generation X, with a little Iggy Pop thrown in."

The band's biggest contribution to the OC sound was introducing the harmonized octave guitar sound. In just a few years, that sound, originated by Racca, would appear on genre-defining albums by the band's younger admirers.

"If it wasn't for these guys," Racca told the *Los Angeles Times* in 1996, "nobody would know what I did."

Rikk Agnew agreed. The guitarist, who was nicknamed "General Hospital" by the Mechanics, learned how to fuse the style he cultivated at home with punk thanks to Racca.

"They [the Mechanics] would come out at a fucking kegger party in Yorba Linda, full of rich, privileged white kids," Ness says. "We would be fucking poking around and then getting in a fight with some jocks and the party would get broken up. It was epic because they [the Mechanics] were coalescing with what I was listening to."

In fact, before forming Social Distortion, Ness served as one of the Mechanics' roadies along with future Adolescents members John O'Donovan and Steve Soto, who would break him out of his house at night so he could practice. During a night out that culminated at a Denny's, Ness got into a fight that summed up the mayhem of those early years.

"Mike got his ass kicked that fucking night," Bill Evans of Naughty Women said. "And he got taken by the cops. But, the thing about Mike—he had that thing where he was going to make it or die trying."

Like the Mechanics, Naughty Women was one of the first punk bands to emerge from OC. Formed by Fullerton High School pals Bill Evans and Robert Larson (who remained the band's only consistent members), the duo attended early punk shows in Hollywood where they rubbed elbows and traded sweat with bands like the Germs and the Runaways. As for their sound, they were influenced by bands like the New York Dolls and blended metal with punk. Yet they weren't fully accepted by the punk scene. They saw themselves as misfits, which included a young Rikk Agnew, and they weren't fully sold on the punk look. Using the Dolls as an example and inspired by *The Rocky Horror Picture Show*, Naughty Women were theatrical, dressing in glitter-glam—more specifically, makeup and women's clothing in the name of provocation and shock value.

After meeting Darby Crash and Pat Smear of the Germs, the band's first show was opening for the LA legends at the storied Hollywood punk club Masque. After that appearance, which saw them never invited back to the vaunted Hollywood venue, Naughty Women had a hard time finding shows, especially in Orange County. In the late '70s, OC was one of the most conservative regions in the entire country.

"People would set us up to play, but it would be a marine bar," Larson said. "Or here, play at this bar and it would be a biker bar. So we're coming out wearing makeup and in our spandex pants and dresses, and doing all kinds of crazy things and have things like dead animals, ripped apart dolls and pornography. So we had a few episodes where we almost got beat up really bad."

Eventually, they started getting gigs in LA with bands like the Joneses, Vox Pop, and the Mentors. Yet, if they played places where hardcore punkers and skinheads frequented, they were not well received. Homophobia was still rampant in the scene, and they were attacked onstage. They had stuff thrown at them, they were beaten up, and people tried to drive them off the road. In one instance, a crowd saw them and instantly tried to beat the shit out of them. No one was seriously injured, but it summed up those chaotic times.

Another bit of Naughty Women's claim to fame is that Steven McDonald of Redd Kross and Izzy Stradlin, later the rhythm guitarist for Guns N' Roses (who played drums for them), were in the lineup for a brief time.

However, after a 1984 show where members were drunk and strung out, Naughty Women called it quits. They only recorded a few songs, mainly for compilations. Though they weren't as widely influential as the punk forebears, Naughty Women also caught the ears of the same impressionable young punks, most of whom were outcasts.

Oftentimes, non-punks hurled homosexual slurs at them.

"Where I went, they immediately equated punk rock with homosexuality," the Adolescents' Tony Brandenburg said. "With that came a lot of really harsh name-calling. I can't say what they were more afraid of. My sexuality or me being a punk rocker."

One of the few punks in early OC who was openly gay was Robert Omlit. The scrawny, five-foot-nine, queer white boy was a fascinating character. He looked like a mad scientist—his Coke-bottle glasses magnified a crazy-looking pair of bulging eyes underneath a massive forehead and a halo of wiry blond hair. In the late '70s in conservative middle-class Orange County, he stood out in more ways than one—as a punk, as a flamboyant, openly gay man, and as a generally odd-looking person. He rolled with a motley crew of equally odd friends that included a Native American friend who was dubbed "Indian Glen," a biker friend aptly nicknamed "Biker Carl," an extremely obese brother and sister named Mark and Kathy Tobin, and a blind guy named Blind Boy Troy.

Omlit's crew always hung out together in a pack that soon included Rikk Agnew. "All these people were neat, cool, and unique but very odd. Hanging out with Omlit and his friends was like a David Lynch movie, like *Blue Velvet* or something," Frank said. "What tripped me out about Omlit was how he was able to have a group of friends that came from completely different worlds and to this day I can't figure out what they had in common, except that they were all weird." Omlit had his own band, aptly named the Omlits, and was roommates with Ness at the infamous Fullerton apartment that would become known as the Black Hole.

In fact, as Evans recalled, the band loved messing with Rikk Agnew—sometimes in a mean-spirited way, other times in a violent fashion.

"Omlit cut Rikk's arm," he said. "We were drinking beer in a van and Omlit had a box cutter and used to tape it to his hands and he scared the shit out of people. He took it and was cutting himself, which is what he used to do, and then Rikk goes, 'Robert, hurt me.' So he grabbed Rikk's arm and held it onto his leg and cut him to the bone. The blood just started pouring out like that. Rikk still can't feel the arm because it went through his whole hand and took the whole index finger off."

"Rikk thought he was going to give him a little slice, not fully stabbed," Frank Agnew said. Omlit ultimately lived a short life, dying in 1991 at age thirty-three. His death was ruled a suicide after ingesting a lethal combination of pills and alcohol, according to *OC Weekly*.

Despite their influence and almost zero recorded music, the band had over forty-five songs in their arsenal, which allowed them to perform vastly different sets at their shows. Yet collectively, their influence on Orange County punk remains steadfast.

Hoogland continues to toil around in Orange County, playing in bands like Poop while Racca also floats in and out of bands. But one thing remains certain: without the Mechanics, the Orange Curtain may have been torn down at some point, but how things shook out would have been vastly different.

A DIFFERENT KIND OF BLUE

fter seeing the Mechanics for the first time, Rikk Agnew
wanted to be in a band and was invited to join his friends
Gordon Cox, Jeff Beahn, and Mike Koerber to form the
Detours in 1978. Cox was an unlikely candidate to be the leader of
a punk band. As Agnew recalls, Cox had long hair, was a jock, and
was even the homecoming king and class valedictorian at Troy High
School.

At first Agnew played drums, but during one jam session when
the guys swapped instruments, Agnew's guitar prowess blew his bandmates away.

"When we heard that, the bass player and I both looked over at
each other and went, 'Oh, my God, we're gonna need a new drummer
now! Rikk's gotta play lead!'" Cox said.

The band practiced at a makeshift warehouse called the Chicken
Coop (a dirty barn-looking shack, so it wasn't just a clever name) on
La Jolla Street near Placentia Avenue. It's where the Detours held their

sweaty practices. The place was owned by a local hillbilly type who was half-deaf and owned the land and rented out spaces on the lot, including the shack where these punk bands held their practices. It was a wood-paneled hut with a metal corrugated roof, one light bulb, and one outlet that accommodated an extension cord where the band members plugged in their amps. The rent was forty bucks—dirt cheap for a bunch of punks who used the Coop for all it was worth.

In late 1977, Cox and Agnew took a "borrowed" car to LA and had their first experience in the big-city punk scene. In the time they'd spend there in the coming months, the pair would hang with the Weirdos, the Bags, and the Controllers and become friends with Brendan Mullen, who owned the Masque. As visits to the club became more frequent, the duo would return to Orange County with stories of what they'd experienced. It would also serve as the impetus for them to write their own songs that detailed life behind the Orange Curtain.

In the spring of 1979, the Detours got their first break.

Rodney Bingenheimer, who previously managed a Los Angeles nightclub called Rodney Bingenheimer's English Disco, became an influential tastemaker at KROQ in Los Angeles. Beginning in 1976, the Bay Area native had a show called *Rodney on the ROQ* that often featured up-and-coming bands from Southern California. Outside of Bingenheimer's program, Orange County punk had no home on the radio. The list of artists who Bingenheimer played first is iconic. Listeners who were on the cutting edge of culture couldn't get enough of Rodney's show.

Just ask Tony Hawk.

Now a skateboarding legend, when he was barely a teen Hawk entered skating competitions across the Southland. But he knew that the further north he drove from his northern San Diego County home, the more excited he'd be to hear the sounds that emanated from the airwaves.

"Rodney had deep cuts and new bands," Hawk said. "We would listen to his show when we could and then when that first [compilation] album came out, I knew the tracklist from top to bottom. Starting with the Brooke Shields intro, that's what led me into learning about all those bands."

Hawk says his early music heroes from the KROQ airwaves included Fear and X from Los Angeles, as well as Agent Orange, the Adolescents, and Social Distortion.

"It was a doorway into a whole new world."

One of the first acts Bingenheimer played from across the Orange County line was the Detours. On his show, he played the band's three-song seven-inch single.

Rikk Agnew left the Detours to play with Social Distortion in 1978. He played with them for a year before leaving with Royer to join another emerging outfit.

<hr/>

Even with the burgeoning Fullerton scene in the late 1970s, there weren't many overly conspicuous-looking punks in Orange County. The area was still a bastion of conservatism.

If you were a punk, you'd wear subtle items to indicate your musical allegiance. As the region's misfits, the punks were targets of the square community. Some felt compelled to disguise their allegiance to this new brand of music, while others, like Ness, did not.

"If you were riding the bus and some kid hopped on a bus with peg pants, a buzz cut, and a fuckin' thrift store T-shirt, you're gonna go, 'Hey, what's up, man? Any bands going on this weekend?'" Ness said. Sensing style was a safety net for punks. "There was definitely a need to unify, especially because it was very dangerous." Punks would be picked on, beaten up, and jumped.

Despite the potential for physical harm, Ness and Rikk Agnew fully embraced that look and style. In fact, before there was even a look, the two were all in on the punk aesthetic.

"Rikk kinda pulled the whole scene together, he never really gets credit for that," Frank Agnew said.

Steve Soto remembered how Agnew would show up at his doorstep one day dressed like a proto-punk in a leather jacket and mascara, and another time, he looked like he popped out of Aladdin's lamp.

"That's how great punk rock used to be back then: There was no uniform; it was just weird," Soto said in 2014. "He was just always a character."

"With the exception of the occasional dog collar, the punk look wasn't uniformed yet in Southern California, not even for Mike," Corvin said in 2004. "He wore a leather jacket and dyed streaks in his hair once, but there wasn't really a look yet, so there was no shit-giving. We just wore what we felt like wearing."

"Fullerton was a very repressed, Republican majority in general," former Social Distortion drummer Derek O'Brien said. "Outsiders who did not fit the perfect image of the status quo had a rough time and were judged harshly. The jocks ruled the schools and if you could not afford the cool cars, did not dress to their code, or fit in to some obvious clique or category, not only did you not get the chicks—you were likely to get your ass kicked and had to watch your back!"

"Everybody hated punk rockers at that time," Ness continued. "The cholos hated us. The bikers hated us. The fucking construction workers and the jocks hated us. It was fucked."

"When I would be targeted, I would be by myself, almost always," Tony Brandenburg said of being a punk. "Even if I was with my friends, there was always the possibility that a car would pull over and attack us."

It was the same in LA.

"You were getting harassed on the streets," Youth Brigade's Shawn Stern said. "So when you would meet another punk or see another punk, they instantly became your friend."

It wasn't just locals. Across the country, organizations like Parents of Punkers (founded by therapist Serena Dank) would implore parents to protect their children from the music.

"When I walked in [to the bar] I was in a fairly good mood," Dank said of punk on *Donahue*. "When I walked out, I was so angry. What happened was it was just body to body and while I was just standing there, I was just innocently looking around, and I got beer shot in my face and obscenities."

On another show, Dank would say that "the message of punk, a lot of it, is there's no future."

Those sentiments were common, especially in conservative Orange County. By the '80s, President Ronald Reagan would call the region "where the good Republicans go to die," making it harder for punks to exist outwardly and peacefully. It made life difficult for Ness and his punk cohorts, even though many of them, like Soto, would go dressed like they were going to school instead of a punk show.

"The Orange County punk scene from my perspective was the rejects from the suburban monolith. It was very white, but there was also a lot of color," Frank Agnew said.

At the time, many of the punkers attended either Fullerton or Troy High School. That meant that at any of these schools, members of the Adolescents, Agent Orange, Social Distortion, the Mechanics, and Berlin were sitting next to you in history class. It allowed for the bands to have synergy and cross-pollinate in the sense that everyone was playing in bands with everyone. If someone was unable to attend a show, they'd know someone who could substitute in an instant. For example, when Danell had a broken arm and couldn't perform, T.S.O.L.'s Ron Emory came to the rescue.

After playing several more house parties that saw the band performing covers, this incarnation of Social Distortion, which also featured Mark Garrett on bass, dissolved. Corvin left the band in 1979 to attend graduate school at Bob Jones University (he'd later become an on-air television reporter). Before the singer's departure, Corvin, Royer, and Ness wrote an instantly catchy song with lyrics about an amoeba.

✖✖✖✖✖✖✖

Dennis Danell's brother, Gunnar, worked the lights at the Starwood Auditorium in Los Angeles on Tuesday nights. The venue was where bands like Fear, the Blasters, and the Germs would play. Punk bands from an already white-hot Hollywood punk scene—acts like the Gears and X—stormed the stage on a nightly basis, looking like ne'er-do-well spawns of Gene Vincent, '50s greasers with eyeliner and attitude. Others looked like UK facsimiles of Adam Ant. Ness remembers one such snotty, new romantic–looking teen looking down on his crew from OC and talking shit. "He said something to me about, 'you fucking punks from Orange County, you don't know shit,'" Ness recalls. "I just told him I'd stick a Les Paul up his ass."

So how did Fullerton become the bedrock of OC punk? When you lay it out on a map of the city connecting the dots between cross streets and clustered points of punk interest, it all makes sense.

What streets like Beach Boulevard, Warner, and Ellis were to Huntington Beach, the streets of Chapman, Commonwealth, and Orangethorpe were to the cradle of blue-collar civilization that provided the geographical template for the punk scene to take hold in Fullerton in the late '70s and early '80s. When Ness turned seventeen, he moved into a one-bedroom apartment in his hometown across from Ladera

Vista Junior High School, which became ground zero for the punks in the area. Behind a rusted white painted gate on 1801 Wilshire Avenue, the rat's nest of debauchery in apartment two on the ground floor was known as the Black Hole—the place where Ness along with his band-mates, friends, and fellow degenerates ran wild, burned through drugs, and congregated before and after shows.

A few blocks down, less than a two-minute walk away, was Dennis Danell's family home. Danell's parents had spent the money to build an accessory dwelling unit on top of the garage, which served as Social D's first rehearsal space. North of Chapman Avenue, near Coyote Hills Golf Course, lived Casey Royer with his family. He grew up a few blocks away from drummer Scott Miller of Agent Orange. Nearby Troy High School was known as the punk rock high school in north OC where most of the main players in the Fullerton scene either attended or were kicked out of. It also provided a meeting ground for Ness and Danell in between cutting class and smoking weed behind the bleach-ers. To the east, across the 91 freeway, a young Steve Soto lived with his family in a neighborhood bordering Placentia and Fullerton.

The Fullerton bands, including the Mechanics, Social Distortion, Agent Orange, the Naughty Women, and the Omlits, among others, all became friends. Whether it was in Hollywood, at the Cuckoo's Nest, or in someone's backyard, the punkers hung out together, build-ing community and tribe.

Eventually, Ness and Danell became friends with other bands like the Middle Class and Eddie and the Subtitles. Born Eddie Joseph in 1949, the Eddie and the Subtitles front man was a little bit older than the rest of the original Orange County punks, just like the members of the Mechanics and the Middle Class. He was born in Reno and moved to California, eventually landing in Fullerton since his brother was a professor at Cal State Fullerton. Before that, he lived in the South

Bay and had been in a few bands (his first time recording was in 1974) before settling with the Rockets. At the behest of his friend John Blair, who said there were fifty bands called the Rockets, Joseph changed the band's name to Eddie and the Subtitles.

As an early OC punker, Joseph met Ness, Danell, and a young Anthony Brandenburg before they were in bands, serving as a big brother figure. "They were really nice people, and I could tell that they were just itching to play music," Joseph said.

"He [Joseph] was a well-seasoned punk rocker by 1978–'79," said Greg Antista, lifelong friend and fellow punk who went on to play with Soto in the band Joyride and other projects.

"[Those guys] were the first link I had to the Orange County punk rock scene," Tony Brandenburg said. "I always looked at him as a leadership person. At first, I was a fan of Eddie and the Subtitles, then he'd go on to manage my band."

After hearing Bingenheimer play bands like the Sex Pistols and the Clash, which reminded him of the bands he liked, Joseph decided that his band would go punk. On top of that, Joseph's main influences came from '60s psychedelic/garage rock bands like the 13th Floor Elevators and the Electric Prunes.

Since there weren't punk rock–friendly venues in Fullerton, Eddie and the Subtitles would head up to Club 88 in Santa Monica. Soon, they'd play shows there with LA punks X, the Alley Cats, and the Plugz. They'd move on to places like the Hong Kong Café, where they'd open up for the Bags and the Go-Go's, and they eventually headlined a bill that also featured the Germs.

Early on, Eddie and the Subtitles were one of the first OC bands to be recognized outside of the region. In a *Los Angeles Times* article titled "New Violence in the New Wave," Eddie and the Subtitles, along with X, were the only two bands mentioned in a piece that pointed at punk bands for causing violence at shows. Specifically, the booker at the Hong Kong Café told the *Times* that they didn't book bands like Eddie and the Subtitles because they were too much trouble.

After they were booted from the Hong Kong Café, Joseph started putting together Orange County punk shows at the Starwood.

"They went over well," Joseph said. "They [the shows] got popular really fast. It was pretty funny, because I remember the guy who booked the place, David Forest, came up to me and said, 'Who is this T.S.O.L.? What does that stand for? What kind of a band is it? Is there going to be anybody here?' I booked T.S.O.L. and Social Distortion. And of course, it was completely packed. And he came up to me afterwards. And he said, 'I will never ever question your ability to put a show together.'"

In addition to his work as a booker and front man, Joseph served as an early manager to those bands and the Middle Class.

He would have parties at his apartment in Fullerton, which was between the 91 and 57 freeways. Chaz Ramirez, who owned and operated Casbah Studios (which would later be the place where a number of seminal OC punk albums were recorded) in an industrial park off Commonwealth Avenue, played bass in the band. Having this space gave Eddie and the Subtitles the ability to record one of the first OC punk singles, "Fuck You, Eddie," which was self-released as a seven-inch vinyl in 1980. Living close by, Joseph was a frequent visitor to the studio.

An amusing moment came when the band's name was mentioned in a fictional ad in a kung-fu movie. It wasn't just a coincidence. The person who created the sound clip, Jon St. James, worked at KROQ. After that, the band purchased two ad spots to air during Bingenheimer's show, and it went over so well that it was played during the day. By the time the band played the Starwood next, some people were calling the box office wondering if Eddie and the Subtitles were Eddie Van Halen's solo project.

After Eddie and the Subtitles recorded *Dead Drunks Don't Dance* in 1983, Joseph left Orange County and returned to Reno because as he saw it, "the punk scene died out" due to overzealous cops. He left music behind to work at casinos.

Eventually, in the late 2010s, Joseph emerged with a new version of the Subtitles after rereleasing those early albums. Though he rarely plays in Southern California (his most recent show was in 2023 at Alex's Bar in Long Beach), Eddie and the Subtitles have found a home in Reno, where they continue to perform.

⬛⬛⬛⬛

As Social Distortion coalesced into a formative band, Ness invited Danell to join the band despite knowing he couldn't play any instrument. That led to Rikk Agnew and Royer leaving.

"I said, 'Have you ever been in a band? I'll teach you how to play guitar,'" Ness said he told Danell.

After they left, Social Distortion was revamped as a three-piece with Ness, Danell on bass, and John Stevenson, a.k.a. John Carrot (because he was a redhead), from Garden Grove on drums.

Their reason for leaving was simple.

"Rikk and I played well and were ready to play gigs, so we joined the Adolescents when Tony Adolescent asked," Royer said.

"They were just a cool, great band," Joseph said of that early incarnation.

"The reason why Rikk and Casey were even entertaining the idea of playing with us was because we had surpassed the Detours in such a short amount of time getting club shows in LA," Frank Agnew said. Within months of performing, the band was playing shows at clubs like the Fleetwood, booked by Joseph. Sure enough, with the addition of their two new members, the Adolescents became a bona fide powerhouse. "We became what I wanted, got as good as the Weirdos," Frank Agnew said. "And Rikk's songs took us to a whole different level."

Ness would find himself in and out of trouble. In 1980, he was at a party and was arrested for spitting on a cop who tried to break it up.

"I let this guy into this party, and he ended up busting us and I was like, 'You fucker!'" Ness said. "So I spit on him, got arrested, and went to jail. I think I was still seventeen, so my mom was going to come down and get me, and the party was at my house so arresting me didn't really do anything.

"I remember getting released from juvenile hall one time and the judge said something and I said, 'Yeah, well you're going to die before I do,'" he continued. "It's like, 'Wow, where does that come from?' Just another day."

✖✖✖✖✖✖

After Royer left Social Distortion, he and Rikk Agnew would join Anthony Brandenburg and Steve Soto to form the Adolescents. The band started in 1979 after the sixteen-year-olds met at an Agent Orange show where they learned they had a lot in common besides their music tastes. Brandenburg and Soto were made fun of for their weight issues (Soto for being overweight, Brandenburg for being underweight and four foot seven) and were constantly ridiculed in high school for their punk rock allegiance.

"He [Soto] was touchy about it because it was a problem," Frank Agnew said. "His parents weren't necessarily big and I think he had a classic eating disorder and he struggled with it his whole life and that's eventually what killed him. His ticker went out because it was being overworked for so long."

Before forming the Adolescents with Brandenburg, Soto played in Agent Orange. Born in Riverside before moving with his parents and two siblings to Placentia, Soto first picked up the bass in the late '70s, his first concert being the Clash at the Palladium. Soto's father, Jim, grabbed the instrument from the lost and found at his city job where it had been sitting for a year. As a Beatles and Paul McCartney fan, the young Soto was thrilled.

Not long after, Soto and his pals Mike Palm and one of his childhood friends started a band called Lyte, which eventually became Agent Orange in 1979. The band's break came a year later when "Bloodstains," a song that clocked in at less than two minutes but was filled with punk fury combined with surf rock, was featured on Rodney Bingenheimer's now-legendary 1980 compilation album, *Rodney on the ROQ*. The compilation, which was released on Posh Boy Records, featured the rising tide of punk bands growing in prominence across the Southland.

The growing success didn't help the band's lineup. Soto asked Palm to incorporate his songs into the set. When Palm refused, Soto left in 1980. "Steve had songs he was bringing to Agent Orange," Brandenburg said. "But Mike was passing off the songs for his own songs. Or at least this is how Steve interpreted it and how he explained it to me at that time."

"Bloodstains" showcased the best of what Palm and Agent Orange offered. In under two minutes, the song's urgency—expressed through a crunchy metal-like riff, pounding surf pattern, menacing Arabian-sounding solo, and Palm's raw lyrics about his life—pushed OC punk forward. The band was the first to fuse surf rock with punk, which added a new element to the genre as it became popular on the West Coast. It became the band's signature song and would later be the subject of a dispute with another Orange County outfit. However, it was and remains an influential moment in merging those two elements, along with being one of the forebears of a movement that emerged in the early '80s: skate punk. This was confirmed years later when the song was included on the soundtrack for the highly influential *Tony Hawk's Pro Skater 4* video game.

In 1981, the band released their debut album, *Living in Darkness*, which was released through Posh Boy Records and was produced by Brian Elliot. When Soto left, the bassist was replaced by James Levesque, and his grooves are present throughout the album. The eight-song *Living in Darkness*, which Palm mostly wrote, featured "Bloodstains" along with three covers: "Pipeline" by the Chantays, "Miserlou" by Dick Dale, and "Mr. Moto" by the Bel-Airs. In 2015, the *Phoenix New Times* ranked the album one of the top ten skate punk albums of all time.

"Chock-full of goodness, *Living in Darkness* contains one classic song after another," Tom Reardon wrote. "There truly is not a bad song on the album."

A year later, they'd release an EP, *Bitchin' Summer*, also through Posh Boy.

That label, founded by Robbie Fields, was the subject of praise and scorn. Over the years, Fields was praised for his ear and for finding and releasing albums by local talent. But in 1979, Posh Boy released a compilation associated with Southern California punk, even though most of the bands weren't from OC. Known as *Beach Blvd*, the compilation is widely considered the record that showcased the hardcore punk movement that was emerging at the time. The songs featured on *Beach Blvd* were recorded and mixed between November 1978 and July 1979 at Media Art Studio in Hermosa Beach. With Fields at the helm, the album featured all original songs except for three. The compilation was divided into several distinctive parts, but they all showcased the emerging hardcore sound. Representing OC, more specifically Huntington Beach, was the Crowd (they mixed surf and hardcore). West Covina's Rik L. Rik, Rosemead's the Simpletones (considered melodic punk), and Negative Trend from San Francisco were also featured. Sped up and more anarchic than their punk predecessors, *Beach Blvd* gave rise to a new variant of punk that the Middle Class pioneered only a few years before.

The compilation was played on *Rodney on the ROQ*, and though the album presented a snapshot of what was coming out of Orange County and suburban punk at the time, it didn't quite paint the full picture.

Fields had a knack for discovering scenes and talent. Compared to other punk labels, he was more likely to give artists their first crack at recording and, in some regard, a taste of the harsh realities of the music business.

A polarizing figure, Fields was accused by the bands of never paying them and acquiring their publishing rights.

"Robbie was a piece of shit," said Michael "Cheez Boy" Brown, who was signed to the label as a solo artist in the early '80s. "And a liar and a thief. But he influenced those other labels to do stuff. Nobody was going to put out my record. Without Robbie, nothing would have happened."

In addition to releasing Agent Orange's early material and taking the band's publishing rights, Posh Boy is known for putting out T.S.O.L.'s seminal first EP.

"I can't speak for the T.S.O.L. guys, but he never paid me a cent," Cheez Boy said. "I'm very thankful for him. At the same time, if he came to my house for dinner, I would make sure I counted the silverware before he left."

After Posh Boy emerged, Lisa Fancher founded Frontier Records in 1980. Located in the Sun Valley section of Los Angeles, Fancher's label released some of the seminal punk albums that weren't from big cities. The label's first two releases were Flyboys' self-titled album in March 1980 and Circle Jerks' *Group Sex*, which featured fourteen songs in just fifteen minutes and is considered a high point in the hardcore move-ment. Frontier's next two releases, which were from Orange County bands, would put it on the map as one of the most important labels for punk bands in Southern California.

⋙⋘

Even as Agent Orange grew in prominence locally, that didn't deter their former bassist. Soto found a kindred spirit in Tony Brandenburg.

Soto cofounded Agent Orange, but he left the band to start the Adolescents with Brandenburg. Most of the kids involved in the early bands knew each other from their childhood sports or skateboarding or surfing.

Brandenburg knew Soto as the bassist of Agent Orange, mean-while, and Soto knew Brandenburg as the first guy he'd ever witnessed doing a stage dive. "I'd see him at shows," Soto said in an *OC Weekly* article in 2005. "Really intense." In what must have been a medieval sort of atmosphere, they plotted out what they thought music should be: "Our voice should be heard," Brandenburg said. "We should no longer be squashed like bugs. So we started talking about the possibil-ity to make a little bit of noise."

"Steve was the one person in my life who I never had an argument with," Brandenburg said. "Here's a person who knew me well enough, when to pull back and let me vent. He knew when to anticipate my behavior [in a way] that other people couldn't anticipate and help me get myself in a place where I could write music in the first place. . . . I started as his student, and I became his peer."

Whereas Soto started on a somewhat more traditional route to a band, Brandenburg's was a bit bumpier.

Born in February 24, 1963, Brandenburg had a tumultuous upbring-ing. As a kid, he moved around a lot before settling in Anaheim in the mid-1970s. Police were constantly at his family's house, and being on welfare, they didn't fit in with the rest of the neighborhood.

"There was domestic abuse and just some really crazy shit," Brandenburg said of the discord at home.

After his stepfather left, his mother raised five kids on her own. It was in that environment that Brandenburg drifted toward discovering live music outside of his family, where he first learned about music through the Beatles and the *Yellow Submarine* record his mother gave him. At first, he started playing music with siblings using the family's organ, and they figured out how to make tape loops.

By the time he reached high school, Brandenburg started writing lyrics and trying to rhyme what he wrote by paying attention to syllabication. Growing up as he did, Brandenburg always felt like an outsider, and it was reflected in his lyrics. "There's a lot in that social aspect of those times that created for me that necessity to lash out," he said.

The first time Soto and Brandenburg spoke was during a blackout by candlelight at a Mexican restaurant in Santa Ana called the Renaissance Café, waiting for somebody to pop up and reset a circuit breaker so the bands could go back on. Brandenburg was an undersized baby bird of a kid with dyed hair and ripped jeans growing up on welfare in Anaheim, and Soto was a heavyset, outgoing nice guy whose dad coached his Little League team in Fullerton. They had opposite looks and opposite lives; they could have sailed right past each other, but it was the end of 1979, and they were both tired of the Eagles on the radio.

Before Brandenburg and Soto started playing, the pair knew they needed a band name. Brandenburg suggested the Adolescents because "that was the beginning of a friendship."

"We would sit there and we would talk," Brandenburg said of him and Soto. "We started talking about starting a band. And we started writing songs from our bedrooms. He would put the bass up against the wall and hold the telephone to it. Then I would listen and write lyrics. And that's how 'I Hate Children' was written."

The song was inspired by an incident Brandenburg saw while riding the bus on the way to El Dorado High School in Placentia, which, at Soto's behest, he attended as he took a regional class for at-risk students who were on the verge of dropping out.

"I saw a man and woman, a young couple with a child who was screaming," Brandenburg said. "The man kind of harrumphed and said, 'You know, I hate children!' We started coming up with lines and just laughing. We actually thought it was a really funny song."

Once Soto and Brandenburg joined forces, their vision of what they wanted their new band to be took shape.

"No one was doing that and the only reason we did that is that we were trying to be middle-class punk, but half the band also wanted to be Black Sabbath," Brandenburg told the *Los Angeles Times* in 2007. "Through the years, it seemed to really echo with people."

First, Rikk (who Brandenburg first met when he was drumming for the Slashers) joined the band as the drummer, replacing Greg Williams. That wasn't for long. "He was too fucking good of a drummer to be able to play without beating the shit out of things," Brandenburg said. So he switched over to guitar.

After Rikk switched instruments, replacing John O'Donovan on guitar, Royer took over on drums. Between the new members (who were slightly older), Brandenburg, Rikk's brother Frank, and Soto, there was instant magic.

"With the addition of Rikk and Casey, we'd moved to the next level," Frank Agnew said. "They were older and more experienced, so we improved quickly."

To their bandmates, the melodic interplay between the Agnews evoked Beatles-esque qualities.

Add that to a fiery live show, and the Adolescents were quickly gaining a reputation as *the* punk band in the area. That reputation would spread quickly to the point that they and Agent Orange were known as two of the best live bands in the Southern California punk scene.

Brandenburg quickly gained notoriety as much for his erratic behavior and lack of social graces as his wiry build and unhinged, borderline psychotic stage presence.

"Agent Orange used to blow us off the stage every time they'd play with us," Descendents drummer Bill Stevenson said on the *Turned Out a Punk* podcast. "And the Adolescents would blow us off the stage every time *they'd* play with us."

In the fall of 1980, the nascent group had a breakthrough. Soto, Frank Agnew, and Agent Orange drummer Scott Miller were sitting at Rikk Agnew's apartment. Rikk played them a song he came up with, a lengthy melodic journey that was unheard in punk at the time. Aptly titled "Kids of the Black Hole," it was a game changer.

"I remember Soto saying, 'This is it; this is the song that's gonna put us above every other band,'" Frank said. "At the time, no one had heard a smartly crafted punk tune with layered guitar melodies and seedy, poetic lyrics of suburban angst and a catchy chorus—or a song that lasted a whole five and a half minutes. It felt like the punk equivalent of the Who's 'Quadrophenia.'"

The final version would make it onto the Adolescents' self-titled debut album known as the Blue Album. The band's frenetic energy was on full display through the recorded version. But before they recorded the song in 1981, hearing Rikk play the song inspired the three Adolescents members.

For now, though, they celebrated. Rikk went into his bedroom with his girlfriend. Meanwhile, back in the main area, Miller boasted how Agent Orange was on the brink of something big due to the opportunities thrown their way. His bragging needled his former bandmate, who wasn't psyched to hear of their success.

In response, Soto unloaded on Miller.

"You know what, Miller?" Soto said. "I gotta tell you something: Fuck Agent Orange! Let's compare Adolescents to Agent Orange. No. 1, you're a shitty drummer, Casey [Royer] is way better than you. No. 2, I'm a 10 times better bassist than [James] Levesque—you kicked me out for that fucker?! And let's go to guitar: the Agnew brothers against Mike Palm? Ha! And singers? Palm's boring, Tony [Reflex] is exciting. And we got better songs!"

Sitting with the two, Frank was happily a bystander to the argument.

As the spat wound down, Soto declared that he was leaving to take a piss, to which Miller responded, leaping up from the couch to get in Soto's face.

"Steve . . . you play HOKEY bass!" Miller declared, hoping that the insult would land.

In response, Soto said, "I play hokey bass!"

And thus, a nickname was born. To many in punk, Soto was known as Hokey.

In a few years, that would eventually stew up a whiplash blend of hardcore and melody into something punk had never heard.

⬡⬡⬡⬡⬡⬡

When Corvin, Royer, and Agnew left Social Distortion, the "Amoeba" song mutated. Keeping his arrangement, Ness rewrote the song's lyrics about a person going to war, which turned into "1945," one of the band's first singles that was released through Posh Boy Records.

"Our singer and drummer would write the songs, but the songs didn't mean anything," Ness told *Flipside* in 1980. "They wrote a song about an amoeba, a little fuckin' stupid little cell."

Originally, Royer and Agnew planned on recording the song with the Detours, their post–Social Distortion band, and keeping Corvin's lyrics. The band recorded an early version of "Amoeba" with Gordon Cox on vocals.

Rikk Agnew and Royer's role in the Detours appealed to Brandenburg.

"Part of the reason we respected Casey and Rikk was because of the Detours," he said.

Now with the Adolescents, the group brought "Amoeba," along with a slew of others, to be recorded. In 1980, the Adolescents recorded the song that ended up on that year's edition of Rodney Bingenheimer's *Rodney on the ROQ* compilation. The song was an instant hit.

"At the time we recorded 'Amoeba,' I didn't really appreciate it because I wasn't aware of that history," Frank Agnew said. And with good reason: he had just turned sixteen at the time. Soto was only seventeen, and the new elders of the band, Rikk and Casey, were in their early twenties.

"There's the perfection of those harmonies and that vocal arrangement and there's nothing like that around," Fucked Up singer/*Turned Out a Punk* podcast host Damian Abraham said.

Their raucous live shows turned them into local legends. Royer had the drumming on lock and brought his big personality combined with a snotty gift of gab as he cracked jokes on the mic between songs. Rikk Agnew and Brandenburg were the showmen, the latter resembling a young Iggy Pop with dyed blond hair at first. With Soto and Frank Agnew holding things down and contributing to the tight melodic structure of the songs, the band was peerless in its ability to execute songs that were well-played and able to whip up a mosh pit on demand.

Onstage, the chemistry worked. Offstage, two of the chemicals in the mix were extremely volatile—Rikk and Brandenburg, who got on each other's nerves and didn't see eye to eye. "Tony has a very strong personality and so does Rikk and ultimately they weren't compatible," Frank said.

On top of butting heads constantly, Rikk's behavior became very erratic due to his drug use. Though Royer was using drugs too, it didn't seem to change his temperament. "He was one of the only guys I knew who could shoot heroin and still be hyper," Frank said. "But he was always easygoing. So his drug thing didn't become a problem." Tony was also doing drugs, but for Rikk it escalated his mood swings that made him unpredictable.

"We were playing at the Starwood once around this era and he went up and performed half the set and then he just took off his guitar, threw it and walked off stage." When he was too high to play well, the band's roadie would stealthily turn off his amp. It got to the point where Frank had to learn all his parts and be able to play lead at the drop of a hat. "It actually improved my guitar skills," Frank said.

A year later, the Adolescents headed into Perspective Sound in Sun Valley to record their first proper album for Frontier Records. Lisa Fancher saw the Adolescents perform at a party that ended with police helicopters and saw instantly that there was something there with the band. Armed with an arsenal of material that included "Amoeba," "Kids of the Black Hole," "No Way," and "Creatures," the Adolescents knew they didn't have time on their side. The group had four days to record the entire album, which was engineered by Thom Wilson and produced by Wilson and Middle Class bassist Mike Patton. Up to that point, Wilson had worked with easy-listening acts like Burton Cummings and Seals & Crofts. The Adolescents couldn't be any more different from them. Wilson captured the raw energy of the band doing their best version of their live set, almost down to the exact order they typically played it onstage.

"He was a really cool guy," Brandenburg said of Wilson. "But I was so full of anger and in frustration, I wasn't the best guest in his studio. But he got a great performance out of me."

Despite punk's popularity, the Adolescents didn't abandon their foundation of melodic classic rock music.

"We never sat there and acted like, 'We're punks, and we hate every other kind of music,'" Frank Agnew said. Despite being the poster children for OC punk, Agnew and Soto weren't afraid to express their love for the Beatles, even as they were readying their debut full-length. "It just wasn't like that."

As close as Brandenburg and Soto were in those early years, Soto and Frank Agnew were as thick as thieves. When they weren't rousing audiences at the Cuckoo's Nest or the Starwood in Los Angeles, Soto and Frank were playing at backyard parties. Instead of performing rollicking punk rock, the pair played old songs on acoustic guitar.

"All these fuckin' punkers with mohawks and leather jackets who slashed themselves on the weekends and rolled in broken glass would all stop and listen to the Beatles," their friend Greg Antista said. "Because it was just good music."

"At the time we were at our peak—playing live, no one could beat us, we were that good," Frank said.

Though they weren't quite sure what would happen once they went in, the end result was magic. That includes the shenanigans that went on during that handful of days.

"One of the first things that happened was Tony grabbed the fire extinguisher off the wall and then fired it into Frank's face," Rikk recalled. "Frank was never quite the same after that."

"Wilson got mad at me, justifiably," Brandenburg said. "That pissed me off, like how dare you get mad at me? That wasn't the right response. How dare you get angry with me for making a total mess out of the studio? So there was that anger and frustration and that desire on my part to break things and to make things not nice."

Wilson worked well with Frank and Rikk and was a lot more involved in the guitar portion of the tracking.

Even as they had their issues, once it was time to lay down the tracks, the band was good to go.

"Everybody knew the songs like the backs of their hands," Brandenburg said. "So when we went in, it was not hard at all to lay that down. It was very exciting." It wasn't lost on Brandenburg that they wanted to reward the faith Fancher and Frontier Records had in them. "To go in and have somebody else believe in something that I was doing enough to invest money was exciting to me," the singer said.

The studio also had a soda machine that featured standard drinks like Pepsi, 7-Up, root beer, and grape soda. The Adolescents weren't interested in those. Instead, they decided to select the button with the question mark on it.

"The fucking curious cat in me just couldn't resist," Rikk said. "Because it was only a quarter I had to see. And guess what? It ended up being a beer!"

Once they realized the machine's secret, the band pumped quarters into it and had their fuel for the session.

"One after another we just got real fucking drunk," Rikk said. "And we're still able to play, you know?

"I don't know about the other guys, but for me, I could get so drunk that I can't even remember," he continued. "But if you listen to tracks or you listen to the live tapes or whatever, they were right on the money."

Despite that, the sessions weren't exactly smooth. Rikk and Tony argued over the vocal recording. By the time Rikk got to the studio, Tony had finished recording. Rikk was unhappy since he thought that Tony rushed his tracks to get them over with so he could go see the Slits that night. Disagreements aside, they both agree that in the end, everything worked out how it should have sonically.

"To me, it is one of the greatest punk rock songs of all time," Soto said of "Kids of the Black Hole." "And of course 'Amoeba' was catchy as fuck, and everybody wants to hear it."

"It was his crowning achievement," Brandenburg said of "Kids of the Black Hole." "Some might say it is Christian Death but I saw that song as people being born. So I knew what went into it. And I think Rikk really, really knocked it out of the park."

Just like "Amoeba," the Adolescents could give Mike Ness an assist for "Kids of the Black Hole." The song immortalized Ness's Fullerton apartment (as it was in Social Distortion's "Playpen"), which became the ultimate hangout for punks in Orange County. Appropriately for the young outcasts, the apartment was a graffiti-covered drug den fueled by parties, sex, and violence.

Pointing to Rikk's songwriting, Soto added that he was "adventurous for punk rock. He was writing stuff that was punk but had a Beatles-esque quality with the guitar harmonies." The songs were written primarily in 1980, with the origins of "Rip It Up" going back to Rikk's time in the Detours.

"'Wrecking Crew' and 'Who's Who' are amazing songs, and that's my brother and Steve's genius right there," Rikk said. "The same with 'LA Girl.' I just happened to write what I wrote because of my pop sensibilities."

The Adolescents was released in April 1981. The track listing was in the exact order they performed the songs live. At the time, Brandenburg hoped one hundred people would buy it. He didn't expect that with this album, the Adolescents would change the sound of punk. Led by Rikk's arrangements, the album showcased the best of the Adolescents and channeled the intensity of their live show. Unlike other bands of the time, they harnessed a faster, more aggressive sound that didn't lose its melody. Rikk's doubled guitar tones and inventive chord progressions singlehandedly pushed punk forward. The songs, written by literal adolescents, became the blueprint for hardcore and even post-hardcore. It was an instant classic, and the band was surprised by its reception.

"When the record came out, people came to the shows knowing all the lyrics," Brandenburg said, "which was really exciting to me that people went through the trouble of learning the words of my songs."

As much credit as Rikk received and deserved for his playing and composition, his younger brother wasn't too shabby, either.

"Rikk Agnew is great and gets too much of the attention in my opinion," Bad Religion's Brett Gurewitz said, "because Frank Agnew is a great guitar player and was the greatest guitar player out of that scene. I used to see him live and be blown away."

The Adolescents pushed punk forward and created a definitive Orange County sound to an audience outside of the Southland.

"In Washington, D.C., our first exposure to punk was Circle Jerks and Black Flag," former Minor Threat and current Bad Religion guitarist Brian Baker said. "It was definitely distinctly different from my first cognizant Orange County thing, which was the Blue Album. We knew that was not from the same part of California as the other bands. We knew that sound wasn't from Torrance or Hermosa Beach. For me, they were the first band I clocked as being from Orange County."

"The melody and backing vocals," he continued. "For me, it sounded more like the Damned so therefore, I liked it. I was attracted to the melody of it. It was more melodic and influenced by the bands that I liked. I mean Tony, Soto, the Agnews, it had it all."

"It felt like Adolescents songs were holding up to the other bands around the world who were doing punk," Guns N' Roses bassist Duff McKagan said.

NOFX's Fat Mike agrees.

"The best song to come out of Orange County is 'Kids of the Black Hole,'" he said.

In fact, Rikk's style developed to be so distinct that the octave chord became known as "the Agnew."

In his retrospective review of *The Adolescents* in 2016, Jack Rabid of *All Music* wrote, "The debut from these five Orange County kids established the mid-tempo, punk-pop 'Southern Cal sound' led by the long, great, pummeling, Johnny Thunders–derived solos of the two Agnew brothers, Rikk and Frank. . . . They're super-catchy, heavy-riffing rock & roll, proving again that punk was the true heir to the likes of Chuck Berry, Larry Williams, Bo Diddley, and Eddie Cochran."

The self-titled album quickly became known as the Blue Album due to its now-iconic cover, which featured the band's name written in red type on top of a blue field.

However, the band was splintering. Fights between bandmates increased, as did their collective erratic behavior. Two months later at a show at the Starwood in LA, Rikk abruptly threw his guitar, walked offstage, and showed up late for the show's second set, which the band started without him. The Germs' Pat Smear filled in.

Not long after that show, the Adolescents broke up. Soto and Frank Agnew were tired of driving to Pomona to practice. Brandenburg quit showing up entirely and moved to Glendora after getting kicked out of his mom's house. And Royer and Steve Roberts were more interested in shooting heroin than playing songs. "Me and Soto just decided let's put an end to this," Frank said.

All of this took place a couple of weeks before the band's first US tour. This version of the Adolescents never made it out of California. Rikk rejoined the Detours for a spell until they called it quits in 1982.

"Who knows what that band would have morphed into had we stayed with it," Brandenburg said.

As for Royer, after he left the Adolescents, he started D.I. (Drug Ideology) in 1983. Royer was no longer behind the kit—now in charge of his own band, he was its front man. The first D.I. lineup included the Mechanics' Tim Maag on guitar, Fredric Taccone on bass, and Social Distortion drummer Derek O'Brien. Just like the bands the members were a part of, D.I.'s sound delved into hardcore. But unlike those bands, this one incorporated elements of the rising genre known as new wave and infused surf-driven guitar rock.

In 1983, D.I. released a five-song self-titled EP through Revenge Records. In just thirteen minutes, D.I. helped shape a new path for melodic hardcore. Songs like "Richard Hung Himself" (which Royer composed while in the Adolescents) and "Guns" had origins as far back as the Detours years, with Gordon Cox and Rikk Agnew receiving songwriting credit on the latter. Close to home, "Obnoxious" referenced the streets of Fullerton, and "Reagan der Führer" was a sharp rebuke of the Reagan administration, which was growing in prominence in Orange County. The songs were dark and had a somber message, but they also incorporated humor.

Rising punk tastemaking magazine *Maximum Rocknroll*, which became known to punks as the *New York Times* of hardcore, approved of the effort.

"D.I. have well-executed, concise songs with interesting but not necessarily innovative arrangements," Ruth Schwartz wrote in her review in September 1983. "There are a lot of obvious influences here—Flipper, Adolescents, Circle Jerks, Misfits—but the witty lyrics and good production make it plenty entertaining."

The one constant in D.I. was its revolving cast of characters. By 1983, Maag was out and guitarist Steve Roberts (who cowrote "Reagan der Führer" with Royer) was in. By late 1983 and early 1984, Rikk and Alfie Agnew were in, Maag was back, and Wade Walston replaced Taccone on bass.

D.I. released their first full-length album, *Ancient Artifacts*, in 1985.

Produced by Thom Wilson, the album was comprised of nine songs that reflected on life behind the Orange Curtain. Songs like "O.C. Life"—penned by Rikk Agnew and previously on his 1982 solo album, *All By Myself*—and "(I Hate) Surfin' in HB" were direct in reflecting the band's disdain for the area at the time.

The solo album was a high-water moment for Agnew. Sometime in 1982, Agnew was trying to figure out what to do with his decent catalog of unrecorded material when he ran into 45 Grave keyboardist Alex Gibson, who told him it was time for him to release his own material. "I didn't know what to do, and [Gibson] was like, 'Rikk, you already play all these instruments. Why don't you just do a whole album by yourself?'"

With the backing of Frontier Records, Agnew drove to Sun Valley's Perspective Sound from Fullerton after work for three straight days to piece together a solo record with Thom Wilson on a $1,500 budget. In just two or three takes apiece, he recorded the guitars, bass, drums, keys, and random sonic flourishes. The end result, aptly titled *All By Myself*, produced a number of great songs that channeled his angst about life in the suburbs and encapsulated the feeling that punks felt. In addition to "O.C. Life," Agnew recorded the angst-ridden anthems "Falling Out" and "Section 8."

At the time, Agnew said he caught a lot of flak for recording on his own and for having the audacity to include the new wave–infused "Everyday." Some even called him a wannabe Paul McCartney and a sellout.

"If I was selling out, I'd have been writing 'Amoeba' every time," Agnew said. "Just because it sounds more accessible or more pop—that's called an artist fulfilling his own needs and progressing and branching out."

Despite the naysayers, Agnew put together a body of work that was perhaps his finest hour as a songwriter. When D.I. recorded "O.C. Life," it showed how versatile and deep Agnew's writing was.

"C'mon, 'O.C. Life'? That's perfect," Fat Mike said.

"D.I. sounded a little like the Adolescents," Gurewitz said. "It makes me think that Casey had something to do with that."

"'O.C. Life' with its bump, bump, bump guitar, it was the sound that was different to me than a lot of other bands," future D.I. guitarist Clinton Calton said. "Rikk and all of the Agnews are savant guitar players."

Once again, the lineup changed with Royer and the Agnews joined by John Bosco on bass and John Knight on drums.

Soon, the *Los Angeles Times* would have several reporters covering the music emerging from Orange County. Mike Boehm and Randy Lewis had a bird's-eye view of what was going on south of the Los Angeles County line. They saw the changes in punk that were taking place, and Boehm's take on the Blue Album reflected that.

Calling the record an "underground classic," Boehm wrote in 1998 that the album's thirteen songs "defined the O.C. punk experience, back when punk was a beleaguered subculture." Pointing specifically to "Amoeba" and "Kids of the Black Hole," Boehm wrote that the "two songs introduced a massed, harmonized 'octave guitar' blitz—an Orange County rock signature."

The album's legacy lives on. "Amoeba" was covered by Blink-182's Mark Hoppus and Travis Barker for the *Endless Bummer* soundtrack and featured in video games years later like *Tony Hawk's Pro Skater 3*, *Grand Theft Auto V*, and *Call of Duty: Black Ops Cold War*.

Other songs from the album have been covered by the likes of NOFX, the Dropkick Murphys, Pulley, and the Briefs.

Despite the Adolescents' rapid ascension and demise, there was no doubt that a punk scene in Fullerton was emerging away from the genre's hubs of London, New York, and Los Angeles.

6

ANOTHER STATE OF MIND

ocial Distortion's first show that wasn't a house party took place at the Cuckoo's Nest in Costa Mesa. The venue was the only punk-friendly place to play in Orange County. However, it often attracted a tough crowd. So much so that Ness had a chunk of his ear bitten off during an altercation. Fighting became the norm for Ness. Before a show in San Diego, Ness punched out a bouncer and subsequently battled the rest of the security crew before police arrived and arrested him.

Soon Social Distortion was featured in underground fanzines, which introduced the band to a new audience.

"If you put out a 45, it's going to be advertised in the magazine," Ness says. "So the kid in Greenville, South Carolina, if he's hip to that magazine he's going to see your band and maybe buy the 45. It was so grassroots, and so underground."

Social Distortion's first 45, *Mainliner/Playpen*, was released in 1981 through Posh Boy. "I remember Dennis had the checks going to his house," Ness says. "So I'd be there when he'd get the mail and we'd say 'OK we got plenty of beer money for tonight.'" As the band started to see its popularity grow, Ness's drinking began to spiral.

Not only did Ness with his small, wiry physique have the gumption to take on big-city punks (or just about anyone after he had a few drinks in him), but onstage his band flung themselves at the crowd with an equal amount of abandon. Rocking a stiffly starched, spiky hairdo with pimple-ridden skin, a sweat- and blood-stained white T-shirt, and a dangly skull earring, Ness led the charge backed by Danell's brooding guitar strumming, a pissed-off Mark Garrett, and hyperactive Casey Royer pounding away on the drums. The quartet bashed out early renditions of "Mainliner" and "Mommy's Little Monster" into the tinderbox of wild, reckless energy found in LA clubs like Club 88 and Madame Wong's.

In 1982, Social Distortion's first firm lineup took shape. Consisting of Ness, Danell, bassist Brent Liles, and drummer Derek O'Brien, the group's hardcore sound developed. Upon the release of "1945," the band quickly started to gain a following.

"I had seen Social Distortion at Fullerton High School when they opened for a local band called La Morte who had all this crazy equipment and a light show at a high school dance/party," O'Brien says. "Social Distortion was a three-piece band then. Their backdrop was a white bedsheet with their logo spray-painted on it, and their light show was one green light bulb. I appreciated their rawness, minimalism, and energy they put into the simple, straightforward catchy songs. It was completely different from every band I had heard and seen up to that point."

O'Brien knew Ness and Danell but was uprooted during his senior year, moving to Creswell, Oregon, with his family. He wouldn't be there long. O'Brien moved back to Fullerton on his own three months before graduation and through his cousin, who was friends with Danell, heard Social Distortion was looking for a new drummer. Upon hearing this, he phoned Danell and soon enough, Ness, Danell, and O'Brien were jamming in Danell's living room.

"I walked in with my long, blond hair and probably some hippy-looking shirt carrying my '70s Rogers chopping block finish drums and said, 'Hi, Mike, nice to meet you,'" O'Brien said. "He looked me up and down and just kind of nodded. As soon as I set up, they just started playing the songs and I joined in, learning as I went. I think I even suggested some intro/outro breaks and backup vocal parts here and there. We went through the songs one more time and then Mike said, 'So you want to play some shows?' I said, 'Sure!' He said, 'OK, you'll need a haircut and Dennis here can help you figure out what to wear.' I said, 'Fair enough, you guys think you could keep your guitars in tune?' They both looked at me like, 'Who the hell is this guy?'"

After a rehearsal, O'Brien was thrown right into the fire. The band started gigging immediately, averaging three shows a week.

"Things immediately took off and this was my first experience with an original band so I just figured that is how these things work!" O'Brien said. "I also had to stop smoking weed so I could tell which song was which!"

As was the norm in the early OC scene, Social Distortion's shows were raucous, violent, and sometimes out of control.

"It seemed like the police tried to shut down many of them, but the shows and crowds kept getting bigger quickly," O'Brien said.

It wasn't just Social Distortion—it was all punks.

"Punk rock was really getting hammered by the police," Eddie Joseph said. "Every time we'd book a show, it would get canceled."

In their early years, Social Distortion was managed by Monk Rock. Born Mark Wilson in 1953, Rock became known for telling it like it was within the OC punk scene, earning him the respect of the bands he came in contact with. His antics were also the stuff of legend. He was a wild man with a big heart and an appetite, like many in Fullerton on the scene at the time, for cocaine. He was the band's first champion and would do anything for them. He booked the band's shows, sold the band's records out of the trunk of his 1960s-era Volvo, and made sure the name Social Distortion was on the tongue of every punker on the scene.

"Monk was a good guy," promoter/musician Michael "Cheez Boy" Brown said. "There was not a negative bone in his body. And he did a lot for that band that would set them on a silver platter for what was to come. He was a fun, good dude."

"There will be many Monk stories themed with hilarious escapades, of which I have my share, but the moments that stand out are ones that are in contrast to the craziness of those early days," Gordon Cox of the Detours said. "We often compared notes on the common auto maintenance issues we experienced with our 1960s Volvo 544s. When the Detours began an exceptionally long hiatus, Monk offered encouragement, saying, 'You've got unfinished business there. It'll come back.'"

"If anything was going on in the '80s shows parties, for a lot of us it started and ended at Monk's house," former Social Distortion crew member Roger Ramjet said. "He was always down for anything."

While most people had fond memories of Monk, there were a few who pointed to his wild personality and appetite for using and selling drugs as contributors to his eventual downfall.

Powered by its placement on Bingenheimer's latest *Rodney on the ROQ* compilation, Social Distortion went out on their first proper national tour in 1982. Teaming with Youth Brigade and Washington,

DC's Minor Threat, Social Distortion hopped in a run-down school bus (which was Rock's idea and showcased his skills as a mechanic) that held the bands, four crew members, and two bands' equipment. The tour, which was immortalized in the 1984 documentary *Another State of Mind*, was a glimpse into what life was like in a touring punk band. Needless to say, those early Wild West years weren't great, especially since the band members in their late teens and early twenties were novices to life on the road. "A tragic comedy," Ness joked.

"Punks are misunderstood," Youth Brigade's Shawn Stern said at the beginning of the film. "Most people, when they think of punks, they think of violent freaks rolling around in glass beating each other up. When I think about punk, I think of the power, I think of the energy, I think of the possibility for change, and that's what punk's all about—change. It's about music by kids, for kids, reflecting the frustrations and the problems that kids face every day."

Stern's quote served as the thesis and mission statement for what lay ahead. Throughout the film, the bands and their fans explain how punk culture in 1982 is reflective of who they are.

"Well, it wasn't exactly our idea to document the tour," Stern said of the quixotic journey forty years later. At first, Stern wanted to release a compilation that included Social Distortion in conjunction with their first album and would showcase emerging bands they were fans of. Having been drug dealers before their punk rock adventure, Stern said they were aware of the business of being in a band. They knew the DIY culture and how to properly build a brand. Unlike many of the punks of that time, they understood margins, marketing, networking, record distribution, and the necessities to succeed as a band—including buying a bus.

Then Adam Small, a former high school classmate of Mark and

Shawn Stern, wanted to shoot a documentary of the band. Small was working for a millionaire who gave him access to filming equipment. He proposed following Youth Brigade on tour, promising to take care of his own expenses.

"My main thing that I said to him is I have no problem doing this," Stern explained. "All I want is that when you go to edit, we be involved in the edit." Simple enough. However, nothing is as simple as that. "Of course, it was a problem at the end," he said.

Stern, knowing Social Distortion would be a good fit due to their inclusion on the compilation, asked them if they'd hit the road with Youth Brigade. They accepted.

"If you watch the movie, we explain what we're doing," Stern said. "I don't know how much some of them really understood the words that were coming out of my mouth, like there's not going to be a lot of money but we'll survive."

From the music to the clothing, they acknowledge the outsider nature of their subculture, which at this point during the Reagan era made them an even bigger target and enemy of the normies. Thus, what Social Distortion and Youth Brigade chronicled in *Another State of Mind* showcased the outsider nature of punks at the time.

"They get pissed off because they have to go to work every day, and I can damn well do as I please," a member of the road crew said, referring to normal everyday people. "It's a big part of why everyone dislikes punks so much."

"If I wore [Sperry] Top-Siders and Polo shirts or something like that, I would define myself as the nice middle-class kid ready to take up where my parents left off," a fan named Jim said. "The fact is that I don't look like that, and that means that I'm not willing to do that. My look is a direct reflection of my attitude."

"The reason why I look the way I do is because I don't like the quote-unquote Brooke Shields look," another fan named Roxy said. "I don't like the All-American girl . . . because I'm not."

Road crew member Marlon Whitfield, the only Black member of the tour, succinctly added why the culture was appealing.

"If I dressed normal, like preppy, I could still get pulled over for being Black and being in the wrong neighborhood, which has happened before," he said. "Being a punk . . . walking around with blue hair or something . . . I had some guy say to me 'Isn't it bad enough that you're Black and you have to go and have blue hair?' He was going to duke me so it didn't matter what I did, because if I was Black and normal, I'd still get fucked with, so I might as well do what I want to do and take my chances. It's part of being a Black person in this country to be fucked with, and it is part of being a punk too to be fucked with because people dislike you."

Both bands' battles against shady promoters (who paid bands in rolls of pennies), a bus that wouldn't cooperate, prejudiced restaurant owners who wouldn't serve them, and eventually the beginning of their spirals have been chronicled. In particular, Ness was headed down a dark, destructive path. His Fullerton apartment may have been immortalized in "Kids from the Black Hole," but Ness's black hole threatened to derail Social Distortion. The documentary of the five-week tour saw the band play around thirty-five shows in thirty-one cities, mostly in places where punk bands never played. The band was living on ten dollars a day, which Monk said "is really cheap" and added that "we're all just doing this for the fun of it."

The goal wasn't to become rock stars but instead to break even. Along the way, the group hoped to build cred along with a story or two as they returned to OC as conquering heroes.

Another State of Mind gave a behind-the-curtain look at what made Ness tick. Sitting on the back porch of a crumbling house in Canada,

Ness describes what a typical day in his life was at that time. It includes rising late, eating, watching shows like *Twilight Zone*, *General Hospital*, *Rockford Files*, *The Mary Tyler Moore Show*, and *The Bob Newhart Show*, eating again, and watching more TV before going out to drink with friends and going to a show. Ness's look would vary during these shows. Sometimes he'd wear a torn shirt with a headband, and at a show in Chicago, he'd sport a button-down over a tank-top undershirt and black pants that would come to define both Ness and Social Distortion later in the decade.

One of the documentary's iconic scenes is when Ness is preparing for battle onstage before the first show in San Francisco. Backstage, Ness prepped his signature getup: spiky hair, guyliner smeared down his cheeks, and earrings in each ear. It's a look that he doesn't just use for a show—it's how he prepares to go outside into the world. Simply put, he said, "It's just my look. A lot of people laugh. To me, there's nothing funny about it. To me it's very fashionable, and it's a look I've wanted for a long time.

"Most guys don't know how to wear makeup anyways. Guys naturally think you're gay 'cause you wear eyeliner and mascara and put a little nail polish on. I like it because it has a little sympathetic view towards you onstage and it looks more natural too because it looks as though you've been crying."

Social Distortion's whirlwind live performances—which included attempting a Pete Townshend–esque guitar jump, immediately crashing into O'Brien's cymbal stand, and nearly falling over—encapsulated who they were at that time. The band's raw power and Ness's charisma added to the growing mystique around the band in the punk community, in particular at the Chicago show where he rolled around on the floor, attributing that blast to a "spirit of energy that you get because the energy of the music just builds and builds and you're going balls out."

"It was the best and worst of being in a band at the same time!" O'Brien said. "Everyone was on each other's last nerve most of the time, and Mike was on his path of self-destruction with drugs and fights, which was difficult. At the same time, we were kids traveling across North America in a school bus playing to not only packed houses but to people who were really into it and excited to see us.

"Also, no matter what fucked-up thing had just transpired— someone just got back from jail or beaten up by a gang or jealous boyfriend, someone just went hungry that day because they were broke and traveling the whole day after promoters stiffed us, or waking up in some junkie's puke all over your sleeping bag or whatever, we would hit the stage with confidence and it would be a great show every time!"

O'Brien does have one regret about *Another State of Mind*.

"The film told a bit of a different story from the filmmaker's point of view and sort of from their own agenda," he said. "I found it entertaining, but I think they actually missed the best stories."

He's not the only one who felt that way.

"There's a lot of shit that was shot in that movie . . . a lot of really great stuff," Stern said. "There's stuff at the Dischord House with Minor Threat. There's shots of all kinds of great bands and great, insane moments that they just left out."

To both of their points, that included the chaos that transpired when the tour hit New York City.

"Something was going down and Mike threw like a half-empty 40 oz. beer, and it hit the wrong guy and shattered his knee," O'Brien said. "So all these punks came running after him and then us as we ran out of this club. They all had chain belts, so they pulled chains out of their belts and boots and started smacking him with chains. He's running down the street, and we piled into the video van because our bus was somewhere else. They're jumping up and down, pounding on the windows and the video guys are just shitting themselves. They never dealt with anything like that before. We're driving down the street with punks literally hanging on the video bus and falling off into the street."

The story didn't end there. When the group ended up at the Misfits' dungeon house (which looked like the Haunted Mansion at Disneyland) where they were going to stay in New Jersey, more chaos ensued.

"We stopped at a restaurant and we were a freaked out, rowdy bunch of kids," O'Brien said. "We were sitting at one table and Mike was sitting at a separate table because they had literally beat the shit out of him. He was covered in blood and shit his pants. None of us wanted to sit by him. We're yelling at him and he's yelling at us. We finally got kicked out and the cops threw us in jail. They told us we were going to stay there and they were going to call our parents and were scaring us until the morning. Surreal moments that you can't make up."

After that, they went to the Misfits' dungeon where they stayed up all day, ate hamburgers, and drank beer.

By the tour's fourth week, things were going off the rails (which happens when you pack eleven guys into a school bus that keeps having mechanical issues, forcing the bands to push the bus to get it to move in Washington, DC). One by one, the road crew turned on one another and deserted the bus to find places to stay or skip town back to Southern California.

"It's like we're getting punished for something on this tour," Danell said in the film. "Like we did something wrong before we left and now this is our punishment."

"This tour has brought out the worst in everyone," Liles said in the film. "Plus, Michael is constantly drunk because he's always had money or someone flowing him brews, which is not good because Michael drinks excessively 'til he falls down."

"I can get as drunk as I want and still play," Ness said in a later scene. Justifying his behavior, he said that he'd been playing half of the band's songs for three years.

By the end, Danell, Liles, and O'Brien left Ness behind, saying they could make more money (and have less hassle) in Southern California. As he attempted to soldier on, Ness was dismayed by what he perceived as his band's lack of faith. He openly contemplated bringing in new members while vowing to keep the band's name and songs before performing his completed version of "Another State of Mind." The tour ended before it returned to Southern California, but its legacy propelled Social Distortion, Youth Brigade, and Minor Threat (which made a cameo at the end of the film).

Another State of Mind, much like *The Decline of Western Civilization* before it, pulled back the curtain on punk rock. To the non-punk world, the appearances of the characters in these films may have portended a societal decay. However, go gently below the surface, and it was easy to comprehend that these were just outcasts who were trying to find their way in a world that refused to accept them.

It inspired a generation of admirers who got a first look at what punk could mean and identified with the bands.

"*Another State of Mind* is the reason I got into music," Vagrant Records founder Rich Egan said.

As off the rails (and financially unsuccessful) as the film showed the tour to be, it provided insight into Ness's songwriting process. Sitting alone with an acoustic guitar, Ness would write and come up with lyrics, including for "Another State of Mind," on the steps at a house in Calgary.

It's something that Brian Baker, who was in Minor Threat at the time, said speaks to Ness's prowess as a gifted songwriter.

"Despite what was going on, even if he [Ness] was sitting on the porch by himself writing 'Another State of Mind,' it was still good," he said.

Baker also remembers that tensions between everyone on the bus were so fractured that he was offered a chance to buy Danell's white Gibson SG guitar with the three pickups. In 2024, that guitar has a value of $33,000.

"Even at sixteen, I got the sense that that was not a great move," Baker said. "I remember being like, 'That's the coolest guitar I've ever seen.' I remember thinking, 'I really want this guitar.' And then kind of going, 'I don't think I can, I don't think this is punk.'"

Over forty years later, despite the band's zigs and zags, the way Ness writes remains the same.

"It was quite an interesting thing to be on," Stern said.

In addition to "Another State of Mind," Ness had been working on new songs that, along with the singles released prior to the tour, comprised the band's live set. By 1983, he felt confident enough for the band to head into a studio to record the songs, and that was a good barometer of where the band was. Produced by the band along with Chaz Ramirez at the Casbah in Fullerton, the session was recorded in two days.

"Social Distortion had a very simple formula and it worked really well," O'Brien said.

The result was *Mommy's Little Monster*. Released and financed in June 1983 through the band's 13th Floor Elevator label, the album, with its unabashed sonic aggression and Ness's snarling attitude, is a fiery blend of melody and buzzsaw guitars. Raw, a bit sloppy, and full of attitude, *Mommy's Little Monster*'s hardcore sound encapsulated the Fullerton scene. Ness's storytelling was vastly different from the punk that was emanating at the time.

"Mike's formula for songwriting and lyrics about personal experiences when most punk bands were heavily political, the time period, the group chemistry of that particular lineup, and some 'first album naïveté' with songs like 'Anti-Fashion' created an undeniable aesthetic," O'Brien said.

Over the years, *Mommy's Little Monster* has come to be widely considered a perfect punk album. Though its tempo is steeped in hardcore, the album's melodic nature sets it apart from what was being released at the time.

"That album is a fucking masterpiece," Christopher Reece, then of the Lewd, said.

Tim Yohannan praised it in the September 1983 edition of *Maximum Rocknroll*. "You've got to know by now what Social Distortion sound like—those distinctive vocals, the harmonies, the rockin' guitars, and melodic hooks galore. Their album is filled with more of the same. Nothing here is too frantic except 'The Creeps,' which really blazes forth. There's precious little exciting punky-pop around these days, but this is one of the rare examples of it," he wrote.

In a review of the 2023 reissue, *Under the Radar*'s Matthew Berlyant wrote that *Mommy's Little Monster* is "one of the greatest punk records ever made." Continuing, he said the album "oozes cool, rebelliousness, and an IDGAF attitude while combining hook after hook."

"I don't even remember making that record. It was just a blackout," Ness said of that time.

Ness was spiraling. His heroin use worsened, and his friends were concerned not just for him but for their own property.

"I had to tell my mom, 'If Mike comes over to borrow any of my equipment, don't let him have it because it'll end up in the pawn shop,'" Danell said.

<hr />

Also in 1983, Social Distortion first met Jim Guerinot, who would play a prominent role in their lives for the next twenty-six years. At the time,

Guerinot was a local promoter who booked shows at Ichabod's, and soon he was booking lunchtime shows at Fullerton Junior College. In February 1983, Guerinot booked T.S.O.L. for one such gig, and the result was . . . predictable.

"It was a disaster for me, I shut the whole campus down," Guerinot said.

Using the student center as a base for the 11:00 a.m. show, the crowd overran the facility, and there wasn't enough security. Soon, there was a perimeter blocking the venue and the show was shut down. Guerinot was banned from putting on shows . . . for three months. After booking the Untouchables, the young entrepreneur caught the attention of many local bands.

Every Monday night at the Commonwealth Pub on Harbor Boulevard, it would be twenty-five-cent-beer night, hosted by *Flipside*. Soon, that became known as punk rock night. Ness would often be bartending, and one night in particular the police were called to the bar. There, Danell would get busted for smoking pot and passing a joint to a cop while Guerinot was nabbed for being drunk in public. As fate would have it, the pair ended up having the same court date.

"I'll never forget it," Guerinot says. "He was wearing a green suit with sandals. He [Danell] was reading *Up and Down with the Rolling Stones* by Tony Sanchez, which I had read. I walked up to him and introduced myself to him as a fan of the band, and I told him I could get the band a gig at Ichabod's for $1,000."

The way the band saw it, Guerinot had industry experience, which he laughs about. But Danell introduced Guerinot to Monk Rock, and after booking another Social Distortion show at the University of California, Irvine, for $1,000, Guerinot became the band's booking agent.

Other characters started to pop up on the scene. One of the most colorful ones was a redhead named Michael Brown. Born in Indiana before relocating to Fullerton when he was ten, Brown lived with his aunt and hung out around Fullerton. When Brown settled in Fullerton, his first three friends were Ness, Danell, and T.S.O.L.'s Ron Emory.

To many, though, Brown is best known as Cheez Boy.

"It's a fucking stupid story," he said regarding the everlasting nickname. "We were on a high school field trip when I was a junior [in 1980]. And a friend's hat blew out on the freeway and I said 'I'll get it.' It was bumper-to-bumper traffic, nothing major. I was running back through the lanes trying to catch up to the truck that we were in. My friend told me before I went out not to do it and I'll get hit by a car and be the cheese boy because you'll get splattered. As I'm running through the lanes, there was this Frito Lay truck that passed me, and the mirror skimmed me. It didn't hurt me or anything, didn't even knock me down. On the back of the truck, it didn't even have the cheetah, it had the rat and he was taking a bite of a Cheeto and it just said 'Cheez.' All my friends were like, 'Oh dude, you are the cheez boy, it's fate,' and it was dumb as shit."

Though he was annoyed at the time, Brown soon embraced his new moniker.

"Then all of my punker friends started calling me Cheez Boy," he said. "When I got signed to Posh Boy and he [Robbie Fields] wanted me to do a solo album, he wanted to call it Cheez Boy."

In time, Cheez Boy became known around the county not only as a booster of the punk bands but as a promoter. Cheez and Guerinot booked a Social Distortion show at the Placentia Boys Club. Even as he promoted shows, Cheez also performed. He says that his band opened for Social Distortion a bunch of times in those early years around Orange County.

When the Cuckoo's Nest closed in 1981, local punkers were left without a local venue. House parties became the norm, as did traveling up to LA to punk-friendly places like Devonshire Downs, the Olympic Auditorium, and even the Palladium.

As much as the young punkers of Fullerton loved the music and making new friends, turning it into something bigger was unfathomable.

"Back then, none of us thought that we could ever make a living playing this kind of music," Cheez said. "The punk rock thing was in a vacuum. You'd go to the same shows and see the same people."

※※※※※

On the strength of *Mommy's Little Monster*, Social Distortion started to play in front of bigger crowds at their own headlining shows. Previously, Social Distortion opened for the Adolescents, T.S.O.L., and even the South Bay's Black Flag. The band's hard-charging live shows made them a draw on the party circuit and at venues across the Southland. Social Distortion was carving out a distinct identity, powered by Ness's lyrics. To the world, the quartet was on the cusp of joining the Adolescents as the biggest band to emerge from Fullerton.

What's more, the band, on top of having a sonic identity with an album that received rave reviews, finally had a visual signifier. Thanks to their friend Mackie "Mac" Osborne, the world was introduced to Skelly, the martini- and cigarette-holding, fedora-wearing skeleton who was a take on the skeletons that graced the *Mommy's Little Monster* cover.

"It [the logo] was an invitation to a New Year's Eve party that my friend had designed," Ness said. "At the time, I saw that, and it just felt like, 'That's it right there. It's life and death, it's celebration.' It just felt powerful."

Even as the band gained a bigger following and grew in influence, things were falling apart internally.

By the end of 1983, Ness devolved into a full-fledged junkie, moving from drinking and smoking weed to shooting heroin.

On New Year's Eve 1983, things fell apart. Social Distortion played a show at Los Angeles's Cathay de Grande. Following the show, Ness asked to be paid in China white so it would save him a trip later that night to score. As his addiction grew worse, the band's performances sank. Ness would mouth off at the audience while the band's live show "sounded like shit." Fans would walk out, and following that Cathay de Grande show, so did his bandmates. With Ness's addiction spiraling, the band's bright prospects suddenly dimmed. Liles and O'Brien quit Social Distortion in the middle of the show.

"If I had a crystal ball at the time, I would have handled things differently but alas, I did not," O'Brien said. "It was the only time in my life I left a band and did not play shows I had committed to. I had some growing up to do and some lessons to learn."

At the time, though, even as Ness's addiction spiraled, he was growing disillusioned with punk rock.

"It seemed like there were a lot of bands coming out that all started to sound the same, look the same," he said. "It became a formula. Now it's like, 'Wait, he's the quarterback of the fucking high school football team and he's singing in a fucking punk band?' It was too much testosterone."

After Liles and O'Brien left the band, Ness and Danell had to find a new rhythm section. At first, Monk tried to get Mike Conley of the band M.I.A. to replace Ness, but Danell was vehemently opposed to that. In early 1984, problem one was solved when they tapped John Maurer, a buddy from Fullerton who they knew from Troy High School, to join them on bass. On a tip from a Circle Jerks roadie, Christopher Reece, formerly of San Francisco–based punk band the Lewd, filled the position behind the kit. Reece had met Ness and Danell when they stayed at the Lewd's house when they played by the Bay.

"The band was pretty fractured at the time," Reece said. "Ness was a full-fledged junkie and alcoholic. They were all doing it like it was the cool thing to do because that's what Johnny Thunders did. Mike was on a downward spiral . . . but I joined the band anyway."

How come?

"Because it was a fucking badass band when he [Ness] was on," he continued. "I saw the potential, but it was touch and go. Everyone went to those Olympic [Auditorium in LA] shows to see if he'd show up or if he'd be dead. I needed to make some rent money, so I hope that fucker didn't OD. He was running with a scummy crowd, a bunch of hangers-on . . . sometimes he was so high he couldn't fucking tune his guitar right. But when he'd have his guitar in tune it would be great. Sometimes it was a disaster, but most of the time it was good . . . sloppy, but good."

Soon, Reece's Hollywood bungalow became Social Distortion's headquarters. Reece said he was the only member with a steady day job waiting tables at the time. When he'd return, he'd see his bandmates on the floor drinking beer.

As sonically energizing as the new rhythm section was, they couldn't get past the one giant obstacle holding the band back: Ness's addiction. He'd be in and out of jail as he struggled with the grip that heroin had on his veins, and the band's reputation among their peers worsened. Ness would pawn instruments—his own, his bandmates', and those of other bands—to fuel his addiction.

"I remember driving through Fullerton with Johnny [Maurer]," Reece said. "We looked at a pawn shop and saw a bass amp in the mirror, and Johnny said, 'That looks like my bass amp.'" And with good reason: it was his bass amp. Ness sold it to a pawn shop to score drugs.

"When I was living with Mike, all my shit went missing," Guerinot said. "I had a change jar, and Mike stole every bit of change with the exception of the pennies. Nickles and dimes were not excluded from his thievery."

As Ness's manners as a houseguest continued to decline, Guerinot had to boot him out—albeit in a passive way that didn't put him on bad terms with his friend.

"I finally figured out how to get rid of him," he said. "I told him that they were going to the guy who owns it, and the guy is paying $300 a month. I said he's going to charge extra because he knows there's two people living here. So I need to get you to give me two hundred bucks a month. He was gone and went off to someone else's place."

Ness was arrested again in San Diego, and Guerinot's girlfriend's brother got him out of jail. It had become abundantly clear to everyone in his life that Ness had to get clean before it was too late. So much so that things almost ended at Cheez Boy's twenty-third birthday party at his Fullerton apartment. The event was ground zero for one of Orange County punk's most infamous incidents.

With many members of T.S.O.L., the Adolescents, and Social Distortion in attendance and copious amounts of beer and cocaine present, the party got out of hand quickly. After a spell of being clean, Ness, who was in jail that morning, scored some heroin and went to Cheez's party with a sixteen-ounce beer in hand. Arriving in his leather jacket and sporting a headband, Ness avoided some of his friends, including Guerinot and Darnell. When Guerinot saw Ness dipping into the bathroom, he knocked on the door and went in when he shot up. He saw how much Ness was using, and warned him that he was using too much. Ness complained, saying he knew what he was doing, but Guerinot reminded him he hadn't shot dope in a while.

Guerinot left the area, and complained to Danell about what was happening. As the minutes passed, Ness didn't come out of the bathroom with Guerinot and Danell waiting for him to come out high. When he didn't come out, they went over and knocked on the door, to no answer. Cheez told Danell and Guerinot not to kick the door in, but Danell had a little knife that enabled him to unhinge the door. Once in the bathroom, they found that Ness had overdosed and was face down in Cheez's kitty litter box on the right side of the toilet with the rig still hanging out of his arm. Guerinot immediately grabbed Ness's tongue to prevent him from choking and saw his eyes roll to the back of his head. He was given CPR by another partygoer while they waited for the paramedics. When they arrived, they went to work on Cheez, who had passed out after drinking a bottle of Yukon Jack. Danell told them they were working on the wrong person, and they gave Ness an adrenaline shot to resuscitate him. Suddenly his eyes popped open and his lungs filled with air as he began to miraculously breathe again. He went from lying flat on the ground to sitting perfectly upright. To the surprise of everyone who remained at the party, the first thing Ness said was "Where's my leather? Somebody stole my leather!" The paramedics took him to a nearby hospital, and he was thrown in jail for being under the influence of a controlled substance.

※※※※※

For Social Distortion, 1985 was a year of major change. Monk Rock, who helped keep the band together during those dark years, stopped managing the band since Ness was so out of control and left Orange County for Las Vegas. That paved the way for Guerinot to become the band's full-time manager. "Monk served that band up on a silver platter to Jim," Cheez said. "And Jim would take them to the next level." Also that year, Ness's heroin habit hit rock bottom. His band's hopes were on life support. But before that, there was plenty of trouble. It became clear to everyone around him that he needed to get clean or else he'd be six feet under. That year, Ness got sober and has remained so ever since.

Even through his spiraling addiction, Ness continued to write. The tenor of his songs changed. Whereas *Mommy's Little Monster* was a classic hardcore album, in the new material, Ness started to lean on the music of his youth.

MANIAC

He looked like Sammy Hagar and he had a joy buzzer all the time. So I'm not going to be in his band."

Those are Joe Escalante's first memories of Steve Jensen, who when not raising hell worked as a birthday clown at children's parties. Jensen, who once dated Escalante's sister, asked if the younger Escalante was interested in playing in his band. At the time, Escalante was something of a musical prodigy. He played drums in the school band and was advanced for his age. He enjoyed humorous, intellectual music, with Devo being his favorite.

"I would answer the door, and he'd have a joy buzzer and a whoopee cushion and all this stuff," Escalante said. Escalante was playing drums in the marching band, and as a one-off he was in a punk cover band called Permanent Damage. His sister told him that Jensen was interested in Escalante bringing his drum skills to the Vandals. "She goes, 'Yeah, he wants you to play in his band.' And I said, 'No, I'm not playing in your friend's new wave band.' At this point, I think I'm so punk and will not be in this guy's new wave band."

At the same time, Escalante was hanging out with T.S.O.L. and their drummer, Todd Barnes. In the early '80s, the Adolescents and T.S.O.L. were battling for the crown of Orange County's biggest band. Escalante was Barnes's drum tech and had hung out with T.S.O.L. since the days they were calling themselves Vicious Circle. He was firm about not joining Jensen. But Barnes told him otherwise and that Stevo was looking for a new drummer.

"'You get in that band, and then you'll have money for beer,'" Escalante recalled Barnes telling him. "Then I saw them at a party and they were great. And I told Todd to hook it up and to be in the band I just saw. I didn't realize that Stevo was Steve Jensen and it was the same band. The day I figured that out, I told my sister to call him and tell him I'm in."

Formed in 1980 out of the ashes of Huntington Beach band Gestapo by drummer Vince Mesa, bassist Steve Gonzalez, and guitarist Jan Ackermann, the Vandals had also featured future momentary T.S.O.L. vocalist Rick Fritch before he was replaced by Jensen. The Vandals quickly became known as an outlier in the notoriously rough-and-tumble, serious punk scene. When Gonzalez also bailed in 1980, Steve "Human" Pfauter was the logical choice to replace him, as Human had played in a band out of the Rossmoor neighborhood of Los Alamitos with Escalante called Jim Jones and the Koolaids.

Unlike their contemporaries, the Vandals incorporated humor into their lyrics, with much of the band's early songs inspired by their personal experiences. But that's what happens when you have a front man who wore a joy buzzer to get a rise out of people.

The Vandals would soon lose Mesa, which is when they sought Escalante's services.

Having played in a band with skateboarder Steve Olson before joining the Vandals, Escalante crossed paths with a group of troublemakers, albeit not by choice.

"My drum set got stolen over at Steve Olson's house," Escalante said. "It turns out it was stolen by Todd Barnes, Vicious Circle's drummer at the time. So I went to get it and stupidly I asked my sister, I go, 'Who is this Todd Barnes guy?' And she goes, 'Oh Jack Grisham gave me this guy's number, here it is.' So I called him and say, 'I heard you stole my drums. I was hoping I could come and get it.' He goes, 'Oh really? Come on over.'"

It turned out Barnes tuned up the drums, so he couldn't give them back. The two agreed on a price and for Barnes to give Escalante money . . . but the plan was when he went to get the money at the rehearsal room behind Barnes's house, they'd beat him up. Wisely, Escalante brought a friend with him, and it turns out they all got along. Barnes wrote Escalante a check for sixty-five dollars, and everything was settled.

Following that incident, Escalante and the T.S.O.L. crew became friends and would remain that way for many years.

"But they were bad actors," Escalante said. "It was a place [Barnes's back house] where you don't want your kids to hang out."

"Lyrically, he needed a lot of help," Escalante said of the clown/front man. "Between me and him, we were writing all the lyrics and we got through it. Usually, I had to write part of a song and let them finish a couple of lyrics. And then sometimes he would write a whole song."

By 1982, the Vandals were snapped up by Epitaph Records, the label formed by Bad Religion's Brett Gurewitz. Connected to the band by Bad Religion bassist Jay Bentley, who was friends with Human, the Vandals were the first non–Bad Religion band to release music on the label. The band's first EP, *Peace Thru Vandalism*, was released that same year to much acclaim and featured production by Thom Wilson. "We all thought he was a legend for doing the Adolescents' Blue Album," Gurewitz said. "Urban Struggle," a song Escalante said was written by Stevo and Ackermann, was a local hit after being played on KROQ by Bingenheimer. Occasionally when it played, the song was a snapshot of the chaotic scene in Costa Mesa where punks and cowboys fought each other in the parking lot that connected the Cuckoo's Nest to Zubie's. The Escalante-penned "Ladykiller" was another song aided by the taste-making LA station. He thought of the song on the way home from his daily drive to UCLA.

"After those, then you're thinking, 'This is pretty easy!'" Escalante said. "But in those days, you could have a hit for the whole year that was like No. 5 or something like that on KROQ. So you think you have a career, but it didn't hit around the country."

Keeping with the theme of fighting at the Cuckoo's Nest, "The Legend of Pat Brown" was about the story of an infamous punker who ran over two police officers and was subsequently arrested.

The EP spread wide and gave punkers from out of town a glimpse into what was happening in Orange County.

※※※※

Not all of the tracks were about the Nest. "Pirate's Life" chronicled what it was like to ride the Pirates of the Caribbean at Disneyland . . . on acid. "Anarchy Burger (Hold the Government)" was the band's most popular song at the time and was an amusing number (as much as it could be) about anarchy. The song later became the subject of discontent between Escalante, Stevo, and Human over its use in the 2002 film *XXX*.

In 1983, the Vandals appeared in the Penelope Spheeris film

Suburbia. The film focused on a group of suburban kids who ran away from home (and squatted in . . . suburban homes) and became punks. Their performance of "The Legend of Pat Brown" was featured, as was T.S.O.L.'s "Wash Away" and D.I.'s "Richard Hung Himself."

"That Orange County hardcore thing became very storied in maybe not a positive way, but certainly in a way of adding infamy to it," said Damian Abraham said. "I remember seeing those bands in *Suburbia* as a kid and being like, 'Oh my God, that's what the scene is. It's like fucking crazy.'"

That early success made the Vandals believe that they'd be propelled to instant stardom. They weren't active in the scene, but that didn't deter fans from coming to see them. Yet massive success for the Vandals never happened. The band had only one major label meeting, and the rep said that he didn't hear any anthems and hits on the record. That was one of the factors that caused this incarnation of the band to stall.

The other was their volatility.

By 1984, Human left the Vandals, putting them in a tough spot as they readied their first full-length album. He was replaced by Eric VonArab for a spell before Brent Turner was enlisted to play in the studio. Chalmer Lumary of the Hated played bass during this time as well. That year, the band released their debut album, *When in Rome Do as the Vandals.* The album was produced by Thom Wilson and joined the ranks as the latest in a long line of OC punk albums.

"He was just in the right place at the right time and super friendly and amenable," Escalante said of the producer, who died in 2015. "Other records that were being produced by Robbie Fields and Posh Boy, those things were sloppy as hell. He had more professionalism to them. And he was a super cool guy, who you wanted to spend time with."

Drugs and the fear of Stevo unsettled the band, especially on the road.

"It was a very, very abusive situation on the road," Escalante said. "At one point, we had a fine that anyone had to pay if you woke up Stevo. It was $50 because while he was sleeping, he was awesome. Once he woke up . . ."

He was also growing more difficult to write with. "He started becoming a megalomaniac," Escalante said. "It came to a point where we had to approach him and say, 'Now you write two verses.' That's how you could get a song done."

The situation was untenable, and it came to a head in Northern California. At the time, the Vandals had another song on the San Francisco radio station Live 105. Playing up there proved to be an inflection point. During the band's sold-out show at the Stone Club in Palo Alto, Stevo passed out onstage halfway through the set. Lumary and Ackermann had to finish on vocals. To make matters worse, when it came time to settle with the club, the band got their money, but they were banned from playing the venue.

The next night in San Francisco at the Keystone was even worse.

"It was really, really so bad to the point where I had to go outside and buy drugs for him because he said he wouldn't go onstage unless you get me speed," Escalante said of his dealings with Stevo. "I'd bought drugs before. But I went out on the streets on Broadway, and I found a guy and I bought them and gave them to him. And he said they're fake. He exploded and said, 'You bring that guy back here or I'm not going to play.' So I find the guy and bring him back and he [Stevo] says they're fake and wants to talk to you. So I somehow get this guy in the club in the back and they hashed it out. Then [Stevo] goes onstage and passes out halfway through the set."

The Vandals were on the rise. They were making the most money they'd ever had and were playing high-profile shows. But their front man's erratic behavior cost them dearly. Following that show, Escalante was ready to quit. To keep Escalante, Ackermann suggested that the Vandals replace Stevo with the Falling Idols' Dave Quackenbush.

"We had always looked at him [Quackenbush] and admired him as a great front man," Escalante said. "And I go, 'Well, if you can do that, then yeah, I'll definitely stay.' So that's what we did. So now, that was good."

Even those in the scene who knew him and liked him said the same thing: Stevo is a maniac.

Guerinot, the rising manager of OC punk bands, was uniquely positioned to speak about the Vandals front man's unpredictability. In addition to managing Social Distortion, Guerinot took on the Vandals as well. The biggest difference between the two bands?

"Social Distortion listened to him and the guys in my band didn't," Escalante said. "That's how I knew it wasn't going to work."

GOLDENVOICE

J n 1981, most club promoters wanted no part of punk rock, especially in Orange County. It wasn't considered a sound or a culture—just a nuisance and a major liability. One of the few who embraced it was a guy named Gary Tovar. The prospect of teenage mayhem didn't scare him, and neither did the raw magnetism of the sound and community that came with it.

"Nobody wanted to do punk rock because there was no money in it, only destruction," Tovar said. "Who wants to be in a business where people give you shit and destroy everything? People would throw a show one time, they'd lose their ass and they'd quit. Then you'd have punk gangs who wanted to dictate what the scene was. And we had skinheads—there were good skins but there were bad skins too."

Tovar, who was twenty years old when he started promoting shows, learned about punk through the heavy-handed crackdown he'd witnessed at punk shows around SoCal via his younger sister Bianca, who was going to local punk shows at the time. Tovar wasn't a stranger to the music that had already landed on the western front of the US. His first time seeing a punk gig was a Sex Pistols show at San Francisco's Winterland Ballroom in January 1978. What he wasn't aware of just yet was how much the punk scene in his backyard was starting to bubble up.

"Punk music needed to be showcased in a better environment, better sound, better lights—but nobody had any money. So what I tried to do was kick the scene and this culture into high gear, and that's what I did. I pushed and I pushed—we would lose money and I still kept pushing."

Tovar grew up in Los Angeles and Huntington Beach, where his family moved when he was twelve. He attended Golden West College and Fullerton College, then moved to Santa Barbara. He chose to start his promoting career there, eventually launching his own promotions company Goldenvoice in 1981, comparing it to "practicing in the minor leagues before I came into the majors."

"Santa Barbara was my training ground for learning how to promote shows. We hit town about the same time [former President] Reagan moved up there, and I wanted to shake the town up a little bit," Tovar said. Goldenvoice, launched in 1981, began with shows in Santa Barbara social halls and community centers because "at that time [punk] was pretty taboo in Los Angeles."

He also chose to kick things off in Santa Barbara because, he said, "at that time [punk] had hit a rough point in Los Angeles" due to burnout over seeing a lot of the same bands over and over again at shows. "People wanted to see stuff they hadn't seen yet or hadn't seen very much," Tovar said. "You can't beat it over the head if you play too much. People get bored with you."

Tovar came up with the name Goldenvoice pretty much right from the get-go, a moniker inspired his work in the marijuana smuggling business. "I got into the marijuana business because I didn't like the marijuana coming in from the Mexican border, border weed was terrible and I wanted to smoke better pot," he said. "My whole goal in life as a marijuana smuggler was to have as much fun as I could and not hurt anybody. I've never shot a gun in my life. We did everything by diversionary tactics." Tovar named his company after a strain of marijuana from Thailand—a moniker that foreshadowed his ties to the strain of weed known by the same name.

"When you smoked it, they said it was like when angels spoke to you," Tovar said. "There was also Elephant ganja, which they say felt like an elephant stepped on you. I figured [Goldenvoice] was more musical. Otherwise, we would be Elephant Productions."

The first show he ever booked for Goldenvoice was T.S.O.L., Shattered Faith, and Rhino 39 at La Casa de la Raza on December 4, 1981.

From the beginning, T.S.O.L. knew Tovar was a bit different from the average concert promoter. "He started paying us more than anyone else in the country would pay us," front man Jack Grisham told *OC Weekly*. "I mean, it pissed people off. Gary really started paying these bands what they were worth."

Despite playing to packed houses, most bands were used to getting maybe $100–$200 for a sold-out show. Tovar was the first punk promoter who paid the bands fairly, Grisham said. "Everybody wanted to be on Gary's shows, and it was only a short time before he was the biggest promoter around."

Tovar was a hustler. And his booking agency Goldenvoice became a conduit to help bands like Social Distortion and the Vandals embark on tours that would help them break out of LA and get exposure across the country. He even went the extra mile for bands who wanted to tour but didn't have their own vehicle by purchasing them a van. That's what he did for the Vandals, Joe Escalante remembers.

The promoter was an early champion of the quirky punk band, to the point where he even wanted them to play in places outside their normal punk touring circuit. He helped get the band gigs in Hawaii when they were still very young. "He met me in Huntington Beach at a parking lot and handed me four plane tickets to Oahu," he told *OC Weekly*. "We had the time of our lives."

Tovar's style of show-promoting was epic to watch, whether from the crowd or behind the scenes.

Jim Guerinot started working at Goldenvoice's Signal Hill office with Dead Kennedys manager Mike Vraney. At one point, he helped book the Dead Kennedys, T.S.O.L., Social Distortion, the Vandals, the Dickies, 45 Grave, and Agent Orange for national tours. They would book bands up and down the coast when Goldenvoice boss Gary Tovar would fly them in from England. Prior to his career as an executive director of artist development at A&M Records, he learned the ropes of advertising and eventually headed the company's now-discontinued booking agency division.

"[Gary] paid me to do graphic design, which I never had done before. I thought he was awesome!" Guerinot told *OC Weekly*. "I gotta tell you, it's really impossible to talk about this without sounding extremely old, but the scene was very small. And Gary, in a weird way, he made it really big. He really, really did. And to seat 5,000 people going to see the Exploited or GBH, that's like the US Festival of punk rock, and this guy was doing it on a weekly basis. And he was selling tickets at London Exchange and Bionic, and he had his own ticketing system!"

Kevin Lyman, the creator of popular mega fests like the Warped Tour, Taste of Chaos, and Mayhem, was a student at Cal Poly Pomona with Paul Tollett when he began working for Goldenvoice in production. "Whatever they needed," he says. "It allowed me to learn a lot about production and touring. Being able to put on shows? That was the coolest thing. Watching Gary, he was always generous with the kids, and he always wanted to put on the best show and something extra for them. Paul and I put on some of the biggest festivals of the country. I put them on the road, and Paul is stationary, but we always try to do something different and special for the fan—and I think that's what Gary taught us."

He recalls seeing Tovar pull money out of his pocket to help kids hanging around outside venues get into Goldenvoice shows. "He was proud of his shows," Lyman says. "That's the thing: He taught me to try to be proud of your shows."

✕✕✕✕✕✕✕

As far as liabilities go, OC punkers had earned their reputation thanks in no small part to a bloody kerfuffle like the one on January 8, 1983, dubbed the Sunset Riots at SIR Studios. T.S.O.L. was headlining the show with support from Social Distortion and Redd Kross from nearby Hawthorne. The riot squad was also outside—a standard sight at punk shows back then—and as per usual they were pissed off and ready to kick some punk asses.

Inside the performance hall at SIR Studios, Grisham had the audience sit down in protest. But what started as an attempt to resist peacefully ended with 2,500 punks pouring into the streets and trading blows with cops in riot gear swinging billy clubs.

"A lot of the riots were due to the fact that a lot of people outside wanted in," Tovar told *OC Weekly*. "All that was polarized. It fed the fire and gave us more. More people wanted to join the fray. . . . But after each riot, kids would call me from different states and say, 'Oh, God, I wish I were there.' The riots accelerated, and that brought growth." About one month later on February 11, 1983, a show at Mendiola's Ballroom in Huntington Park, a 450-capacity club headlined by the Exploited, with Channel 3, Youth Brigade, the Vandals, and Suicidal Tendencies, turned into an infamously bloody brawl that was shut down before the Exploited even hit the stage. Forty-one punkers were arrested and ten police officers were injured in the roughly hour-long brawl that resulted in $25,000 in damage to surrounding business and a local church.

But Goldenvoice's run at the Olympic Auditorium—a massive building in Downtown LA that has since been converted into a Korean church—seems especially memorable for fans who attended early Goldenvoice shows.

Dating back to 1951, the Olympic had been a destination for rhythm and blues concerts. Prior to punk hitting LA in the '70s, the giant venue on Eighteenth and Grand was a hotbed for hard rock of the day, hosting shows for Mountain, Jack Bruce, and Ten Years After.

It was used more extensively as a musical venue after 1980 when Tovar started booking monthly punk concerts from the likes of GBH, the Exploited, T.S.O.L., Suicidal Tendencies, U.K. Subs, Circle Jerks, the Dickies, Dead Kennedys, the Vandals, and many others. Black Flag was the headliner for an infamous 1981 New Year's Eve show.

In late 1983, Tovar said he wanted to get a building where he could fit everybody in and close the door behind them. While inside, the activities at the show wouldn't get busted up by the cops.

"Get everybody inside, close the door behind us, the police are outside, I always said if you're gonna get beat up, I'd rather you get beat up by your own people," Tovar said of what was going on inside the Olympic Auditorium.

It was a perfect storm: an arena past its prime, a wild scene looking for a home, and a promoter crazy enough to make it happen. At the peak of that period from 1983 to 1985, Goldenvoice put on the biggest hardcore shows in the world.

The Olympic's height in August of 1984 also happened to coincide with the 1984 Olympic Games coming to Los Angeles with a series of shows that made headlines for their massive draw both in crowd and police presence.

According to Tovar, half the Olympic shows did over 5,000 people; meanwhile, the biggest punk shows in New York were doing shows with no more than 1,200 to 2,000 at the time. "We were four to five times as big as New York City and there were way more people in a smaller area," Tovar said. "And our people had to drive."

San Clemente to the Olympic is seventy miles. Santa Barbara to the Olympic is ninety miles, then you had West LA, different parts all over SoCal all piling in their cars to make a long freeway pilgrimage to this dingy, scary, massive hub of punk culture. "Just imagine people coming from every side," Tovar said. "Orange County punks, Thousand Oaks punks, west side punks, punks in the two valleys, San Fernando and San Gabriel, South Bay, they came from all over."

The Olympic Auditorium shows, which only happened once a month for approximately two years—twenty-five shows in all—sketched an early template for much of the format of modern festivals that feed the counterculture around the country today. Utilizing a chain of thirty record stores from San Clemente to Santa Barbara as well as punk clothing stores like London Exchange in OC to sell tickets to young punks buying records and T-shirts every week, Tovar created a business that catered to a scene he saw emerging from all corners of California. "It allowed us to really measure the size of this scene—it helped us figure out how many punks were really out there."

When the hardcore scene kicked in, the violence surged. Instead of wanting to see a band play, kids came to fight. "I would always breathe a sigh of relief when nobody got killed," Tovar said. "Because the potential was there."

Tovar is particularly known for helping introduce UK acts like Siouxsie and the Banshees and the Damned to SoCal audiences. He'd fly bands in stateside and then usher them to San Diego, Phoenix, Sacramento, San Francisco, and Fresno. He didn't stop at punk—he also introduced a wide swath of underground, goth, and speed metal acts via Goldenvoice. However, Tovar admits that the tastes of many California punk crowds carried with them a more nationalistic ideology that favored American bands over their European counterparts.

"I did a lot of English bands. I did shows with these bands in California, but a lot of the crowds just wanted American bands—they didn't want these limey bands. They rejected a lot of the European acts, anything that wasn't American," Tovar said. "San Francisco did not embrace the leather jacket Europeans."

Admission at the Olympic was affordably priced at $7.50 ($8.50 at the door), with the bulk of the audience ranging from twelve to twenty-one in age. The 12,100-square-foot building was practically dead center in the middle of LA, pulling in punks from all over the city and the suburbs, including Orange County and particularly Huntington Beach. Tovar's lineup hinged on bands like T.S.O.L., Bad Religion, the Dickies, Circle Jerks, and Dead Kennedys drawing crowds of thousands on a monthly basis.

"The reason people loved the Olympic so much was because the massive crowd was like an energy force," Tovar said. "People liked small clubs, but there's something about 5,000 punk rockers in their own world packed into a place that was very exciting, and the bands knew it. . . . I wanted it to be a gathering point for every section of town—let's all meet in the middle right there and shut the door behind us and have our own little punk world for a few hours."

Though it was a staple of the punk scene for a couple years, Tovar's red-hot venue eventually burned itself out. The wild punk shows at the Olympic started to die down by the end of 1985 due to lack of demand and the sheer amount of violence and unruly fans that flocked to the shows.

"It was really scary, the neighborhood was scary, the audience was scary, my own audience scared the shit out of me most of the time," Frank Agnew recalls. "That's why I was glad I was in the band because I knew I wouldn't get my ass kicked."

"Most of the time I thought it was just good energy," Tovar told the *Los Angeles Times* in 1992. "But when it started getting violent I stopped doing the Olympic. It started to become a gladiator ring: who could be the toughest guy in town." Despite the violence, Tovar still regards the era of the Olympic as a "spiritual experience."

"I thought that somebody had to pick up the mantle and forward this movement," Tovar said in the documentary *18th & Grand: The Olympic Auditorium Story*. "I think we took it as far as we could go. The peak of punk rock is like a shooting star, it's just there and then it's gone."

A few years after the Olympic era vanished for Tovar, so did his freedom—the result of his double life.

Until he was arrested in 1991, most bands, musicians, and employees at Goldenvoice had no idea Tovar was trafficking marijuana as far back as a decade prior to throwing shows. It was the funds from the drug trade—reaching the double-digit millions—that supplied the company with the seed money it needed to function in those early years.

"I stacked the bills, I put on big bands and spent money on quality sound and lights. I wasn't making any money on those shows. I was hoping I would, though—but it took too long, people were too slow," Tovar said. "And the bands were too young, they had no money, some of them weren't even old enough to have a job—that made it very difficult."

From the outside, Goldenvoice seemed like a fast-growing concert empire, but the reality was not so glamorous. The company struggled financially in the early days, and any money lost from shows came directly out of Tovar's pocket. "I lost $3 million to $4 million over eleven years—that's 1980s dollars now," he said. "I had a lot of money, but it was like $300,000 to $400,000 a year."

Tovar relied on the weed business to keep the concert business going. "I had two worlds," Tovar said. "I had my Goldenvoice legit world, and then I had my marijuana-smuggling world. But in the middle of the marijuana world, people were going down, and I knew it was only a matter of time before something happened to me."

And then something did happen. In 1991, Tovar was arrested by the feds.

Tovar, who was forty at the time, was sentenced in October 1992 to seven years in federal prison for marijuana trafficking.

He pleaded guilty in November 1991 to four charges of participating in a ring that tried to buy marijuana in Arizona for distribution in California and elsewhere.

Prosecutors had been pushing for a sentence of twelve and a half years. "I was hoping to get less, but it could have been worse," Tovar told the *Los Angeles Times* over a jail phone in Maricopa County in Phoenix at the time. "I thought everything went as well as could be expected."

Nine people were arrested in the case following federal and local investigations in Tucson and Mesa. All were convicted or pleaded guilty. Tovar was the last to be sentenced. He pleaded guilty to two counts of conspiracy to possess marijuana with intent to distribute, one count of attempted possession of marijuana with intent to distribute, and one count of operating a continuing criminal enterprise. Authorities implicated the ring in attempts to acquire a total of 162 kilograms (about 357 pounds) of marijuana that was to be sold in California and elsewhere.

In June 1992, some musicians whose careers Tovar helped build performed at a benefit concert at the Palladium to help pay his legal bills. On the bill were Social Distortion, Porno for Pyros (fronted by former Jane's Addiction leader Perry Farrell), Thelonious Monster, the Meat Puppets, Tender Fury, and Firehose.

Guerinot, who by then was managing Social Distortion, said when asked to have Ness and the band play to support Tovar, there was no question they'd do it despite having recently played the Palladium just a few months prior.

"Time and time again, Mike Ness was in jail, and time and time again I was going to Gary to get money to bail him out," Guerinot told the *Times*. "It didn't take half a second for us to know we were going to do [the benefit]. He'd always been there for us."

"He was one of the first to bring in some of the big punk bands from overseas, when no one else would bring in bands like PiL," Dean Naleway, co-owner of Triple X Entertainment, a punk-oriented Los Angeles independent record company whose highest-profile release has been the 1987 debut album by Jane's Addiction, told the *Times*. "He pretty much cracked the whole thing wide open. If it wasn't for him, a lot of us growing up in the area wouldn't have been able to see some of these bands. None of the bigger promoters would consider taking a chance with these bands because of the violence that might occur, and nobody wanted to house a bunch of punk rockers."

Before he served his sentence, the founder signed over ownership of Goldenvoice to the two men responsible for how we know the company today: Paul Tollett and Rick Van Santen.

Tovar had met Tollett when he was nineteen at a Bad Manners show at Fender's Ballroom in Long Beach. He started working for Goldenvoice in 1986.

"I remember the first time I met Gary," Tollett told *OC Weekly*. "I was walking past this alley, and I look and just see these two good-looking dudes with great hair talking to each other."

The "good-looking dudes" he was referring to were Tovar and Mike Ness.

Years before cofounding Coachella, one of the world's biggest, most respected music festivals, Tollett was a fledgling promoter, hustling for small ska shows around Pomona. He had also done a stint passing out flyers for Revelation Records, which moved from the East Coast to Huntington Beach to help breed the new epicenter of hardcore. Tollett had heard of Goldenvoice and decided to chat with Tovar about his upcoming shows in the city, and Tovar offered him tips on where to properly publicize. Tollett began distributing flyers for Tovar at shows and stores and dropping off tickets at record stores.

"When Gary first started doing ska, I go, 'Okay, I gotta go talk to him.' I wanted to work for him. So we hit it off, I felt—you should verify this with Gary," Tollett told *OC Weekly*. "But we had fun right out in the beginning."

Van Santen started working for Tovar at age twenty specializing in publicity, booking, and advertising. On the side he also managed the band 45 Grave. Early on, Tovar recognized that Tollett and Van Santen made a good team. "When I left, I made sure I put the two of them together," he said.

The two became inseparable from 1988 to the time of Van Santen's death of flu-related complications in 2003.

Years later, Tollett still described Tovar as more of a friend than a boss. "He never acted like he was my boss—we were just together," he told *OC Weekly*. "I didn't know it, but he was obviously the guy in charge. He didn't treat you like that. I hope that was passed on to me with my staff. I hope they don't think of me [as their boss]. I just want to be their friend. People doing shows together."

He continued, "[Tovar] was always drive-drive-drive. I liked it. But the thing I liked the most—and I think this is probably what I picked up—I liked how he built shows. Stacked the bill, stacked the deck, understood the bands and how they fit in with other bands. Which ones would resonate with people when they saw it on a flier. If I had to point to anything to this day, one of the No. 1 things that relates to how Coachella works, it's understanding the music first."

Even today, Tovar, nearing seventy, is still a fixture at shows all over LA. You can still find him popping up low-key in shades and a T-shirt or hoodie, floating among crowds of fans decades younger than him. Guided by the punk rock spirit, Tovar's attraction to the new and the worship of music for music's sake are what keep him out and about, regardless of whether he's still part of the day-to-day Goldenvoice machine he created.

Going from the creator of a live music juggernaut to now becoming another die-hard face in the crowd who still gets embraced and recognized when he pops up at shows, Tovar said his sacrifices for the punk scene are a part of his life he would never change.

"I got treated badly by people who wanted to own the scene like it was something to own, and people thought I was owning the scene and I was just trying to put it on. I knew it wasn't gonna be forever," he said. "I knew it was a shooting star and I tried to put on the best shows I could when the timing was right. . . . I liked bringing joy. Music is a way to express your feelings. You show your feelings through music. And to this day, people love Goldenvoice because we helped the bands do that. Folks who were there back in the day realize now that that early punk rock era was the best time of their life—and it was. Because they had a concert company that didn't care if it made money. Do you know what kind of advantage that is?"

THE REBOUND

y the end of 1984 into 1985, the Orange County punk scene was beginning to splinter and go underground.

There was a big difference between the punk scenes in Hollywood and Orange County. When the Orange County punks headed up north, the LA punks took it to mean there was some methodical, evil plan for the OC to come into the scene and ruin it for them. The way the LA punks saw it, they were open-minded and accepting of everything, when in fact they were dismissive of their counterparts. Not every OC punk was innocent by any stretch, but they were dismissive of their rivals' disgust toward them.

"The people in Hollywood were gonna jump on anything," Joe Escalante said. "Whatever trend came in, they'd hop on and then they'd stop. They'd have some snide, cynical thing to say to me because my punk band is still playing. The guys in Orange County, they're just bored and they see the chaos. It was more impressive because they weren't art students like in Hollywood. They were suburban kids who didn't have a gripe so much other than boredom. And recognizing something that looked fun and pissed people off. And the Orange County people liked to piss people off." As punk bands rose in local popularity, the media soon caught on. Though advantageous at the time, Grisham says it was ultimately the first wave of punk's undoing.

"Journalists destroyed it, too," Jack Grisham said. "What they did is they started classifying what was happening. Instead of like letting it happen. They started saying, 'Oh, this band is a punk band. This band is a hardcore band. This band is a goth band.' They started putting these bands together in boxes and then the bands went into their area. So now that big bitchin' fucking stew has just been separated. Now the scene is getting destroyed. Before, it was a big umbrella of sound where the Go-Go's would play with Black Flag. It was really fucking open-minded.

"*Maximum Rocknroll* was a big one that fucking did so much damage to this thing," he continued. "A lot of it was the fucking intellectuals. I hate to say it but they fucking destroyed it."

Grisham's experience in LA ran contrary to what the bands up the freeway preached in their lyrics, and it angered those punks. Not that he cared at all.

"You're mad at me for throwing bottles at the police?" Grisham said. "What the fuck, man? It's like, are we the fucking opposition or are we not? They were right. We were exactly what they said we were; we were fucking violent, and we were out of control. But it's also what kept this music going. It's also what keeps people buying their records right now. We ruined the party, and they didn't like it. They had this safe little pogo party going on, and Orange County crashed the party.

"Here's the thing," he continued. "They didn't like us, but they sure as fuck didn't mind us keeping that music going. I sure as hell didn't see them saying 'please don't buy our records.'"

✕✕✕✕✕✕✕

When Grisham, drummer Todd Barnes, and keyboardist Greg Kuehn all left T.S.O.L. in 1983 to form Cathedral of Tears, it set off a chain reaction. The Adolescents splintered, the Vandals endured lineup changes, and T.S.O.L. reformed without Grisham and instead with Joe Wood on vocals, and all of this happened to varying degrees of success.

Wood, who grew up bouncing back and forth between Cerritos and Long Beach, got into punk and started playing in bands around 1977. One of three kids, he said he grew up mostly without parents, couch surfing while his older brother, who became the breadwinner of his family at a young age, looked after his mother and sister. He learned guitar from an uncle who he said was a member of the Aryan Brotherhood. "He was unfortunately one of my only male role models there for a while," Wood said. The soon-to-be front man came from a musical family and used his artistic background to learn to play guitar well enough "to get girls." Early self-taught vocal lessons were mostly just him singing into a hairbrush in the shower. But it was a show at the Masque in the late '70s watching the Germs play that made him think he could have what it takes to do a bit of what the shambolic Darby Crash was pulling off onstage.

"My friend cut all my hair off before we went to the show, and as they were playing I grabbed him by the arm and said, 'Man, we can do this—I can play that good.' I was watching 'em play bar chords, but it wasn't about how good they were, it was just the attitude, the movement."

When he started playing with Ron Emory and Mike Roche, Wood was into blues and hardcore punk, and he expanded his sound to meld searing blues solos and Americana with aggressive four-chord smashing to create a band he dubbed Joe Wood and the Loners. "People always wanted to put you in a box, but I could never fit all my pieces in there," he said of his eclectic style. Around that time, after the breakup of the original T.S.O.L., Emory started sitting in with Wood's band, followed soon after by Roche, who met Wood at a party where the Loners were playing. After they were done, Roche approached Wood about playing in a new project with him and Emory.

Given the legendary status of T.S.O.L. even after breaking up, Wood happily obliged, and they started looking for drummers. The crew decided on Mitch Dean, who'd been the replacement drummer for the original T.S.O.L. in the past. Armed with a fistful of songs like "Flowers by the Door" and "Nothin' for You," which Wood said he'd written while he was in the Loners, a new configuration of T.S.O.L. was slowly taking shape with a much different sound than it had in the first Grisham era. Emory's guitar licks played a crucial role in the sound, Wood says, which helped in the development of roughly sixteen songs that the band quickly wrote to play shows.

No one in the band with Wood was necessarily trying to hijack the T.S.O.L. name, but as Wood said, there were business interests having to do with record labels looking to cash in on the band that made the use of the old name basically inevitable. At one of the band's early shows opening for the Dead Kennedys before ever marketing themselves as T.S.O.L., the white-hot San Francisco punk band's manager caught their show and was impressed—enough for him to make the band a proposition. "He said, 'Hey, if you guys call yourselves T.S.O.L., I'll get you a record deal right now and get you on the road in no time,'" Wood recalls. The twenty-three-year-old Wood was too ignorant at the time to realize the hell he was signing up for when he said yes. "I didn't know fucking shit about any of that stuff. And I still don't really. I'm not a business guy. I didn't get into this wanting to take the name T.S.O.L. I didn't think that would ever happen until right then when it did." Wood said he did not expect to be Grisham's replacement. But once he strapped in and took the stage, there was nothing he could do to stop that perception.

From the minute the new version of T.S.O.L. plugged in to play and their new front man took the stage, fans of the old band were dumb-founded or at the very least knew something was very different. The new songs were now crunchier and bluesier with a dash of new wave, a noticeable change from the sneering nihilism and breakneck speed-up pop songs of old T.S.O.L. This sound, both hard and soft throughout each song, also had more of a metal vibe, and the throaty gravel tone of Wood's vocals toed a razor's edge between Billy Idol and Jim Morrison. Of course, fans who had no idea who he was were caught off guard.

From the beginning, Wood said he got his ass handed to him by fans of the original band. "Half the people liked me, half the people hated me." Though he was technically the new front man, the core of the band remained Emory and Roche calling the shots and direct-ing things, Wood said. The changing tide of the band during its metal metamorphosis proved to be a tough road to travel.

The singer recalls getting his ass kicked and having to fight multi-ple times during his six-year tenure with T.S.O.L., though he says that whether it was the songs of "Change Today?," "Revenge," "Hit and Run," or "Strange Love," he stands by the music he made with the band. "I suppose it's none of my business what other people think of me as what I think of me," he said. "I thought that I wrote better songs and that my shit was good. And I believed it and I lived it. I lived my songs. I still do."

The band's metal years, often derided by fans of the old (and now current) T.S.O.L. as the era that dragged the band's name through the mud, were not easy for its members despite having a deal with respected LA label Enigma Records. And let's not forget the music video moment that introduced the band to the world when Guns N' Roses drummer Steven Adler donned a torn-sleeved T.S.O.L. shirt during the grainy, black-and-white video for megahit "Sweet Child O' Mine." Wood still carries a tinge of regret when remembering the cheesy cover photo of 1987's *Hit and Run* with the band's black leather jackets and teased-up, hair metal 'dos staring coldly into the camera. "To this day I regret it," Wood said. "At that point we had tons of people working for us and a record label to please, I was strung out on dope, I didn't give a shit either way, that was kinda my attitude. I was wearing Roche's clothes in that picture. I never had my own clothes—I was poor the whole time."

They ended up playing with the LA sleaze metal superstars, but things fell apart fast.

"We went on the *Appetite for Destruction* tour with Guns N' Roses," then–T.S.O.L. member Mitch Dean said. "After we played four dates of the tour, their management called our management and said either T.S.O.L. stays in a different hotel for the rest of the tour or leaves the tour. They thought we were a bad influence on Guns N' Roses, and they were right because we were well-connected. T.S.O.L. fell apart because we were so dysfunctional."

By the end of the '80s, Emory left the band, and Roche was the only connective tissue to that band's past. The new incarnation of T.S.O.L. still drew huge crowds, in particular in Brazil and Argentina.

By 1989, Grisham (who was playing with his new band Tender Fury), Emory (involved in his band Lunch Box), and Barnes were enticed to play a reunion show as T.S.O.L. But a roadblock stood in their way: Roche, who still played in the Wood-fronted version of the band.

In December of that year, a one-night resurrection of the ghost of T.S.O.L. took the stage at the Celebrity Theatre in Anaheim with rising OC bands the Offspring and Cadillac Tramps opening. Following weeks of internal wrangling, the active T.S.O.L.'s Wood and Mitch Dean withdrew their opposition to Roche's participation in the December 29 reunion show by the band's original lineup.

"I'm trying to get away from all the petty things and just get back to music," Roche told the *Los Angeles Times*. "We're going to play a really good [reunion] show, and the night after I'll start doing some shows again with the new T.S.O.L." They went on to play more shows over the next few years as LOST and Superficial Love.

In 1999, minus Barnes, who died of a brain aneurysm at the age of thirty-four earlier that year, the original core members sought to revive T.S.O.L. Despite claiming to have the rights to the name, Wood acquiesced and gave Grisham, Emory, and Roche—the classic version of T.S.O.L.—the name back.

"Roche came to me after getting out of prison for a couple years because of his dope habit and said, 'I wanna do T.S.O.L. again,'" Wood recalls. In response, Wood agreed, but only if he had the band's naming rights in Brazil. "I'll give you the band, the name, just give me Brazil, that's all I wanted," he said. The two parties verbally agreed to these terms, Wood said. However, after resuming the Grisham-led version of the band, Roche and company later wound up touring and making a quick run to Brazil in 2013. Today, though, Wood still plays with his version of the band under the name Change Today, and the battle of the two T.S.O.L.s still causes occasional confusion in the crowd.

"It's weird," Grisham said. "Their music [Wood's T.S.O.L.] does well online. We've kept that name going so they can never play. When T.S.O.L. plays, they expect to see us. But, sometimes the crowd will yell out songs that were from the other band. I just wish at the start, they would have fucking changed the name."

※※※※※

After 1983 and the initial boom, punk went underground and faded but didn't disappear. College afternoon shows at Cal State Fullerton and UCI were still prominent, as were some unorthodox shows.

Being that this was Orange County, there were bound to be punks who weren't exactly anti-authority. Specifically, in 1985, the Vandals headlined a Young Republicans–hosted show at Cypress College with support from Circle Jerks, the Dickies, the Vandals, D.I., and Plain Wrap.

"We were like, 'Eh, that's fine with us because they're Orange County people,'" Escalante said. "Our parents voted for Nixon, although my parents are Democrats, so we didn't care."

"I've always been a fairly conservative person myself," Keith Morris of Circle Jerks told the *Los Angeles Times* at the time. Not quite "Wild in the Streets." "Growing up, I was self-employed and my dad was in a small business. To me, the Republicans were for business in general, although lately they've swung to big business. But basically, the Republican party always stood for the employer and the Democrats stood for the employee. And being in a band is a business."

That said, Morris justified the Circle Jerks' appearance by pointing to the strength of the lineup and how the band had a number of shows in Orange County canceled, not to mention the fact that the bands had run into difficulty playing shows in the area.

"I'm not really a political person myself," he added. "Our main reason for doing the show is because of all the bands that are playing. We'd still do it if it was for the Democrats on campus. If it was for Young Communists, Young Socialists, or Young Fascists, we would have backed out."

"I like the Republicans," John Knight of D.I. also told the *Los Angeles Times*. "I think they are better, more open, more in tune with what is going on today. Rikk and Casey might shoot me if they heard that."

"It was one of the best shows we'd ever played," Escalante said.

Following the show, *LA Weekly* published an article criticizing the bands performing at the show. The bands responded either with ignorance or, as they stated in the buildup, by expressing that they didn't care about the organization's political leanings.

"They said nothing, compared to the shame of the Vandals, who knew and openly have supported Ronald Reagan or something like that," Escalante said. "I'm sure me and Jan did that somewhere. But that's part of being from Orange County. Chances are you come from a Republican family."

✕✕✕✕✕

Also in 1985, Mike Ness emerged as a new man. After years of addiction he got sober, and in the process gained a new perspective. He got a job painting houses. Though not the most riveting of gigs, being out in the sun all day was healthy for the singer. While on job sites, Ness's fellow workers would play oldies on the radio. With his foundational knowledge of classic rock, Ness was reinvigorated by hearing artists like Chuck Berry through this lens.

As he continued working during the day, it gave him motivation on how to bring Social Distortion forward. Even during his darkest days of addiction, Ness never gave up writing. As his sonic relationship with classic rock flourished, the songwriter had a new perspective to bring to his lyrics. Gone was the live fast, die young element that informed *Mommy's Little Monster*. Now in his mid-twenties, Ness was ready to live and was able to see things clearly for the first time in years. Focused and reinvigorated, he took this into the newly configured Social Distortion lineup.

"I thought that lyrically I was being honest and writing about real-life things," Ness said. "That's where I saw a connection. Billie Holiday singing about whiskey, heroin, and bad men . . . that's punk rock! So I felt it was important lyrically to hold on to that punk attitude but musically, venture off into a little Americana."

As Ness stayed on the straight and narrow, which he has been ever since, his energy was channeled in a new way. Sober for the first time in twelve years, he was more in touch with his feelings, which gave him more to write about. Wading through his fears and personal discomfort allowed him to grow as a songwriter and a human. His hunger for success remained, but sobriety allowed him to channel his talent in a vastly different way.

"I don't know where I got the work ethic," Ness mused, "but as soon as I stopped committing petty crimes and going to jail, it's amazing how much energy I had."

It wasn't necessarily easy, and challenges awaited. Less than a year sober, Ness crashed his motorcycle and was badly injured.

"He had asphalt on his leg and arm and everything," Christy Danell-Walker said. "Dennis got the call and somehow, Dennis got into the emergency room with him. He saw that Mike was begging them not to give him painkillers and told the doctor, 'You can't give him anything. He's an addict. You can't give him anything.' And they just start taking a wire brush and brushed out all the asphalt and shit out of his forearms."

Yet despite that pain and other potential brushes with painkillers, Ness endured and resisted any temptation. Danell's loyalty and friendship during Ness's darkest times weren't lost on him.

"Dennis really suffered the brunt with my addiction," Ness said. "I'd call him up dope-sick and say, 'I'm getting ready to just jump in front of a moving car right now so I can go to a hospital and get some fucking pain meds or something.' I don't know if I'd actually have done it but it's sad that it sounded reasonable in my mind at the time."

After he got sober, Ness had to relearn how to have fun without substances.

"I had a new set of friends in the program," he said. "It was important for me to have fun and then also learn to not take yourself so seriously."

Perhaps more important to Ness than his newfound creative burst was ensuring that Social Distortion was not pigeonholed as just a punk band. Ness was focused on playing better and being a better musician and implored his bandmates to do the same. He'd seen what had happened with his peers and how the roots music that he was reconnecting with informed their sound . . . and their look.

"It just became very important to me that that was American roots music," Ness said. "I'd seen bands like X, the Cramps, or the Gears bringing a rockabilly, '50s greaser vibe to the punk scene. I was rethinking things and wanted to bring that into our sound."

Over the next few years, Social Distortion plugged away. The band played all around Orange County and LA, with some weekends spent performing in Arizona and Northern California. Their national profile disappeared for a stretch as Ness came out of his drug fog. At these shows, the band debuted songs that would comprise their second album. The punk scene was mostly dead in the Southland, and Social Distortion had to find other places to perform (in addition to the usual house party scene), including up the coast in Santa Barbara, and they steadily built a following there.

Before Ness got sober in October 1985, the band recorded an early version of the *Prison Bound* album. Ness hated the recording because he was using drugs at the time.

Social Distortion wasn't the only band still swimming through these lost years for punk.

In 1986, D.I.'s sophomore album, *Horse Bites Dog Cries*, which was actually recorded a year earlier at Fullerton's Casbah Studios with Chaz Ramirez producing, came out through Reject Records.

However, the band's time with this iteration was limited.

Rikk Agnew would leave D.I. in 1986, and along with his brother Frank, he rejoined the Adolescents. Royer didn't leave D.I., but he returned to the Ads as well. The Blue Album's seminal lineup played shows and even laid down a pair of demos with "The Liar" and "Peasant Song."

"When we did that second go-round, the past was left where the past was, and there wasn't any bitterness," Brandenburg said.

After just a few months, Frank Agnew left the band and Alfie Agnew took his slot. Then in August, Royer chose to focus on D.I. and parted ways as well. He was replaced by Sandy Hanson.

The Adolescents weren't the same, and they knew it.

"I think that when Casey left, the band lost a major part of its sound," Brandenburg said in the liner notes for *Live 1981 & 1986*. "Casey always played this kinda surf beat. On top of that, he was a major part of the vocal attack. When Casey left, the band . . . changed."

At the end of 1986, Alfie Agnew departed and headed to college, and in was Dan Colburn.

The band toured with the new lineup and released *Brats in Battalions* in 1987. That year, Brandenburg and Colburn left the band, and the Adolescents were effectively done (outside of a Blue Album reunion show at Reseda Country Club in 1989), unable to fulfill the promise of the Blue Album lineup and that record. The band was never quite able to put it all together.

"I was interested in other things [I had joined another band, the Flower Leperds], and the Adolescents touring cut into my school work," Brandenburg said in the live album's liner notes.

The Flower Leperds released three albums between 1988 and 1990 and matched the Adolescents in success and name recognition. Over the next few years, the Adolescents splintered into different factions. Soto was involved in various other projects, including with Hanson, and Frank Agnew founded Joyride, and later, 22 Jacks. He would be a constant presence in the scene in the years to come.

Rikk Agnew rejoined Christian Death for a spell before releasing solo albums under the Rikk Agnew's Yard Sale moniker.

As for Brandenburg, he formed Sister Goddamn, which released two albums in the 1990s.

One thing was certain. The groups had varying degrees of success and could draw crowds, but they were Adolescents no more.

✕✕✕✕✕✕

As sobriety settled and cleared his mind, Ness continued to plug away. Social Distortion spent time in the studio in 1987, recording the songs they mastered while performing. Those songs were vastly different yet still retained the same songwriting sensibilities of Social Distortion's early material.

"By the mid-'80s, a lot of the bands were starting to sound the same and stereotype themselves with these ridiculous rules of what was and wasn't punk," Ness said. "The reason I got into punk was because there were *no* rules and you could do whatever you wanted."

Released in January 1988, *Prison Bound*, the ten-song collection released through Restless Records that was produced and engineered by Chaz Ramirez at Casbah Studio in Fullerton, remains a high-water mark in Orange County punk. The machine-gun fury of *Mommy's Little Monster* was left behind, but its urgency was channeled in different ways.

In a review posted on *AllMusic*, Vincent Jeffries said of *Prison Bound*, "Slower and more song-driven than their previous disc, this sophomore outing is an absolute triumph. The epic stories of hard living and regret that became Social Distortion's trademark fill *Prison Bound*'s tracklist."

In conclusion, Jeffries wrote that fans of the band who may have missed *Prison Bound* should "pick up this gem and are encouraged to do just that at their very first opportunity, as the list of West Coast punk offerings more influential than *Prison Bound* is extremely short."

The album saw Social Distortion take a massive leap forward and influenced a new group of fans.

"I fucking loved *Prison Bound* when it came out," said Chris Shiflett of No Use for a Name and later Foo Fighters. "'Prison Bound,' I mean that's a country song even if it's punk rock. That record really had a huge influence on me."

It wasn't just Ness's growth as a songwriter that influenced the Santa Barbara native. In 1986, a fifteen-year-old Shiflett's band opened for Social Distortion and noticed a major difference between this Social Distortion and *Mommy's Little Monster*–era Social D. The scraggly, early punker look from the '70s that Ness channeled was out as well. In was a look that channeled '50s greaser culture.

"It's silly to talk about, but that was when their look became that thing," Shiflett said. "It was fucking baggy pants, a wifebeater, hair slicked back and we all just thought that was the fucking coolest thing in the world. I used to have long hair, and I fucking brought a picture of Mike Ness to the fucking barber and said, like, give me *that*. I just got the full-on short back and sides, you know? Even then, if I saw him [Ness] fucking wear overalls or something, then I'd go out and fucking get a pair of overalls and a wifebeater under it."

As much as Ness became a style icon within a sliver of the punk world, it was his words that allowed Social Distortion to blossom.

"He became a really great storyteller," Matt Pinfield, a music historian and host of MTV's *120 Minutes*, said of Ness's transformation. "And it was really evident."

At the time, Pinfield was the music director of an alternative radio station in New Jersey. He and Ness hit it off instantly.

"I got a phone call at the radio station that Mike wanted to come in," Pinfield recalled. "He wanted to promote the show at Fastlane and I was like, 'Fuck yeah, man!' I loved *Mommy's Little Monster*. But I had already heard something off *Prison Bound* and it was perfect for the time. Mike was really ahead of his time."

The two's bond and friendship would carry on to the present day. Over the years, Ness performed on *120 Minutes,* and more recently in 2023 he appeared on Pinfield's *New & Approved* radio show on KLOS in Los Angeles, where he opened up about his tonsil cancer diagnosis. But back in 1988, Ness and Social Distortion were breaking out of California and touring the US, and having radio support on the other side of the country helped Social Distortion garner attention.

Eagle-eyed fans noticed that the *Prison Bound* cover featured several things that were unusual to the band. First was the Social Distortion font on its cover. Laughing, Ness gives credit (or blame, depending on your point of view) to the album's photographer.

"The lettering on the front cover was the same as the Hell's Angels," he said. "He was helpful in making an album cover that had an edge to it."

Looking even closer, under Social Distortion, the cover said the band was from LA despite the members never being from LA or having associated much with that scene. But alas, it ended up being an accident that confused first-time listeners and new fans.

What couldn't be confused was the album's sound. Though some songs clocked in at under four minutes, a number that would have turned punks pale at the beginning of the decade, *Prison Bound* was defined by its progressive way of infusing blues, rockabilly, and roots music with punk. The album included a cover of the Rolling Stones' "Backstreet Girl" and crystallized references to personal struggles. However, the album's title track (with a call-out to one of Ness's heroes,

Johnny Cash, and "Walk the Line," which was a preview of things to come) clocked in at nearly five and a half minutes and caught the attention of Rodney Bingenheimer and KROQ. "Prison Bound" was soon in the station's heavy rotation as one of its most-requested songs.

Tough lessons from the *Mommy's Little Monster* era were learned, and Social Distortion was better for it.

"We had gotten calls from guys at some independent labels and they were talking the language," Danell said. "At the time we didn't know anything about the industry and they're telling us, 'We'll meet you down at the Harley Davidson shop and buy you guys four new Harleys.' And I had called my manager going, 'I want a bike so fucking bad.' And he goes, 'Nope, don't settle for the immediate gratification.'

"We would have been looking good for about six months until the bikes started breaking down," he continued. "And then we would have had to sell them to pay the rent, and three years down the line we'd have no motorcycles and still have to do three more albums."

The song was played so much that even the band members couldn't avoid it.

"I was driving home from work in my '77 Monte Carlo," Ness remembered. "It ["Prison Bound"] came on the radio at a red light and I just blasted it! I couldn't believe that it was being played on the radio right then. I thought, 'Maybe someday I can quit my job painting.'"

As instructive and informative as the painting job was for Ness in reconnecting with the sounds of his childhood, he wasn't the only musician fixing up houses.

Jonny Wickersham, who was born in Oceanside but moved to Mammoth at a young age, found his way to Orange County as a teen. From childhood, Wickersham had a desire to play music.

He and Ness, who is five years older than him, first crossed paths when he was sixteen. At the time, Wickersham was living with his father and his father's girlfriend in Costa Mesa. A friend of his had a half-pipe and would hang out skating on the street. A few days after seeing Social Distortion and the Vandals play at the Pomona Valley Auditorium, Wickersham couldn't believe what he saw: Mike Ness in the wild.

"I think I was sitting on the curb or sitting on my skateboard or something," Wickersham said. "Then some dude came rolling up on a ten-speed. Like handlebars up, full-on stoner style and was primer black. It was one of those things that you'd ride it and leave it somewhere—it was your transport. So there's this dude cruising, all black clothes and bleached hair. We were like, 'Oh, fuck! It's Mike Ness!' We're young, little punkers over here at the skateboard ramp, and Ness looked at us and spat and kept going. I'll never forget it."

It turns out there wasn't much to forget. Maybe a minute later, Wickersham and his friends saw Ness pull up a few houses down, drop the bike, and walk through a gate. The young sleuths figured out that the house was where Ness was staying at the time, and they'd go up to him whenever they'd see him.

"We loved them," he said. "Social D were the kings of Orange County."

His love of Social Distortion and the Adolescents was one of the reasons that Wickersham, who soon was nicknamed Jonny Two Bags, started delving into the punk scene.

Now a few years later, Wickersham, who was battling addiction issues of his own, was painting houses to earn an honest wage. To his shock, he saw Ness on the same job site.

"We were both painting fucking houses and it was pretty trippy," Wickersham said. "There was this one dude that hired us one time. We still laugh about it because we were down in Laguna Beach painting some house and the boss put us to work. He outlined our day and then as far as we knew he split, he was this old fucking Marine. What he had done was fucking gone to a fucking another hill and was watching us. He comes back later and shouts at us, 'You lazy motherfuckers!' The whole time we were sitting around smoking and talking, listening to the tunes on the radio."

Prison Bound took off and as their peers in Orange County faded or broke up, Social Distortion's profile increased, and they were finally fulfilling the potential they flashed earlier in the decade. They toured the country, and the songs were positively received. Never one to rest on his band's praises, Ness continued to write. Right before *Prison Bound* was released, Ness wrote two songs that would change the band's fortunes.

With "Prison Bound" a radio hit and the band's song structures evolving, the major labels suddenly had an eye on Social Distortion. It's something that wasn't lost on the band.

"That's when they [major labels] went, 'Fuck, how did nobody sign that band?'" Reece said. "We're fucking KROQ's No. 1 most requested band! Of course, labels started sniffing around and they wanted in on it. And that's how that Sony deal came about."

And with good reason. A sober Mike Ness was writing songs not just at a prolific pace, but with a sensibility that had escaped the band during their wild early days. That didn't stop his bandmates from having a good time. While Danell, Maurer, and Reece were out, Ness channeled his energy elsewhere.

"I would just stay in and write a song," Ness said. "And that's how I got my satisfaction."

Unlike other bands, Ness preferred to write and work out songs live before heading into the studio. In 1987, Ness wrote "Ball and Chain," a song he called a "punk rock hymn."

"I like that 'Ball and Chain' means something different to everyone who listens to it," he said. "But for me, it meant asking for help from a higher power and something greater than myself. It's a spiritual song, and I think people relate to it because everyone has struggles, and the ball and chain is obviously the struggles of people's lives and trying to overcome them."

Ness also wrote the autobiographical "Story of My Life," a nostalgic look back at what was and how quickly things had changed in their lives, moving past in the blink of an eye. For those close to home, it was easy to hear Ness ruminating about how Fullerton had changed and how things like gentrification had started to chip away at the city's character. Specifically, he points to how Farrell's, a pool hall that used to be at State College and Chapman, became a 7-Eleven. Yet as his storytelling continued to blossom, Ness still wasn't fully confident in his ability to connect with the band's audience, even though *Prison Bound* expanded the idea of what punk was and what direction it could go in. As for the sound, it swung and had a rockabilly edge unlike anything the band recorded before or anything that was popular at the time.

"When I was writing songs such as 'Story of My Life' and 'Ball and Chain,' I wasn't sure people were going to like them," Ness said. "I knew I did, so it was a huge risk-taking thing because these weren't stereotypical punk songs."

"That was when we were touring in the van and we played them [the new songs] at soundcheck," Reece said. "We'd play around with them [the music] and he'd write some lyrics and he'd [Ness] make a song out of it. That was the process. Everyone contributed to what they thought the song should sound like. The chemistry of those four guys made the songs happen."

As the success of "Prison Bound" spread, Social Distortion hit the road. At one point, the band played twenty-seven consecutive shows. With funds still fairly tight, Reece served as the band's tour manager on top of his drumming duties.

Once Roger Klein signed Social Distortion to Epic Records in 1989, they knew it was go-time.

"When 'Prison Bound' came out, I thought the lyrics were so personal, so full of pain, but there was some hopefulness there too," Klein told the *Los Angeles Times*. "Before knowing anything about [Ness], I figured he had to be talking about what he knew. . . . There was a sense of honesty that really bowled me over."

"This was my shot," Ness said of what was to come. "This was a major-label record, and I had a shot to carve a direction for the future of this band and what I wanted this band to sound like in 30 years."

"Mike was in full swing," Reece said. "They met and told him to write another album and he did it. He didn't want to play *Mommy's Little Monster* when he was thirty."

Working with producer Dave Jerden, Ness was more involved in the album's production than before. He was concerned that Epic would try to meddle in the band's sound, but having a smallish major label budget kept the band off its radar. With his bandmates' support, including Danell's, who was into the American roots that Ness was exploring, the songs that were worked out in sound checks were finally ready to record.

Also, with the major label money, Ness was able to quit his painting job and focus on Social Distortion full-time. But he didn't lose his edge.

"Some of that rebelliousness and attitude and snarl never really leaves us," Ness said. "I talk about the changes I've come through, but a lot of the characteristics we establish as children stay with us."

In March 1990, Social Distortion's self-titled major label debut was released. The ten songs that comprised the self-titled album picked up where *Prison Bound* left off. They were tough tales about what might have been or the struggles of getting by—topics Ness knew all too well.

"When I wrote this album, I never realized I'd write songs that would change people's lives through the hard times and the good times," Ness said. "I'm just a singer and a guitar player, and I'm grateful these songs have become timeless. People would listen to the lyrics and say they're not hardcore. I was like, 'Really? Because they're about real life.' Besides, what's more hardcore than real life?"

"I had no idea if fans were going to like 'Sick Boys' or 'Story of My Life' or 'Ball and Chain' because they weren't typical punk songs," he continued.

The songs took off.

"Everything about the production of the self-titled record, it still has every bit of edge, from his voice to the instrumentation to delivery," Pinfield said. "He grew into this unbelievable songwriter, this guy could really express himself, you know, through lyrics and talk about his own vulnerabilities and the things that he had been through. It had all the punk ethos and this amazing storytelling, yet there was still that danger and that edginess."

Despite Social Distortion reaching the biggest audiences of their career, things weren't going great internally. Once the stakes got bigger and more money was involved, the issues that were lingering before bubbled to the surface.

"Everything's fine until the money starts rolling in," Reece said. "It's fucking one for all, all for one. Then come the fucking lawyers, fucking management and then the pressure from the record label and that's when the management starts going around doing the divide and conquer shit."

Despite the problems that simmered, the band was at their best.

Having a hit song helps. "Story of My Life," the album's second single, was a hit. Its music video, which sees the band performing in a warehouse as clips from LA and Orange County are spliced in, was in rotation on MTV.

This was all part of a strategy that Guerinot knew would pay off for the band.

"People used to tease me," Guerinot said. "We know your big plan: KROQ, [MTV's] *Buzz Bin* and worldwide. If those all connected, you had the world on lock."

"We'd go to a hotel bar, and they'd have MTV on, and it would be 'Hey, that's us!'" Reece said of the surreal experience. "That changed everything overnight. We went from being a bar band to everyone fucking knowing us because we were on MTV."

The album was Social Distortion's first that landed on the *Billboard* 200 charts, peaking at number 128.

"Look at all the singles that came off it," Pinfield said. "People forget that 'Let It Be Me' was the first single. There were just so many great songs on that record, start to finish. It's just one of the greatest records of that era."

Still, some local grumbles lingered about the hard-earned success Social Distortion was receiving after over a decade of grinding.

"I wasn't going to buy into that [criticism]," Ness said. "Like, you're not supposed to become successful at it? Because I fucking hated painting houses. There was a little sense of satisfaction, but there was no applause, not like being onstage."

Social Distortion was also the band's first album to receive the RIAA's Gold certification. Amid the growing influences of punk and alternative, the album won the band new admirers with its fusion of those genres.

Songs like "It Coulda Been Me" saw Ness looking at friends who died or went to prison. Knowing he could have been another sad statistic, Ness also used the song to show how he'd grown in a relatively short period of time, leaving crime and drugs in the past. "It's very important to remember where you come from and that you can easily go back," Ness told *Rolling Stone* in 2015.

The album wasn't complete without a cover song. In this case, it was Johnny Cash's "Ring of Fire." At the time, Cash wasn't quite considered the king of cool. Not that Ness cared. The legendary singer-songwriter had a monumental influence on the punk's songwriting with tales of outcasts and outlaws roaming around and doing as they pleased as they wrestled with consequences. Thus, for a guy who implored that he got into punk because there were no rules, he couldn't care less about the flak he received for covering the Cash classic.

"People should realize that a good song is a good song," Ness said. "I remember some of my friends, or someone I was an acquaintance of, I was talking about, 'I'm gonna record a Johnny Cash song on this record.' He was like, 'That's not very punk.' And I was like, 'Don't tell me what is punk and what isn't because you're going to lose that debate.' Secondly, I don't like confines and that's *why* I got into punk. So I'd call it the punk rock police when I heard something like that."

After a barren decade, Social Distortion's cover put eyeballs back on Cash for the first time in a while.

"I want to give all the credit to Rick Rubin for what he did with Johnny Cash," Ness said. "But I do know that us putting that out opened the door for that. And that feels good."

The big hit that subsequently became Social Distortion's signature song was "Ball and Chain." The mid-tempo song, which swung unlike any other of the band's songs, was the emotional touchpoint of the album. Like "Story of My Life," the song was filmed for a music video (in downtown LA) that received heavy airplay on MTV.

It was due to this new exposure that the music resonated far beyond Southern California.

"I remember hearing it when I was eleven years old and knowing that it doesn't sound like anything that's going on right now," the Gaslight Anthem's Brian Fallon said of the music. Despite Social Distortion's inroads surrounding *Prison Bound*, having the MTV cosign enabled the band to reach kids in New Jersey, including Fallon. The band's eclectic sound didn't hurt.

"It was everything I liked all in one sound," he said. "And the musicianship was different."

As the album began to sell and they became recognizable, Social Distortion were rock stars. After grinding for years, the band's faith was rewarded, and things changed far beyond what they expected. They went from scraping around Orange County to hanging out with Robert De Niro at Grammy after-parties, a far cry from dust-ups at the Cuckoo's Nest.

With their self-titled album, Social Distortion left their Orange County contemporaries in the rearview mirror. At the beginning of the 1980s, Social Distortion was arguably the third-biggest band in the county behind the Adolescents and T.S.O.L. by some distance. As those bands splintered and crumbled amid personality clashes and drugs, Ness and Danell persisted, and by the end of 1990, they kicked open a door in a way that few thought was possible. Yet even bigger things were about to come for Social Distortion and Orange County.

"So much has happened in five years in all of our lives," Ness said at the time. "Becoming sober and painting houses to rubbing elbows with your heroes. For me, especially, it seems almost like I've started life all over. I feel totally grateful."

10

THE BOYS FROM GARDEN GROVE

Following an October 1983 riot at a Social Distortion show that they couldn't get into in Irvine, Bryan "Dexter" Holland and Greg Kriesel decided to form a band (Holland started on drums before moving to guitar, and Kriesel helmed the bass). The two, who were friends and teammates on the Pacifica High School cross-country team, weren't exactly the most popular kids in school.

"A real unglamorous sport," Holland said. "Cheerleaders ignored us. We'd run three miles, then puke at the finish."

That's not including their academic pedigree. To say they were nerds would be generous.

"It's a pretty geeky thing to be in the math club," Holland said. "And what's worse, I was the president."

As much as the guys liked punk and were excited to form a band, they still had a reputation they were trying to shake. After all, Holland was Pacifica High School's valedictorian in 1984.

"Punkers would, like, ditch class, smoke in the parking lot and get bad grades," Holland said. "The punkers thought we were geeks."

Though they'd been jamming together for a year, hearing T.S.O.L.'s *Change Today?* (after Holland grew up with a steady diet of Creedence Clearwater Revival, KISS, David Bowie, and Elton John) and seeing Social Distortion served as the impetus to turn those jam sessions into something real. Calling themselves Manic Subsidal ("Terrible name! Worst name ever," Holland quips), the lineup was filled out by singer Doug Thompson and drummer Jim Benton. They kept the Manic Subsidal name for a year before quickly realizing that, besides being a mouthful, it didn't look great on the back of a leather jacket.

In 1985, they recruited Kevin "Noodles" Wasserman to play guitar. The other members had ulterior motives for wanting the guitarist to join them: he was over twenty-one and could buy alcohol. At the time, Noodles and drummer James Lilja—who grew up in the same neighborhood as Holland and Kriesel (later immortalized in "The Kids Aren't Alright") and was friends with Noodles's older brother Darren—were playing in Clowns of Death, a name they took from Oingo Boingo.

Just like his new bandmates, Noodles wasn't exactly the homecoming king either.

"I would've been the one upside down in the garbage can," he said. "I used to have kids flushing my glasses down the toilet."

Formed in 1984, Clowns of Death featured Noodles, drummer James Lilja, and others. The band started playing in Noodles's parents' living room. Previously, Holland and Kriesel were a two-man operation. But soon, the pair, who were friends with Lilja, went to Noodles's place.

"It was like the room exploded when we did our first song together," Holland said.

They agreed with Holland that if he would play with them

(Holland, Kriesel, and Lilja were classmates at Pacifica High School in Garden Grove), they'd join his band in return. Soon, they'd join forces in Manic Subsidal. Thus, Clowns of Death performed a grand total of zero shows.

"We almost played a party. We tried to play Jughead's Dump," Noodles said. "She saw the flyer, and then canceled the party. She knew all of the punk rock people we knew would show up and was like, 'My parents' house would get trashed, I can't do this!' And it turns out Dexter's songs were good and our songs sucked. We knew we wrote garbage."

The reason why? Despite being "nerdy," the group had friends with names like "Lizard" and had some other shady friends who caused the party to be called off. "I wasn't one of them, I just liked being around them," Noodles said. "Looking back, she was damn straight right."

"There was a rebellion against whatever the homogeneity of Orange County was because it was this weird feeling," Holland recalls. "I don't remember any of us being overtly political, but we were bored."

Just like Clowns of Death, the first time the Offspring played together was in Noodles's living room.

"When the volume just went, a song kicked in, it was like this huge rush," Holland remembers. "It was like, 'Whoa, this is the hottest thing ever.'"

In search of a new name, the band came up with a number of options but ultimately settled on the Offspring.

"I don't know if anyone was blown away with the name," Holland says. "But we all acquiesced."

"We all had these names we all felt really strongly about, but nobody hated the name [the Offspring]," Noodles says.

By 1986, the Garden Grove band had a newly minted moniker and a stable lineup, and they were starting to write and record their own songs.

Lilja would attend UCLA with a premed focus, and Holland would go to USC to do the same. The group would get together on the weekends and learn new songs. The band would go on to play their first show in Santa Cruz at Club Culture. "We drove all the way to Santa Cruz to open this crappy show," Noodles says.

"It was so hard to get a show," Holland said. "Then we got a show in Santa Cruz and it was like, 'Hey, no problem!' It was 400 miles away and we were stoked to get a show anywhere."

"We weren't allowed to do the Sunset Strip," Noodles said. "We weren't allowed to play the Roxy or the Whisky. We were relegated to the back-alley places in the industrial parts of town. But all that was changing."

The next day, the Offspring would play an afternoon show at the San Francisco punk venue Mabuhay Gardens (which would close in 1987).

"We were terrible, we were so bad," Holland said. "Like if James made a mistake, he would stop for a second and figure out where it was. Noodles broke strings constantly. He broke a string during the set and didn't have any strings because they were in the car. So he had to stop and he left us on the stage for two minutes while he ran to the car. It was a complete disaster."

The band would eventually play a show with New York hardcore outfit Agnostic Front. However, Agnostic Front wouldn't perform due to skinheads and other problems.

"The fire department was next to the hall," Noodles said. "People were throwing beer bottles over the wall until the fire department had it shut down."

"Punkers weren't smart back then," Lilja said.

"The amazing thing about this particular show is that James, for some reason, had a video camera, which were not easy to come by in the late '80s," Holland said. He "captured the whole thing, the whole day. What's so cool about that is when things finally happened for us [after they broke through], people were like, 'These guys aren't real punk blah blah blah.' I like being able to go to that and say we were kinda there from the beginning. No one helped us out and we got the video to prove it."

The band steadily honed their craft and would play generator shows in the desert (including one in the Mojave with Fugazi in the lineup), along with wild house parties, including one where attendees took sledgehammers to the house's wall to make a handy new window so more people could see the stage. Looking back, the band said it was one of their greatest early shows.

Lilja eventually left the band first to attend medical school.

"The scene was kind of dying in a lot of ways," Lilja said of his decision to leave the band on Holland and Noodles's *Time to Relax* podcast. Seeing Nazi punks at a show didn't help either. "The scene was just getting nasty and mean. It was less musical and more angry and I had my share of that. It was too much."

He became a renowned oncologist, leaving punk rock behind (at least at the time).

"I liked the classes and I liked being a student," Lilja said. "The sciences—I'm a big proponent of the sciences—it was like you're learning the mysteries of the universe. Everything is a little epiphany when you learn something."

However, before Lilja was replaced by Ron Welty in 1987, the emerging band received a much-needed boost. The Offspring pressed one thousand copies of "I'll Be Waiting," the first song they'd recorded (featuring Lilja on drums), with "Blackball" as the B-side on their Black Label records. On a whim one Sunday night, Holland made the twenty-five-minute drive from USC in South Los Angeles to Pasadena to deliver a copy of the single to Rodney Bingenheimer. Holland learned that bands could drop off their demo or single at the back door of Bingenheimer's home and that he would answer if someone rang the doorbell. When Holland arrived, Bingenheimer didn't answer, but someone else did. Holland passed along the band's seven-inch, hopped back in his car, and headed back to USC thinking nothing of it. He hoped for the best but didn't expect anything to happen.

Two hours later in his dorm room, Holland tuned in to KROQ and received quite the surprise.

"'So I just got this record from this band called the Offspring,'" Holland said while imitating Bingenheimer's iconically tepid voice on the radio. "And he actually played it!"

It began a long-running relationship in the band's formative days that would help establish them as a presence on Southern California radio.

At that point, the band was growing a successful name, getting played on local radio, and scraping together the beginnings of punk rock credibility.

There was just one problem: outside of their parents' garage, they had nowhere to play in SoCal. Options at the time were anemic at best. The Cuckoo's Nest? Long gone. The Olympic in LA? Too sketchy for some angel-faced suburbanites. The Longshoreman's Hall in San Pedro was the site of their first beatdown at a Dead Kennedys show. The only viable silver lining was Fender's Ballroom in Long Beach, which had just opened, and they were probably underqualified to play (and the venue let them know it when they tried to book a gig).

The Offspring ran into problems trying to get conventional shows. They sent their cassettes around but were told in no uncertain terms that punk bands were out and hair metal reigned supreme.

That left only three solid local options for the Offspring—the

VFW Halls, local bowling alleys, and the ever-so-cool community rooms run by the Knights of Columbus. (Los Angeles's Anti Club was an option as well.)

"That [going to the halls] was just some kid going in and duping the owner because the owner isn't punk rock," Holland said with a laugh. "You know, hundreds of unruly jazz kids ready to cause damage? He thinks, 'OK, whatever.' Then it would be moving on to the next thing—the next victim, I guess."

At the time, backyard parties were also an option. Unlike other OC bands of the mid-'80s, the Offspring weren't dabbling in hard drugs. They preferred to hang out and knock down some beers, which made parties an ideal place to play. But they had to have their ears to the ground—and they were often one-time-only affairs. And bands couldn't risk playing late . . . or else.

"If you were lucky enough, you wanted to make sure you could set up and play before the cops came because that was inevitable," Holland said. "They'd come at some point, and only half the bands that were there got to play . . . they were also so much fun. People are just there wanting to have fun. You know, there were no rules. Everybody was drinking, having a good time."

When the rest of the band aside from Noodles finally turned twenty-one, they were able to experience the cool-kid punk scene—the sweat-drenched chaos of Night Moves club where bands like Social Distortion and 45 Grave had already reached local hero status, the pinnacle of punk at its West Coast birth. Their brand of catchy, melodic songs wasn't what the hardcore punk audiences wanted to hear in the beginning. They were looking for the soundtrack of bloody brawls and anarchy. What the Offspring did was different, and they knew it.

Holland was acutely aware that the LA punk scene wasn't going to offer them a place in the sun. For them, the promised land by the Bay was the emerging punk haven of 924 Gilman Street in Berkeley.

"It was very, very weird for us until Gilman Street came along," Holland says. "That was a total game changer."

Having first been introduced to the venue when they were perusing magazines at Zed Records in Long Beach, the group discovered Gilman Street. They heard (and read) strong positive reviews of the shows and of the venue itself in *Flipside* and *Maximum Rocknroll*.

"Egalitarian." "Punk rock utopia." "A cool place to hang out." These are a few of the succinct words used to describe the DIY venue. It was welcoming Northern California culture at its best.

"It was kids putting on shows for kids," Noodles said.

Free from the stench of capitalism that accompanied pay-to-play shows in Orange County, Gilman Street allowed the Offspring to sharpen their skills in front of like-minded musicians and fans.

Soon enough, the band had a bigger following in the Bay than they did at their home base. With that, the Offspring would travel up north every three months to play shows, but it didn't come without some stress.

Since he was older than his bandmates and not a full-time student, Noodles had to worry about paying the bills. He first took a job as a substitute janitor at night so he could go to school during the day. Then he was eventually promoted to assistant janitor, which was a full-time job. "For an eighteen-year-old kid [at the time when he started], it was good money," he said.

"You got your foot in as a substitute!" Holland joked. "You can't just walk in and be a custodian."

While Noodles went the blue-collar route right out of high school, Holland—who was always a wiz when it came to science and math—went the college route, earning a scholarship to USC as a premed and his bachelor's in biology, a master's in molecular biology, and eventually a PhD in the same field.

Once a month, the band would get together to rehearse or play shows—wash, rinse, repeat.

Their first album was released in March 1989, a year after Holland graduated from college. The self-titled album was recorded in Santa Ana at South Coast Recording by Thom Wilson and was released on the indie label Nemesis Records, which boasted extreme metal band Brujeria, San Diego punk group Pitchfork, and Orange County hardcore outfit Uniform Choice on its roster. Unlike the other groups, the Offspring showcased their brand of melodic punk that differed from the hardcore bands they admired that had emerged from the region earlier in the decade. "Elders" was a song set higher on the guitar and the first that Holland sang in a higher vocal range, which gave the song an urgency that he would carry with him to future Offspring songs.

Wilson taught the band what it was like to explore sound in a studio space and instilled in them the importance of recording live. He also told them why he thought punk rock songs didn't vary from band to band and didn't have dynamics. It informed how the Offspring would thoughtfully go about crafting their songs.

The songs carried the DNA of their heroes like the Damned, with stabbing guitar tones and jolting time signatures like the Adolescents. Songs like "Out on Patrol" and the previously released version of "I'll Be Waiting" were carried by Holland's clean, angst-ridden vocals. What the music lacked in catchy hooks it made up for in energy. The band said that "Beheaded" is their version of T.S.O.L.'s "Code Blue." That song is the only one where Holland collaborated on lyrics with Lilja, showcasing the pair's warped sense of humor.

It would be several years before they perfected the art of melding aggression and pop hooks in a way that would make them one of the highest-grossing punk bands of all time, selling millions of records and touring the world. But for a debut effort by a local punk band, the self-titled debut checked many boxes, including pissing off OC's conservative elders.

The album's last track, "Kill the President," didn't score them any points with diehard conservative cable access host Wally George, who had the band on his show *Hot Seat* to "talk" to them about the song. It wound up being the shortest interview ever.

"I wanna tell you guys, you're from Orange County, but I think you are totally disgraceful," the ghoulishly white-haired George said with his trademark menacing glare. He then proceeded to pull a Sinead O'Connor move by smashing the LP in front of them and tearing up the cover as the crowd of conserv-o-teens (including one in a Bad Religion T-shirt of all things) jeered. The band looked on and laughed on camera for a few minutes, egging on the crowd before being escorted offstage as George destroyed the vinyl on camera.

That quick appearance on KDOC was just about the only press they got for the record—not quite enough to land a real manager, even the guy who later became their manager, Jim Guerinot, who at the time was with A&M Records in addition to managing Social Distortion. The band remembers hitting him up for the first time and being surprised to actually get a response. It was a "no"—but at least he wrote them back.

Throughout this time, the Offspring played a variety of punk shows in the area. Sometimes they'd land on a straight-edge hardcore show, which couldn't have been a worse fit. The Offspring guys liked to drink beer and had long hair, which didn't go over well with that group. One such show saw them play with Hard Stance, featuring Zack de la Rocha on vocals.

"They called us fucking hippies," Noodles said. "Then we started playing and four or five songs in, they shut up. Eventually, Zack came up to us and said, 'Sorry we were dicks.' I think they thought we were going to be a worse version of the classic rock band that played before us."

Before he was rocking with Rage Against the Machine, de la Rocha was a member of Hard Stance. The group formed in 1987 and was a straight-edge hardcore band. Their shows were known for being rowdy within Orange County's hardcore scene at the time. People would mosh, jump onstage during the set, and break bottles, which for their home base of Irvine was out of control. At one such show in Heritage Park, cops showed up and shot tear gas at the crowd.

Hard Stance expanded out of Orange County, playing shows in San Diego before ultimately splitting in 1990. After leaving Hard Stance, de la Rocha played guitar with melodic hardcore band Farside.

Farside pushed the sound and look of what fans thought hardcore could be. Farside singer Michael "Popeye" Vogelsang would wear science goggles and was armed with the unhardcore weapon of an acoustic guitar.

"People were like, 'What the fuck is this shit?'" Farside bassist Bryan Chu said. "Once we started playing, more girls came to the shows. It was interesting."

Hardcore as a whole wasn't known for attracting female audiences, but in Irvine, there was a fervent love of the music. With their boundary-pushing sound and embrace of hardcore, Farside became a popular band that was known for an always-shifting sonic style. They signed with Huntington Beach–based Revelation Records and released three albums, becoming one of the Orange County hardcore bands to become popular outside of the region. Ultimately, they'd split in 2000.

As for de la Rocha, after his brief spell with Farside he joined hardcore band Inside Out, and he eventually left to play in a band with his longtime Irvine bud Tim Commerford. The two learned about punk rock by listening to the Sex Pistols' *Never Mind the Bollocks, Here's the Sex Pistols* in sixth grade. They carried that punk rock spirit and a love of hip-hop forward to form Rage Against the Machine with Tom Morello and Brad Wilk in 1991.

xxxxxxx

Things weren't necessarily easy on the touring front either. The Off-spring's first national tour following the release of their debut album wasn't well-attended, with a total of six people watching them play in New Jersey. Sparse crowds were the norm. It wasn't until 1994 that the Offspring would draw more than fifty people to any given show on their own.

There was a show at the Copacetic Cafe in Riverside where the Off-spring played with Guttermouth and Pennywise. Much to their surprise, the promoter asked the Offspring to go on last. However, the venue emptied out after Pennywise, leaving only a few people left in the pit.

It wouldn't be until a few years later that Brett Gurewitz would invite them to join his well-respected punk label. Signing to Epitaph wasn't cut-and-dry.

"We learned about the labels through *Maximum Rocknroll* and *Flipside* in the ads," Holland says. They would send their demos to the labels, rarely getting a response or feedback. In time, they became friends with some of the guys at *Flipside* who were fans of theirs, like Kirk Dominguez. In 1991, the magazine put out a compilation titled *The Big One*. It would feature bands from Northern California on one side and Southern California on the other. Asked by *Flipside* to contribute and given an offer they couldn't refuse of $500, the Offspring were in.

The sessions took place at Gurewitz's Westbeach Recorders in

Hollywood, and he'd engineer the Offspring's contributing track "Take It Like a Man."

"He [Gurewitz] did a couple of songs with us," Holland says. "And he seemed like he was cool."

Things went well, but they could have gone better had Holland taken the R2-D2 approach to playing against Gurewitz's Chewbacca in a game of chess. Gurewitz told Holland he wanted to start a punk rock chess club.

"I really wanted them to sign us [to Epitaph]," Holland says. "So it's like, shit, I should probably let him win, right?"

"You didn't let him win," Noodles adds.

"Nope, sure didn't!" Holland exclaims. "I couldn't do that, but I wonder if it made him respect us more."

"I think that they've always had a little bit of resentment that I didn't sign them when they first sent me their demo, which I thought was OK, but a little derivative of T.S.O.L.—and there's nothing wrong with that," Gurewitz said. "I was just one person. I was running Epitaph out of the back of my recording studio, which was my livelihood, and I was working two jobs, and I didn't have any employees. I could only put out so many records."

A few years earlier, Gurewitz saw an Offspring show at Hollywood venue Raji's. While he liked what he heard, he decided to pass on signing the band. Holland and Gurewitz had built a rapport and stayed in touch.

After their match, Holland wasn't invited to join the punk rock chess club, and it would take a few more years before the Offspring signed to Epitaph in 1992. By then, Holland had not gotten into medical school and was working on his PhD.

"By the time they sent me the demo for *Ignition*, I had another employee and put out a few more records," Gurewitz said. "I was able to do it. And I thought the demos were better and they'd gotten a little bit of momentum going with the first record."

The band recorded demos and, when complete, would pass them along to the Epitaph boss. Nothing would come of it until an unexpected endorser convinced Gurewitz to sign the band on the strength of one of those demos.

"Brett came to our show at the Anti Club [on Melrose Avenue in Los Angeles] when he decided to sign us," Noodles said. "I remember him sitting at our table, and he said something about how his son Max loved [their demo of] 'Session.' That's why he signed us."

"I might have said something like that, but that was probably me making conversation," Gurewitz said. "At that time, my son would have been like three years old. So I think I was just trying to connect with them on a human level."

THE PUNK ROCK ROADHOUSE

inda Jemison was born in Anaheim in 1964, and her childhood home was just a few miles away from Disneyland. Growing up in the resort and theme park's shadow, she and her siblings used to climb the tree in their front yard to watch fireworks explode in the sky over the Magic Kingdom, which typically felt like a world away from reality. She grew up lower middle class: "My mom raised four kids on a middle-class salary, my sister pretty much played mom to me when my mom was working, so going to Disneyland was a once-a-year thing if we were lucky, even though we were so close."

Her first recollection of music came from watching her older sister, who became a singer and regularly performed in plays before joining a band at age fifteen. One time while lingering around the band as they were rehearsing, Jemison was haphazardly pushed into music when the band's bass player didn't show up to practice, prompting the drummer to fill in on the low end. They ended up asking Jemison, who'd never touched a kit before, to play drums. "So the drummer said, 'Get behind the drums, Linda, I'm gonna play bass. Here's what you do . . .'" Within five to ten minutes Linda picked it up, and "a monster was born." Her mom bought her a hundred-dollar, no-name wood-paneled kit and made a compromise with her—it was this bottom-shelf crappy kit for now, at least until she had continued playing for a year, and then her drums would be upgraded. She was instantly hooked, listening to any of the music her brother and sister were into, mostly mainstream rock and disco. The table was set for her to continue as a typical teenybopper until punk rock came into her life at a party in 1979.

"I went to a party one day with some friends and met all these punk rock people, and brought some of them home with me," Jemison said. "And they stayed the night and they kind of just brought me into their clan. And I went from Bee Gees posters to Sex Pistols posters, within just a couple of weeks."

But it was more than just the posters that invaded Jemison's life. She started playing in punk bands with menacing names like Humane Restraints and Convicted. It only lasted a short time before she became disillusioned with the music business ripping off bands. But after taking a short break from music, she moved over to the business side, promoting shows and toy drives during Christmas.

In 1989, Jemison and her ex-husband, John Mello, bought the Doll Hut, a tiny, blue-collar roadhouse off the 5 North freeway and Manchester Avenue—at 107 South Adams Boulevard in Anaheim, to be exact. Up to that point, the bar had mainly just been a small hangout and a place for railroad and lumberyard workers in the area to play pool, shoot darts, and sip a frosty glass of beer while eating pickled eggs. The bar's name was already immortalized by Anaheim hard rock band the Pontiac Brothers on the title track to their 1985 album *Doll*

Hut. When they realized the bar was suddenly up for sale, Jemison and Mello bought it for a whopping $32,000.

"The whole idea was to slowly transition it into bands without the city knowing too much about it, not making too much of a splash, but it happened pretty fast," Jemison said.

Oftentimes on a late weeknight, the bar's inherited crowd turned over from manual laborers to punks looking to get loud, drink, and listen to music. "Then slowly as the sun went down, we kind of turned it over and all the musician vampires kind of crossed over," Jemison said. That daily crossover of clientele was the catalyst for many unexpected friendships between the punks and a few open-minded daytime stragglers who were intrigued by the culture of frenzied, angst-ridden tunes performed onstage. "It was very weird to say the least, these old guys in their sixties and seventies pounding Coors Lights sitting next to a guy with a mohawk, talking about motors and engines and things like that, so the music definitely brought people together," Jemison said.

The catalyst Jemison said inspired the Doll Hut was the closing of Commonwealth Pub in Fullerton. Known as a major hub for early punks in OC, its shuttering suddenly left a lot of musicians with nowhere to go. "We thought well, you know, we're gonna get them to come here," Jemison said of the Hut. The bar opened its doors in August 1989 with twenty-five-cent-beer night—that's right, a glass of draft beer for twenty-five cents. They didn't charge a cover for the first year and a half. "So you could come in, drink a beer for 25 cents, and watch a band play," she said. "Maybe not the best bands because we couldn't pay them. It was like a rehearsal room at that point."

When they eventually started charging a cover, more established bands came through and started to pack the little roadhouse—Social Distortion, Bad Religion, and Brian Setzer all dropped by to perform after they'd made it, helping Jemison raise money for holiday charity drives. Then there was the Offspring, who were just a baby band when they started coming in playing Monday nights before breaking big years later.

During her tenure, the record industry started to come calling—agents from William Morris and ICM would routinely ask Jemison to get bands on their rosters to play there. "I got a rapport with them that if I would book a band they just signed that nobody knew about and put them on a really good bill, they would kick me down some decent bands. So it became a very interesting relationship—they would say, 'We got a gig in LA but we needed a gig in Orange County. Can we send it down to you?'" she recalls.

As the late '80s began a new epoch that fostered hair metal and then killed it in favor of grunge, punk in OC felt like the outlier in a world that migrated from spandex to plaid, seemingly overnight.

On the Sunset Strip, it was all the hair bands and Guns N' Roses, so it was like a different planet. The Doll Hut was a strange place that did punk, rockabilly, blues, and some country. "Our music scene didn't touch any of that stuff that was so popular. We made a safe haven for people that didn't fall into that kind of popular stuff that was on the radio. And they were having trouble getting booked at the Whisky and the Roxy and those kinds of places because they weren't booking punk or, you know, alternative or rockabilly or blues or any of that—it was just a very weird time," Jemison said.

Despite its small stature as a tiny roadhouse off the I-5 freeway, the Doll Hut was seen as hallowed ground for bands who were on the fringes of what was popular in the rock scene in SoCal, and in particular, Orange County. It was a hub for the scene that Jemison wanted to foster. It was also, in all its rugged, sticker-covered glory, a place where bands who'd broken up could find home again onstage, albeit in different projects or permutations of bands they'd once played with.

Chief among them was the Adolescents. By the late '80s, the band had splintered, with Brandenburg and Soto having parted ways along with the Agnews, who'd also gone their separate ways in other bands and side projects.

Soto, who continued to play in Legal Weapon, Joyride, and Manic Hispanic, met Jemison in the late '80s and eventually started working at the Doll Hut, first as a door guy and a booker and then as the club's general manager in the early '90s. Jemison remembers hitting it off with Soto immediately, and they soon became close friends.

"I remember when, first time I met Steve was at an Adolescents show and it was amazing," Jemison says. "I was thrilled because I saw them when I was in high school. And I didn't know Steve back then but I was a fan [of his music]. He fell in love with the bar immediately. And we became friends very quickly."

Soto was there for Jemison during a tumultuous time for her and the bar. In 1990, she and Mello split up, and the bar was like the child in the middle of a nasty divorce.

"There was a period where I wasn't there because we were legally fighting over the bar," she recalls. "For a while we tried to run it separately—I had nights, he had nights. And whoever's car was parked out front, they knew who was running it."

After a short legal battle, Jemison won ownership of the bar, wrestling it away from Mello—but at a cost. When she set foot in the bar again after months of court hearings, she returned to find that the inside was completely destroyed. "The walls were slathered with orange paint with words like 'Linda is . . .' you can imagine the names," she said with a sigh. On top of that, the carpet and pool table were destroyed, the barstools had been torn up, and a river of sewage was running out the back door.

The situation was dire, but the punk rock spirit of OC had a way of becoming its own safety net for those who'd fallen on hard times. Especially a venue owner who'd given bands in the scene a place to play.

"This was the miracle, that all the people that believed in what I was doing, everybody came together, and we painted it and cleaned up the bar," Jemison recalls. "We did a fundraiser for a new PA system, bought new barstools, got new carpet, painted, and redid everything. And that's when one of my friends said. 'You have to call it Linda's Doll Hut because everybody has to know he's gone. It's a fresh start.'"

After battling her way out of an ugly time, by 1992 Jemison said she was able to really breathe life into the bar and bring Steve Soto on to help her run the place. "It was as much his club as it was mine," she said.

For his part, Soto's mixture of kindness and road-tested wisdom made him an ideal partner to book bands and regulate situations before they turned into major problems. The two had a friendship that often spanned hours talking about music and the often chaotic punk scene that both were exposed to through shows.

"I always like hiring musicians. So 99 percent of the people that work for me were musicians," Jemison said. "I remember he came over to my apartment in Orange and we just sat up until like three or four in the morning, just talking and listening to demo tapes and just you know, cracking each other up. And it was just like this instant friendship. . . . It was like I just inherited one of the best brothers you could ever have."

With Soto came his family of punk rock people, who were a gift—including Michael "Gabby" Gaborno and Warren Renfrow, two of his friends who were steadily becoming local rock stars with the Cadillac Tramps and later Manic Hispanic, a Chicano-fied punk rock cover band that was born out of the Doll Hut and had its first show there.

The Doll Hut gave Soto an avenue to be a player in the scene again. Whether it was playing shows there or booking them, he saw the little bar as a springboard whenever he needed a place to start his next project. "It just was a really great place for creativity, you know. And people just love to come and listen to him. He told the best stories, you know, he's a very, very good storyteller," Jemison said.

Despite having to work day jobs to support himself when he wasn't touring, Soto's connection to music always ran deep. As someone who'd endured one rocky experience after another in the Adolescents, Soto knew what it meant to create an environment for bands to grow. "He felt the same way about musicians that I did, let's give him a break, let's help him out. You know, let's take his band that doesn't draw, put them on a bill, and then they'll get exposed. And then they can start creating a fan base."

By the mid-'90s, punk started to grow in different directions, morphing into a hybrid of sounds that drew in more people and widened the possibility of what sounds could work within the scene. One of the biggest offshoots around the time Social Distortion saw another peak in popularity as a refurbished Americana-style punk band was the countrified rock known as cowpunk.

Meshing the spirit of Hank Williams and Patsy Cline together with the aggression of the Ramones or Sex Pistols, this was a sound that grew roots in OC and led to promoter Bill Hardie creating the Hootenanny Festival in 1995. He had some help from Jemison, who fostered a big portion of that emerging swath of bands in the punk scene.

"[Hardie] came to me and said, 'Look, you book all these bands, I want to do this festival thing. I don't know what to call it, but I want you to help me book it,'" Jemison said. She wound up working on the festival for nine years, booking her own side stage and mainstage acts up until she sold the Doll Hut in the early aughts. It was a partnership that led to some one-of-a-kind, even head-scratching line-ups for years.

"Bill just had the promoter's mind, but he didn't have a rapport with bands. So I had a huge hand in that for the first nine years," she said. "You'd go see Jerry Lee Lewis, but Social Distortion would [be playing the same stage] one night, [and on another night] it was Chuck Berry and then the Cramps. You know, so that really great mixture of rock 'n' roll. That was like, that was really what the Doll Hut was.

"You had legends like Chris Isaak playing with hardcore punk bands, or the Stray Cats with Steve Earle. Half the time I would book these bands just because I wanted to meet them. . . . I was a little selfish in that respect."

But because these bands started sharing festival stages together, it led to more mutations onstage—with rockabilly fans checking out punk bands and punkers getting a taste of rockabilly or psychobilly nights. "It just seemed to be kind of like the melting pot," Jemison said.

As its evolution progressed, punk acquired many different genres, which resulted in naturally eclectic lineups and naturally eclectic music. All of it came along at the time when rock radio was having a major moment that was focused on Orange County.

12

BADFISH

orn on Presidents' Day 1968 in Tustin, from the beginning, Bradley Nowell narrowly missed sharing the same birthday as his dad.

"Doctors in the old days played golf on Wednesday, so they took the day off," Bradley's father, Jim Nowell, said. "My birthday was on Wednesday [February 21], and Nancy was in the hospital, so instead of inducing labor on Wednesday, they did it on Thursday and missed my birthday by one day."

Ever since he was a kid, Nowell was attracted to music. Growing up in Long Beach's Belmont Shore neighborhood, Nowell loved to surf and sail. His parents divorced when he was ten and he went to live with his mother, but she found him too difficult to raise, so he moved in with Jim. Nowell's father played in folk bands in the '60s.

From an early age, Nowell was different from other kids. He tested as a genius and didn't have any trouble in school. He was an honor student in high school and later made the dean's list in college. He was also linguistically gifted, which allowed him to pick up Spanish—a skill that would serve him later in life.

As his father recalls, a month-long sailing trip to the US Virgin Islands when he was eleven sparked his interest in playing music.

Wherever the Nowells stopped, there'd be a bar and music emanating from it. At one location, there was a group of local musicians playing Bob Marley songs. After hearing those songs and learning to play a reggae rhythm later on when some of the locals stopped by their boat, Nowell was hooked.

After this trip, Nowell became enthralled by reggae, and when his father played other genres for him, it sent him on a journey where he tried to play all types of music and infuse them into his own.

Nowell started his first band, Hogan's Heroes, as a teen with Michael Yates and Eric Wilson. By 1986, Nowell went off to college in Santa Cruz. But it wasn't for long. He'd return to Long Beach to attend Cal State Long Beach.

"Everybody loved him," Jim Nowell said of his son. "He had a lot of charisma and certainly wasn't a loner, but he was just as happy sitting around reading a book. They were always nonfiction, history and philosophy. He read all the great books, and we'd discuss them. I thought he was extremely smart, much smarter than I was."

<hr/>

A child of divorce, Bud Gaugh grew up all over Long Beach and the east side of Lakewood. When his father finally settled in Belmont Shore, Gaugh was tired of hopping from house to house and ended up staying there. It was there that he met Eric Wilson.

At the time, Gaugh was already playing drums. Fast friends, Wilson and Gaugh learned how to play from Wilson's jazz musician father, Bill. Unlike Eric (who played guitar) or his brother Gary, Gaugh was very teachable and instantly took to playing drums. With Bill's encouragement, he learned how to play the drums in a jazz style formally.

Gaugh's parents didn't approve.

"My parents were into classical music, and jazz music was fucking noise," he said. "They hated it and were so upset that I was playing jazz."

The pair were soon introduced to rock. Gaugh's father took him and Wilson to see the Who at the Los Angeles Memorial Coliseum. As much as they liked the Who and their early attitude, it wasn't the headliner who caught the pair's attention. Instead, it was the opener: the Clash.

Hearing the Clash was the pair's gateway to punk. Soon, they'd head to Zed Records, the first Southern California store to stock punk and hardcore releases. Bands like Black Flag, Bad Religion, and Descendents were instant purchases. The legendary shop owned by Long Beach Wilson grad Michael Zampelli was first located at a stucco shack with a startling Union Jack paint job and then at the 2300 block of East Seventh Street, a location replaced by a short-lived reggae record shop. Punk stars were known to hang out at Zed's, checking out the latest releases by other acts that helped them understand the music. The Misfits came by several times as well as members of Black Flag, Mike Watt of the Minutemen, and later artists like Courtney Love and the Offspring. They would all drop in to buy records and hang out. It opened the door for hardcore bands and ears of new fans.

"Without Zed, I don't think Orange County hardcore shit is happening," Farside bassist Bryan Chu said.

When he was at his mother's house, Gaugh saw the local punk scene emerge. She lived two blocks away from Jack Grisham, so Gaugh was exposed to T.S.O.L. parties early on. Back at his father's house, he was hooked by seeing the Falling Idols, Secret Hate, and the Crewd.

In the story of Sublime's twisted roots of punk, reggae, ska, hip-hop, and a plethora of local bands that inspired them to get onstage, chief among their early influences was a band of upperclassmen from Long Beach Wilson. Formed in 1981 out of the ashes of a previous band called Red Alert, the Falling Idols was composed of mostly grade school and high school friends who went to Long Beach Wilson—drummer Greg "Mudd" Lowther (who played in countless bands), bassist Trey Pangborn (who later joined the bands Long Beach Shortbus and Long Beach Dub Allstars), guitarist Ross Fletcher (who took over John Flynt who was previously in Red Alert), and singer Dave Quackenbush (who later went on to join the Vandals). The band released a full-length album and a five-hundred-copy EP on their own label, BSC Records. They also appeared on the Bemisbrain compilation album *When Men Were Men . . . And Sheep Were Scared*. Brad Nowell had the tape and wore it out learning a lot of the songs that he used to play on acoustic guitar while attending UC Santa Cruz.

The official punk band of Long Beach around the time of Sublime's formation was All Day. Bassist Randy Bradbury, who went on to join the Falling Idols and later Pennywise, was in the band briefly along with an even quicker stint from drummer Josh Freese, Joel Bratton (the singer from another notable LBC punk band, Rhino 39), and many other local musicians who all thrashed together at a hardcore tempo with throaty vocals and blistering guitar solos.

Even as he and his bandmates got more and more into punk, it didn't stop Gaugh from playing in the semi-professional Long Beach Junior Concert Band. However, through a friend, he met the drummer for the Crewd and was invited to check out their show at Madame Wong's in LA. To Gaugh's surprise, his father allowed him to go, and it happened to be the night that the Crewd opened for Black Flag.

"People were jumping off the walls and off the fucking monitors," he said of the show. "There was no place safe, and the whole place broke out and was fucking badass. We got to do this!"

Jack Grisham of T.S.O.L.,
Ukrainian Cultural Center,
October 15, 1982 *(Credit: Dina
Douglass)*

Social Distortion's Dennis Danell and Monk Rock in 1983 *(Credit: Dina Douglass)*

Stevo and Jan Ackermann of the Vandals *(Credit: Dina Douglass)*

The early era Vandals lineup performing live *(Credit: Dina Douglass)*

A blonde Joe Escalante behind the drum kit *(Credit: Dina Douglass)*

Steve Soto in the crowd *(Photograph by Edward Colver)*

Mike Ness of Social Distortion *(Photograph by Edward Colver)*

The first-ever photo of the Adolescents, at the Scout House, Yorba Linda, California on March 1, 1980 *(From Frank Agnew's Personal Collection)*

Robert Omlit, Kathy Stevens, and Mike Ness in the Cuckoo's Nest parking lot, 1980 *(From Frank Agnew's Personal Collection)*

Steve Soto and Casey Royer of the Adolescents with Chuck Dukowski and Dez Cadena of Black Flag at the Starwood on January 7, 1981 *(From Frank Agnew's Personal Collection)*

D.I. recording at Casbah Studio with Chaz Ramirez, 1985 *(From Frank Agnew's Personal Collection)*

Jack Grisham burning a newspaper *(Photograph by Edward Colver)*

Social Distortion backstage at the Cuckoo's Nest *(Photograph by Edward Colver)*

Warren Fitzgerald of the Vandals and No Doubt's Gwen Stefani at Board in the O.C. *(Courtesy of Lisa Johnson Rock Photographer)*

Social Distortion with Jerry Lee Lewis at the Universal Amphitheatre in Universal City, California in December 1987 *(Courtesy of Jim Guerinot)*

No Doubt in Hawaii, 1996 *(Courtesy of Lisa Johnson Rock Photographer)*

Rikk and Frank Agnew at their parents' home in 1989 *(From Frank Agnew's Personal Collection)*

Andrew McMahon performing with Something Corporate at the Warped Tour *(Courtesy of Lisa Johnson Rock Photographer)*

Ian McKaye and Mike Ness reuniting for the first time since *Another State of Mind (Courtesy of Shane Trulin)*

Mike Ness performing with Social Distortion at FivePoint Amphitheater in Irvine, 2018 *(Courtesy of Dick Slaugher)*

Jim Guerinot with Gary Tovar and Paul Tollett of Goldenvoice *(Courtesy of Jim Guerinot)*

Rebel Waltz's Larry Tull and Jim Guerinot with No Doubt in front of Dexter Holland's plane. *(Courtesy of Jim Guerinot)*

The Offspring at the Warped Tour *(Courtesy of Lisa Johnson Rock Photographer)*

Dennis Danell with his son, Duke *(Courtesy of Christy Danell-Walker)*

Bradley Nowell with his son Jakob, and Lou Dog *(Courtesy of Lisa Johnson Rock Photographer)*

Along with their friend Dave Moore, Wilson and Gaugh formed their first band. At first, Wilson played guitar. That would disintegrate, and Wilson and Gaugh formed the Juice Bros and later Sonic Garbage, mainly playing house parties in Long Beach. They'd also check out parties on the west side, seeing bands like Secret Hate.

Long Beach was full of promising bands, but they couldn't get their shit together.

"They were terrific, but they all had drug problems," Jim Nowell said. "A lot of these bands just fell apart. Guys from some of these bands are still living on their mothers' couches, you know, twenty, thirty, forty years later. Nothing has changed and some of them never got past that."

<hr/>

When Gaugh first met Nowell through Wilson, he had a feeling that Nowell didn't have much street sense and was innocent.

"I would live with one parent and then the next parent, so I would go away from my dad's, and I'd meet some other musicians and start a band over there and jam with them," Gaugh said. "Then hang it up and go back, and so Eric was always introducing me to new musicians every time I'd come back and he's like, 'Hey, you got to meet Brad.'"

He agreed and when they plugged in at Nowell's father's garage, the sound wasn't what the drummer anticipated.

"He started strumming this stuff on the guitar, it's like, this sounds kind of puss, dude," Gaugh said. Then, they realized they had a mutual admiration for Descendents. Finally, when Nowell started singing, Gaugh's opinion of him changed.

"It was like, fuck, he can play the guitar and he can sing! Dude's got a fucking voice like a fucking bird."

As the trio got going, their blend of sound, which included punk, ska, reggae, and hip-hop, represented Long Beach's eclectic nature.

The area was a melting pot of culture and music. So much so that you might have heard Cal Tjader on one corner, Marvin Gaye on another, and Stevie Nicks on a third.

"Our sound was like driving through Long Beach," Gaugh said.

After mulling over some names, the trio decided on Sublime after Nowell's girlfriend at the time saw it in the dictionary. They liked the undertone of being subliminal.

They'd practice at Nowell's father's garage at his house in Belmont Shore. Through Nowell, Gaugh was introduced to reggae drumming.

"Brad's like, 'Here, check this out,' and boom! He starts putting in some stuff and that has fucking good groove to it, and he's like, 'If you like this, you gotta check out dub music!'" Gaugh said.

Growing up on psychedelic rock bands like the Grateful Dead, the Jimi Hendrix Experience, and Pink Floyd, Gaugh appreciated the musicianship of the dub bands. From there he realized that dub was the next step on his music journey.

The trio bonded over their music and became close friends.

"It was so much fun," Gaugh said. "He [Nowell] was so refreshing. Him turning us on to new music and going down to the record store. It was so much fun playing this new stuff."

Once they were ready, the trio, now known as Sublime, hit the Long Beach party circuit . . . this time as performers. The shows instantly caught fire in Long Beach. Playing keggers was the norm, as were marathon three-plus-hour shows when the cops didn't bust them. Sets at Fender's Ballroom, the Nugget at Cal State Long Beach, Club 5902, and Chester Drawers in Newport Beach became frequent appearances.

Sublime enjoyed playing the party circuit far more than driving up the freeway to Hollywood.

"We'd get everybody out there dancing, and then throw in some punk rock," Gaugh said. "Then they'd bring the grills out to cook.

Then we'd get out there and play a couple jammy songs and get everybody dancing."

Formal shows didn't have the same energy, recklessness, and crowd that the parties attracted. And they were put on bills with bands that were sonic opposites.

"It sucked for us because it was all this hair metal," Gaugh said. "They had leather jackets and long hair and they're putting on makeup and shit in the fucking dressing room. We show up and we're in flip-flops, board shorts, and tank tops."

Plus, Sublime's Long Beach fan base didn't make the forty-mile trek with them, leaving the band to play in front of a crowd that didn't understand what they were about.

Sublime was comfortable playing to crowds who lived by the beach instead of up in the city.

"The skate-surf scene seemed natural," Gaugh said. "Skaters are always the fuck-ups and are always the cool kids, which is why we gravitated to that stuff. It was just hang out, have a couple beers. Toes in the sand, Corona in hand. That was how life operated."

From an early age, the Sublime members were already embedded in the drug scene. Gaugh took mushrooms when he was in junior high school, and later acid, and he would get pot from his mother, who had moved up to the Lake Tahoe area. Back in Long Beach, Wilson also dabbled, taking PCP, drinking, and smoking pot. Gaugh eventually started using heroin and meth. Initially, Nowell lagged behind his bandmates but eventually caught up, surpassing their usage.

But in the late '80s, Nowell didn't want to have anything to do with Gaugh's partying.

"Me and Brad had arguments about it," Gaugh said. "So I left and I went to go clean up and I remember they came out. I was probably sober for about five or six months."

At his mother's insistence, he left Long Beach on a mission for salvation and self-healing in the arms of what she described as "a rock 'n' roll church." A branch of the Set Free Church in Northern California was a place where bikers, cholos, rockers, and everyone in between would congregate. At the time, he was flat broke and living in his car.

He was on a mission to detox through music and a little bit of worship. While kicking his meth habit, he got into Bible study and started listening to God-fearing rappers perform hip-hop praise music at church, putting their spin on songs like "O.P.P." ("Who's down with G.O.D.?!"). Though it might've seemed corny to him before this moment, for the first time his heart was open to change, and Set Free offered an alternative to the life he was living.

As he was detoxing, the band drove to see Gaugh while he cleaned up. They had a van and were ready to go on tour. Despite their pleas, Gaugh wasn't ready and didn't trust himself to be out on the road and tempted to use.

After a year away, Gaugh returned to Long Beach but not to Sublime. Despite Nowell telling him when he returned to give him a call, Gaugh's spot in the band was far from secure. In fact, upon his return, it was nonexistent.

His throne behind the kit was now being warmed by Kelly Vargas.

"All right, well, you know, can I crash on your couch for a week until I get a job?" Gaugh asked Nowell.

With his life now more or less back together, he was looking to find a new rhythm in old surroundings.

"I lost my way there for a little bit and had to take a break," he remembers. Nowell, at the time, was upset at his bandmate for getting in deep with "the cheap man's cocaine," but Gaugh couldn't understand why, and they'd constantly butt heads over his drug use.

During that time, through Nowell's Cal State Long Beach buddy

Michael "Miguel" Happoldt, the group found free studio time off-hours to record at Cal State Dominguez Hills.

The timing worked out for the non-Nowell members since they all had day jobs. They had to sneak through the school *Mission Impossible*–style to ensure they could get into the facility without anyone catching them.

"He got it," Gaugh said of Happoldt. "He knew the sound that we were looking for."

Happoldt, a Florida native, moved to Long Beach in 1988 with the prospect of pursuing a career in the music industry producing records. At the time, he remembers the SoCal scene being awash with hardcore punk bands like Suicidal Tendencies, T.S.O.L., and Rich Kids on LSD (RKL) crossing over into metal. Everything else was pretty much a bunch of grunge band soundalikes. As a scene in the middle of OC and LA, Long Beach felt like a bit of a redheaded stepchild. Both areas on either side had better clubs and places to play. Long Beach didn't have much, but they had Fender's Ballroom and some other small places that would do shows here and there. "But they would just get wrecked," Happoldt said.

"Long Beach back in the day was really wild—it was a cheap place to live, and it was where Orange County people moved to be wild. So when I moved here, the reverberations of the old days. The Vandals were the Godhead, they were the biggest thing ever. And they hadn't really come back yet. So they were still living on the old memories."

Though there was definitely a scene in LBC, it wasn't as strongly supported as OC was, Happoldt says. The feeling of it being a more nostalgic way of life was creeping in after the early '80s had passed, but there were still a lot of traces to be found in the records kids dove into in dollar bins at record stores. Young sonic archivists like Happoldt and his buddies who would become Sublime dug deep to find vinyl scraps of what had come before their time.

"I mean, to a lot of people back then punk rock was still the Damned," he said. "The Damned were still coming over to the US once a year and playing Irvine Meadows—they still come here to play, hopefully they never stop."

Despite having a record store that was a magnet for bands and fans of punk rock's glory days, by the late '80s, it felt like it was all over. It would take evolution on the part of the younger generation that was starting to make noise to bring not only aggression, but evolution to the stage and the studio and kick-start the genre that inspired them to pick up instruments and join bands in the first place.

When Happoldt met Nowell, the two were students at Long Beach State. Happoldt was living at a party pad on Third and Coronado. One of his roommates who was fairly tapped into the Long Beach scene suggested one day that Happoldt meet another homie of his named Brad who was in a band called Sublime. With the trio already garnering a reputation as one of the big bands around town, and with Nowell already assuming the role of the classic popular guy on campus at Long Beach State, Happoldt already sort of knew who they were.

He was more than just popular, though. Nowell was actually cool. And not cool in a lame sort of generally acceptable nice guy way—cool in that he knew his shit. He often walked around with a cassette mixtape in his pocket of whatever he was into at the time. If he heard something amazing on the stereo at somebody's house, he had to have it, and then something else had to come off the mixtape to make space. He was constantly updating, erasing old stuff, and searching for the new. His low-key attitude and demeanor made him an everyman even though he was unarguably extraordinary just based on his sheer amount of interests and what he was good at—he could sail, skate, snowboard, surf, and play punk rock and reggae. He would even sometimes mess around with freestyle jazz and was bilingual, speaking

English and Spanish. In other words, he was the kind of guy you wanted to be around.

Mark eventually introduced Happoldt and Nowell at a party, and right away they started nerding out on each other's eclectic music tastes, darting from conversations about punk bands like Flipper to reggae legends Eek-A-Mouse and Barrington Levy. "He was like the original DJ too in that he wouldn't just say, 'I like Eek-A-Mouse,' for example, he would name the songs," Happoldt said. Given their mutual love of music, they decided to plan a recording session together. By now, Happoldt had transferred over to Cal State Dominguez Hills and was taking recording classes.

"Part of that was I was supposed to bring bands in. And so that was it. I just said, 'You want to go record for free?' And then that's sort of how we did it," Happoldt said. "We did a session and just kind of kept going from there."

Those sessions, which rarely started before 7:00 or 8:00 p.m., typically went late into the night and on into the early morning as Happoldt and the band cracked beers, rolled joints, set up mics, and pressed record on what would become a handful of early Sublime tunes.

More than just a friend or a producer, Nowell was looking for a coconspirator to help him and his bandmates get the sounds that were bouncing around in his head recorded onto a two-inch tape.

Oftentimes, recordings he did in studios with other people would sound too clean—nothing resembling the shambolic, soulful riddims and ghostly reverb of "Roast Fish & Cornbread" recorded by Lee "Scratch" Perry on the sweaty soundboard of Black Ark studio in Kingston, Jamaica.

"We wanted whatever was going on there. But no studio here was gonna want to distribute it because they wouldn't want to put their name on it," Happoldt said. "'They' think people would say you don't know how to record!" On top of his budding recording know-how and desire to learn Nowell's sound palette, Happoldt was being introduced to Jamaican legends like Scientist, King Tubby, and Mad Professor by the Sublime front man. "Since I was studying recording I was like, okay, so the snare is going through the flanger and it's playing to the repeats. And so once I figured that out, I was dubbing out a bunch of stuff, but more like alternative like Love and Rockets or Bauhaus before them—that was their attempt at dub," Happoldt said. "I didn't know how to do it like reggae where everything's in time—with real dub you're subdividing time."

Nowell and Happoldt would take their recording, songwriting, and freestyling to the club and perform those songs at the end of Sublime sets and later on at backyard parties they would throw. At the end of the night, they would play songs from N.W.A., Ice Cube, and Eric B. and Rakim (just the drum and bass lines) and take turns passing the mic to freestyle for hours between Opie Ortiz, Marshall Goodman, and others who were part of the Sublime crew.

The Sublime sound was built on the house party vibe—a raucous kegger experience with all your friends who pushed the fun as hard as it could go until the cops showed up with flashlights around 9:45 p.m. Every kid from Wilson and Long Beach Poly would stuff inside a house, typically the one where Happoldt lived on Third and Coronado, and people would park five blocks away to blow off steam, slam brews, and try their best to get laid. "We were just kids walking down the street with beer and carrying on. All the kids and all the parents grew up that way too so they didn't care. It's Friday night, Saturday night, like what are the kids supposed to fucking do?" Happoldt said.

With this energy, Sublime patiently crafted and backyard party-tested the songs pieced together to become the band's first full-length release. Titled *40oz. to Freedom*, released in June 1992, this 22-track album was the culmination of the years of sonic experimentation as Nowell worked to elevate his songwriting from basic slam pit fodder to eclectic poetry that tried to find a way to artfully cram his world of disparate musical influences into one album, or sometimes even one song.

"The punk rock thing is the energy you know, Sublime, that's who we—were but musically we were trying to do something a little bit more astute and really taking cues from like the Specials," Happoldt said of the band's evolving style. "The two things the Specials' first record and *40oz. to Freedom* have in common is that every song was backyard-tested or in [the Specials'] case pub-tested. People write all these songs and make a record, but how do you know anyone is gonna like any of it? *40oz. to Freedom* was made from the list of songs that were the most popular [at the backyard parties]."

In their process of becoming a popular band, controlling the pulse of a party, seeing the looks on people's faces, and hearing the hoots and hollers when they crushed a song's performance from beginning to end was Sublime's ground-level foray into market research. It paired with Nowell's intense desire to absorb feedback from his friends and fans who watched him onstage. "He was really unabashed and very open to self-criticism," Happoldt said. "If a song sucks, why would you play it again?" The front man was also outspoken about what he liked and didn't like about the world of pop music that surrounded him. Seeing music videos of the bands that were popular back in the day often stoked his competitive fire, which sometimes presented itself in the form of stoner humor but with a tinge of smoldering intent behind it.

Happoldt and Nowell often spent time eating shrooms and watching MTV for the simple pleasure of laughing at music videos from polished bands of the '80s like Haircut 100. But Happoldt recalls catching Nowell staring at the screen with a scowl on his face. "He's like, 'I just think I'm fucking better than this guy,'" Happoldt recalls with a laugh when he talked about Haircut's bottle blond singer Nick Heyward. Happoldt, who carried the distinction of being the band's fourth member as their producer and sound engineer, was quick to give him a reality check. "I can tell you right now that's not the game," he said. "The game is getting a recording to show that you're better. The proof is in the pudding. We got to get a recording that showcases how you can sing and how good Eric is as a bass player. How innovative all this shit is."

Meanwhile, the songs from *40oz.* were the result of endless performing for friends and fellow Long Beach locals who saw them evolve from a scrappy punk band into a sound that defied definition. "Musically, we left almost all of that [old punk sound] behind—even the hardcore songs on *40oz.* are kinda like, the way Marshall plays, it's almost a little bit jazzy or something. It's all sort of still kind of funky," Happoldt said.

Sublime showed off their songwriting chops while paying tribute to their wide-ranging influences. The album included six covers, including a breakbeat-driven version of the Grateful Dead's "Scarlet Begonias," a slightly more revved up rendition of Descendents' "Hope," a notably more funk and reggae-flavored take on "We're Only Gonna Die" by Bad Religion, and "54-46 That's My Number" by Toots & the Maytals. Sublime's version of the Toyes' "Smoke Two Joints" was one of their first songs to receive radio play and showcased not only their hilarious instincts when it came to sampling lines from the 1970 Russ Meyer film *Beyond the Valley of the Dolls* in the song's intro but even a—for lack of a better word—subliminal ode to Eazy-E's "No More ?'s" and Freddie Jackson's "Rock Me Tonight (For Old Times Sake)" that ends the song with Nowell's soulfully boozy caterwaul. Originals like "Let's Go Get Stoned," the groove-laden "Badfish" and the ska-driven "Date Rape" (which would have an unexpected second life years later) showcased the layers of Nowell's budding songwriting.

It was in this arena that Sublime thrived by learning how to control the intensity of the party with their music by toggling back and forth between reggae and punk. The strategy was similar to that of their big brothers the Falling Idols, who used mild, groovy, acceptable surf rock to open the doors to gigs. They'd play a few surf songs and gradually ratchet up the speed until they were playing punk, and once tables were starting to rattle or get flipped over at the yacht club who they'd scammed into booking them, they would go back to playing surf. So, too, did Sublime use reggae to get crowds grooving before whipping them up into a mosh pit frenzy, only to cool things back down again.

It wasn't new to them. They'd seen the Clash. And they had seen Murphy's Law—another hardcore band with reggae breakdowns that often goes uncredited as a huge Sublime influence. Over time, the coalescence of sounds and the party scene would make the band immortally cool as long as young people were gathering to rage and relax at the same time.

"They'd mix different genres in the same song, and they'd change the tempo and the genre and everything," Jim Nowell said. "I think that's what made them different and also was something that other bands wanted to copy."

THE BREAKTHROUGH

The success of Social Distortion introduced the band to a new audience unfamiliar with their earlier work and the long climb that marked the previous decade. Excited to bring in these new fans, Social Distortion hit the road—first as a headliner and then, in a bit of a breakthrough, opening for Neil Young and Crazy Horse alongside Sonic Youth on the 1991 *Ragged Glory* tour. Social Distortion was now lumped in with a new echelon of bands on the twelve-week arena tour.

"That was more dues-paying," Ness said. "Maybe we've got 300 fans [in the crowd] in Cleveland or whatever town it was at that time."

On the surface, Social Distortion and Sonic Youth seem like strange bedfellows. Sonic Youth emerged from the New York no wave music and art scene in the 1980s, and their noise-drive, experimental style was far different from Social Distortion's punk. But what they both had in common, besides the support of Neil Young, was that they were always eager to move forward to make the music they liked. Haters be damned.

In Ness, Sonic Youth's Thurston Moore found kindred spirits. During that tour, the two front men bonded. Moore was well aware of the Southern California punk scene.

"There would be pictures of him [Ness] in *Flipside*, and I was curious about them because Ness had his hat on with hash marks under his eyes," Moore said. "I knew there was something going on with these guys, but wasn't quite sure. When we found out that they were going to be on the Neil Young tour [in 1991], I was like, 'Really?' I was super excited."

Moore admired Ness and Social Distortion. Both bands, though they would shape a legacy that made this one of the best tours of their careers, had to fight to win over Young's audience. Each night, they battled as maybe hundreds, if not a few thousand, milled about on their way to their seats, not paying much attention to what was happening onstage. Each band knew what the other was going through.

"We were both getting a lot of heat from those audiences," Moore said. "Social D was always on before us and so they were playing to no one. They would come out and do their business and then they would go on their bus and we would come out and we would try to be as provocative as we could be. Putting our amps in front of people's faces that they just sat there and they could flip the bird at us and, and then we'd go on our bus or we'd go on their bus and watch TV with them or play a game and vice versa."

"Well, they're not going to go be in the front watching you," Ness said of the openers' fans or lack thereof. "There's a guy in the front row, literally in a tie-dye shirt yelling 'Cinnamon Girl' when you're playing."

Unlike his bandmates who generally kept to themselves, Moore took to them.

"I would go record shopping with Mike," he said. "It was really interesting because he was so generally into the vernacular of working-class

American voices. I was really impressed by that. He wanted to hear a real voice of American consciousness. And he was a good dude."

One moment from that tour stuck out to Moore. At the tail end of the first Persian Gulf War in February 1991, the tour stopped at West Point, New York, to play at Eisenhower Hall, which is where the United States Military Academy is based. Throughout the tour, Young would play "The Star-Spangled Banner" a la Jimi Hendrix, and Sonic Youth would provoke the crowd by playing Black Sabbath's "War Pigs." When Young would pipe the same Sabbath song, it would go over a little bit better, but not great.

When it came time to play West Point, Moore and his bandmates, and even Young, were slightly worried about what the reception would be.

"It was all young military recruits in the audience," Moore said. "And I could tell Neil was a little anxious about going out there and making any kind of commentary about the Gulf War, George Bush, or whatever. But Social D came out and they had all decided to wear military fatigues. And they came out and the audience went nuts. They just killed it. And we came out and we stunk up the place. Then Neil came out, and everybody just sort of sat there. These young military recruits were like, 'Oh, yeah, this [Young] is a famous rock person.' Neil came by our dressing room later and he's like, 'Well, that was an interesting one.' And he was just like, 'Social D was the only band that they wanted to hear tonight.' Social D came out and played to the American troops with dignity and rocked their night.

"I saw Mike being like, 'I'm not gonna go out there and push these guys,'" he continued. "'These guys are dedicated to what they're doing. I'm going to go out and we're not going to push their buttons.' There was something about that."

Playing to that crowd was in some ways similar to the hostile crowds Social Distortion faced at their earliest shows in LA and Orange County. Battle-tested, but certainly not road-weary, the band soaked in the experience of performing with two all-time bands.

For Ness, that experience involved becoming a better guitar player.

"That [time] was right when I was searching for my guitar tone," he recalled. "He [Young] had a fucking monster tone and it was so good. Every day, I would pick his tech's brain [Larry Cragg], and that's why I play the mid-'70s Les Pauls with P90s in them now. And I found my tone after that."

After watching Young and Crazy Horse perform every night, Ness realized that he was upset with Social Distortion's performances on that tour.

"I had picked my friends to be in a band, and musical ability came second," Ness said. "Then what I started to realize is like, we're not all we can be. Dennis was my best friend and my best moral support, but he wasn't the best guitar player. We weren't able to play with each other and bounce off stuff and push-pull. That's when I really had to reevaluate things and tighten things up."

Otherwise, things went so well on that tour that when Young returned to the road on his next tour backed by Booker T. & the M.G.'s in 1993, he tapped Social Distortion to open for them.

※※※※※

Back in Orange County, the Vandals were about to experience a renaissance, and they had a dinosaur suit and a teenage drummer who played at Disneyland to thank.

For a spell in the mid-'80s, the Vandals would play anywhere for $1,000. They were uninspired, and battles over the band's direction raged internally.

Following a number of lineup changes in the late '80s, the band still managed to pump out another song that took off on KROQ. "Shi'ite Punk," a Jan Ackermann/Dave Quackenbush–penned song off 1989's *Slippery When Ill*, was an uptempo rocker that was an outlier on the album, which leaned more toward cowpunk. Ackermann didn't want to write any more traditional punk songs, and the disagreement over the band's direction caused Escalante to enroll in law school at UCLA. He was still in the band, but it took a backseat to his studies.

Seeing bands like Pennywise and Doggy Style, though, inspired the Vandals to keep going. Watching the latter band, Escalante first encountered Warren Fitzgerald, who was wearing a dinosaur suit onstage. More intriguing to Escalante was Fitzgerald's use of a wireless guitar.

"He's on top of a table," Escalante said of seeing the guitarist Fitzgerald perform. "There was this couple on a date and he's just dancing on a table and freaking them out playing guitar. He is the funniest guy I've ever met in my life."

They pursued and eventually enlisted Fitzgerald to play guitar alongside Ackermann before he departed the band in 1989. Ackermann would join Stevo and Human to play with former T.S.O.L. drummer Todd Barnes in S.N.I.V. (Stevo's New and Improved Vandals), which led to a legal battle between the Escalante-led Vandals and the new outfit that would eventually be settled.

As for the Vandals, Escalante moved to bass in 1986 after speaking with Ackermann. ("I thought he was going to say no," Escalante said. "But he was very generous about it.") And there was an open position behind the drum kit. Before he enrolled at law school, he spent three years as a substitute teacher in Long Beach while hoping the Vandals would take off.

Punch-line humor made the Vandals unique, but it took a power-house behind the drums to make them great.

Josh Freese grew up in a musical family in Placentia. His father,

Stan, was the musical director at the Walt Disney Company for over forty years, which entailed putting together the Disneyland band. He started playing drums when he was eight, and by the time he was thirteen, Freese was one of two drummers who performed in Polo, a top-forty cover band at the Tomorrowland Terrace stage where every summer, he'd play four shows a day every day. After three years of doing that, a happy accident (depending on who you ask) occurred.

The Vandals were finishing their rebuild, with Quackenbush and Escalante adding Fitzgerald to the lineup in 1989. Quackenbush and Escalante frequented Disneyland and thus, they had seen Polo perform. They were impressed with one of the musicians.

"There's two drummers: an acoustic drummer, and an electronic drummer," Escalante said. "And we don't know either, but we're focusing on the acoustic guy—he's insane, they're all insane! But then, someone found out that the drummer was in Twisto Frumpkin. And we're like, 'If he could be in Twisto Frumpkin he could definitely be in the Vandals!' Warren and Dave went to see [a popular Long Beach band at the time called] Twisto Frumpkin and they found him."

But that's where the plot thickens.

"When they came back, they said, 'We've got good news and bad news,'" Escalante recalls.

"Oh, really? What is it?"

"We found the drummer, and he said he'll be in the band."

"So what's the bad news?"

"It's the electronic guy, not the acoustic guy."

"It's not the guy with the blazer and the no shirt and tie, and mullet haircut?" Escalante asked incredulously.

"It's cool, though. He loves Devo. He says he'll be in the band because we were about to record with Devo, and that is his favorite band in the world." He was fifteen.

Freese's mom gave him a ride to that first practice, and after he left, the trio mulled over what to do.

"I'll tell you what I think," Escalante told his bandmates. "All we're gonna have in our lives is to talk about how we were in a band with Josh Freese."

Freese tells it a little differently.

"I met Warren through a producer friend of mine beforehand," Freese said. "He was filling in as the Vandals' guitar player temporarily before it turned into a lifelong thing. And then he told me they needed a drummer and I was like, 'Oh, cool!' And then when he told Dave and Joe, they were like, 'That's the dude who plays in the cover band at Disneyland,' and then he brought them to a gig I was playing in Costa Mesa and that's where it happened."

When Freese joined the band, he thought that the Vandals were all on drugs, fucked up, and making dumb decisions. What he found was the opposite. The band were "all really smart, sharp, responsible guys," he said. "Not in a bad way, but I look back and we were all sort of snooty or high and mighty and were like, 'Look at all of these fucking losers getting arrested.' We looked down at people doing dumb shit."

With Freese now in the fold, the Vandals released *Fear of a Punk Planet* in 1990, initially through Enigma Records. "We had more energy," Escalante said. "It was like, 'Let's make a record for no reason.'"

Once the record was completed, Enigma Records said they had no money for the Vandals, and the album was shelved. And in a chance call from the studio, Escalante was told the band's masters were just sitting around and someone needed to pick them up. So he did. He got in contact with Triple X Records, which was willing to fight with Enigma for the album, and they ultimately succeeded.

"As the new guy, I was just stoked to be playing drums and super stoked that [Devo's] Bob Casale was going to produce it," Freese said.

"Somehow, on our cheap budget, we were able to afford him, and I completely fanboyed out on him the entire time."

"It was still a dark period for us as far as the shows we were playing," Escalante said. Still in law school, Escalante wasn't as focused on the Vandals since he didn't see a viable, commercial path forward and thought they were limited with what they could do.

Fear of a Punk Planet continued the Vandals' blend of punk and comedy. Having new members gave the band a path forward.

"There was no business, but we were going to make a record that sounded good and had songs that we like, and to celebrate our new drummer, and our new guitar player," Escalante said. "And so that's what we did."

Additionally, the album featured guest spots from Dweezil and Moon Unit Zappa, Scott Thunes, and . . . Kelsey Grammer. For the first time in a few years, the Vandals' lineup stabilized and would remain this way for years. It brought the band back from chaos and would set them up for moderate success in the years to come. The album was a welcome return to form and set the tone for the humorous pop-punk albums that would emerge later in the decade.

Of the album, *AllMusic*'s Victor W. Valdivia wrote, "Even if the constant juvenile humor grates after a while, the Vandals are still more composed and entertaining than most." Continuing, he said, "*Fear of a Punk Planet* may be just a well-played punk album, but for gloriously un-PC punk fun, it's difficult to do better."

The band released a video for their single "Pizza Tran," which ended up being aired on local TV and received moderate radio play.

"That record was cool because I'm in the studio with my new friends, in my new band I'm playing with, and the songs were fun and funny," Freese said of the album.

In 1992, Escalante graduated from law school and went to work in CBS's television department. Through the success of *Fear of a Punk*

Planet, Fitzgerald and Freese were able to have careers outside the band. The former spent three years in the 1990s as Oingo Boingo's guitarist and later as a film composer. Meanwhile, Freese became a hotly sought-after studio musician. Meanwhile, Quackenbush had his own successful alcohol distribution company.

"The Vandals were never successful enough for it to be our only band," Freese said. "But the Vandals were always home base, and they always had an open-door policy for me and were always cool about it. The funny thing is everyone had their shit together."

"Finally it's happening," Escalante said. "I wish it would have happened when I was nineteen, but now I'm thirty. Then you're on a tour bus for the first time in your life. Why didn't this happen when I wanted it to happen?" At the time, Escalante was working in CBS's television department.

When the Vandals did play, they leaned heavily on their post-Stevo material in order to weed out their old audience. And whenever the Vandals performed, they kept the audience on their toes. The unpredictable nature of their performances kept fans coming back not just for the songs, but for the band's antics.

In 1994, the band released *Sweatin' to the Oldies: The Vandals Live,* which focused on the band's catalog except for *Slippery When Ill.* Prior to this release, the band stopped playing songs from their '80s years.

Thanks to the rising tide of humor-driven pop punk and No Doubt's cover of "Oi to the World," by 1998, the Vandals were more popular than ever. They released *Hitler Bad, Vandals Good,* which was their best-selling album, even though its name nearly didn't happen.

"Quackenbush said, 'There's no way—we cannot have a record that starts with Hitler,'" Escalante said. "'We just can't.' And that was the end of it."

Instead, the album was going to be called *Hurray for Everything.* Until it wasn't.

"We're flying to Australia, and Blink-182 comes up to us and they say, 'Dude, I heard you were gonna call your album *Hitler Bad, Vandals Good*,'" Escalante said. "I showed them a cassette with the new title, and they said they were going to use that title if it was cool. So I told Dave, since they stole all of our jokes, 'Are you really going to let this happen? They're going to sell a million albums with that title.' And he goes, 'Alright, we can do it.'"

Hitler Bad, Vandals Good fit in well with the emerging pop-punk scene. The Fitzgerald-penned "My Girlfriend's Dead" (which Dexter Holland called "another great example of wackiness and is one of their greatest songs" and contributed himself to the album with "Too Much Drama"), a tune where the narrator doesn't want to admit he got dumped so instead he tells everyone that his ex-girlfriend is dead, was one of the album's highlights.

"Sometimes you want that awkward silence of something you don't want to talk about and it's a strategy to find your way there for a taboo subject," Fitzgerald said.

In punk and hardcore magazines, the rising Orange County bands like the Offspring and No Doubt credited the Vandals for influencing them.

"We felt very welcomed by all those people," Escalante said.

By the time the Vandals started playing the Warped Tour, they felt comfortable playing "Urban Struggle" because it was the young punks, not the violent ones who marred their earlier shows, who wanted to hear the song. Ultimately, they'd blend the earlier songs with the Quackenbush era.

<hr />

It wouldn't be long until the Offspring went into the studio and got to work on their second album, which would lay the foundation for successes to come.

The album, once again produced by Wilson, wasn't a punk album in the traditional sense. However, times were beginning to change. Starting with its cover art, which could have easily been something the Cure used, *Ignition* was a bit different sonically, especially on slower songs like "Dirty Magic." That song was unlike any of the others on the album and was included because the Offspring never wanted to be compartmentalized as a punk band. They faced some resistance when informing folks it would be included on *Ignition*, but they weren't deterred and believed it was a great song.

Signing to Epitaph was a big deal to the Offspring. And in those early days, they relished every moment, even if they only had ten days to record the whole thing. They didn't even have time to make a demo—they wrote the songs that comprised the album and went into the studio to record.

"There's a part on 'We Are One' that goes on too long," Holland said. "But we didn't know until we got in there [the studio], and once you record it, you can't do anything about it."

"I remember on 'Take It Like a Man,' Wilson cut out half the tape . . . the solo section," Noodles added.

As they were learning how to write, the Offspring knew that their songs needed to take the energy and vibe of punk and translate it into good, catchy songs that had strong grooves.

"I remember when we finally got *Ignition* out and we got our first CDs, it was mindblowing," Noodles said.

The band was at Holland's house and used his five-CD disc changer to listen to what they created. "It was like, 'Yeah, man, we're a real band!'" Noodles recalled.

As the band tested out the new material around LA and Orange County, fans would watch by the tens. Even with the sparsely attended shows, the band never stopped believing. After each show, they'd hop offstage and run their merch booth, hawking swag. At one such show at the Anti Club, the band would make a lifelong friend who would play a big part in their career.

At that time, Whittier native Jason McLean was nineteen years old and loved punk rock. He'd check out shows across the Southland, and his friends' band always played with the Offspring. Though he'd spoken with them before casually, he didn't know them well enough beyond a few pleasantries and facial recognition, if that. And on this night, familiar with *Ignition*, he implored the band to play his favorite cut: "Blackball." Due to the intimate setting (i.e., not a lot of people in attendance), an admittedly drunk McLean heckled the Offspring throughout the set until they finally gave in.

"They weren't playing it live," said McLean. "Finally, from the stage, Dexter said, 'Listen, dude, if we play 'Blackball,' will you shut the fuck up?' And I said, 'Yeah, totally.' So they played the song . . . then two songs later, I was going, 'Play it again!'"

After the show, McLean chatted with the band at their merch booth and a friendship emerged. Playfully, the band started calling him Blackball. Soon enough, Blackball and the Offspring hung out, and Blackball, who worked at a box manufacturer, offered to help Holland move and provided him with boxes to do so. "I guess it could have gone the other way and they could have gotten a restraining order against me," Blackball said jokingly.

For the next year, the Offspring toured behind *Ignition*. Opening for NOFX, the band was exposed to a wider audience for the first time. In the beginning, though, NOFX singer Fat Mike wasn't psyched about their sound.

"When I first heard them, I thought, 'This is the worst drummer I've ever heard in my life,'" he said. "Epitaph wanted us to take them on tour, and I don't think they ever told the band this but they gave us $5,000 to pay for our bus in Europe to take them. So they didn't get paid. And the label paid us."

Adding insult to injury, the bus had twelve bunks and there were thirteen musicians. Needless to say, it's easy to figure out which band's members would have to catch some shut-eye on the floor.

"It was whoever went to sleep last didn't get a bunk," Fat Mike said. "Sometimes it was Ron, but most of the time it was Noodles."

"I did a lot at the beginning, that is true," Noodles confirmed.

"We were getting hazed a lot on that tour," Holland said. "But we were learning a lot from them. We were observing. They were, you know, they had way better equipment than we did. And they had, they had banter onstage. And they had a rapport with the audience. They were a few steps ahead of us at that point."

That tour was a brutal run of thirty-one shows and thirty-five days, yet the band learned a lot.

"We also saw that they [NOFX] were actually making a living at it [punk rock]," Holland continued. "We're like, 'Oh my gosh, so here's a band that can actually make a living.' That was *something*."

Even at that early juncture of the Offspring's career, their songs were catchy enough to have crowds singing along.

"I remember going to Italy on that tour, and there were kids singing the 'whoa, whoa, whoas,'" Noodles said. "I was like, 'How do these kids in Italy know this [*Ignition*]?' It was rad."

It didn't help back at home in Orange County. The band was still bigger in Berkeley, and despite Social Distortion's newfound major label success, the punk scene in Orange County was still shaking out of its late '80s malaise.

"We thought there was really a ceiling, which was, at that time, Bad Religion," Holland told *Us Weekly* in 2004. "They [Bad Religion] sold whatever it was, maybe 100,000, maybe 200,000 even? And that was just insane. But nothing even close to what might be considered a punk band or a pop-punk band had broken at that point. So we really thought that that was as high as it could go."

After the Neil Young tour, Ness's songwriting hot streak continued. That culminated in the 1992 release *Somewhere Between Heaven and Hell*. The album's cover featured a purple background with Ness doing his trademark leap that he did during the band's live show.

Social Distortion's self-titled album introduced them to an audience far beyond Southern California. At this point, their impact on Orange County was undeniable. They surpassed their contemporaries and were showing a new younger generation that being a band in Orange County wasn't the death knell it once was perceived to be. It showed that great Southern California songwriting wasn't necessarily happening only in LA.

"They had a lot of hits," No Doubt's Adrian Young said. "That still felt like that was legit. They meant what they were doing and you could tell."

Even with radio support and MTV playing their videos, Social Distortion was still an afterthought compared to their national peers. With Epic's headquarters in New York, the band was able to work mostly without label interference. That also enabled neglect and a lack of understanding of how much momentum the band had. As they recorded between June and October 1991 at El Dorado Studios in Hollywood once again with Dave Jerden producing, Social Distortion was firing on all cylinders.

The album was another step forward with its blend of punk, rockabilly, and American roots music that Ness had explored since he got sober. Autobiographical songs like "Born to Lose" demonstrated the personal growth Ness experienced as a songwriter and how relatable his lyrics were. Ness continued with themes of down-on-their-luck characters and how they go through life knowing as much. "The songs had depth and space to them," Brian Fallon said.

Sales-wise, thanks to the success of Social Distortion, *Somewhere*

Between Heaven and Hell was the band's best-selling album out of the gate. It peaked at number seventy-six on the *Billboard* 200 and eventually went Gold.

The album's first single, "Bad Luck," was a firecracker of a song that perfectly encapsulated the band's rugged swagger. "Bad Luck" peaked at number two on *Billboard*'s Alternative Airplay charts, and number forty-four on the Mainstream Rock chart. Even with that success, Ness still had a chip on his shoulder. At a show at the legendary punk club CBGB in February 1992, Ness said of "Bad Luck" that it was "the one that all the radio stations finally got hip to Social D. It only took them twelve fucking years."

Even so, Social Distortion had trouble getting a budget from the label to shoot music videos. The band had to shoot the album's three videos, "Bad Luck," "Cold Feelings," and "Born to Lose," in one day, with Guerinot having to foot the $29,000 bill before the label eventually reimbursed him.

Somewhere Between Heaven and Hell was released to another batch of positive reviews.

"Ness' love of country music is more pronounced here than ever," Mike Boehm of the *Los Angeles Times* wrote. "SD's singer-songwriter starts with the essence of a good country song—a simple story that communicates an emotion, coupled with a melody that makes you want to hum along—and applies his distinctive, chest-cold sneer of a voice, some nice high harmonies, and Social Distortion's engine-blast attack."

Continuing, he said, "The result is the band's catchiest, most consistent album. Like Neil Young & Crazy Horse, whose molten twang this album recalls, Social Distortion has found a satisfying, uninhibited way to apply rock's noise and thrust to country roots."

Boehm also wrote that the album had no weak tracks, and while the album didn't break new ground, it had a distinctive sound and was "smart enough to sing only about what it knows, and it knows how to pummel the body while seducing the ear."

As pleased as they were with the critical praise, Social Distortion received plaudits from a source who would change the trajectory of their career.

Having moved to Los Angeles at the beginning of the decade, Bruce Springsteen was leading a quiet life in the Hollywood Hills, having recently started a family away from the madness of his New Jersey home. As the Boss was on the cusp of releasing *Human Touch* and *Lucky Town* at the end of 1992, he sat down for an extensive interview with *Rolling Stone* to promote the releases. In that conversation, the topic of new music came up.

"I like Sir Mix-a-Lot," Springsteen said. "I like Queen Latifah; I like her a lot. I also like Social Distortion. I think 'Somewhere Between Heaven and Hell' is a great record, a great rock & roll album. 'Born to Lose' is great stuff."

"That was big for us," Ness said.

What began as a mutual respect blossomed into a friendship between the two front men. Over the years, Ness would be invited to perform with Springsteen and vice versa.

Fresh off their latest album's release, Social Distortion hit the road for an extensive coheadlining tour with the Ramones.

However, tensions in the band mounted. The album's cover art rankled some members, who grumbled that Ness was becoming the superstar while others were being left behind. Frustrations also abounded that the band's all-for-one ethos that marked their return in the late '80s was being forgotten.

By the end of 1993, after years of relentless touring, Social Distortion went on hiatus.

"We needed a break," Ness said. "Then we had to do some court battles to retrieve some of our early recordings. Not only were they not in our possession, where they rightfully belonged, but worse than that was their unavailability to the public. So we had to retrieve them, package them up and put them out."

In October 1994, after years of the band's most stable lineup in its history, tensions boiled over when Chris Reece announced he was leaving Social Distortion after a decade in the band due to creative differences. Drumming for Social Distortion became a job.

"It was my decision pretty much," Reece said at the time. "But there were a lot of issues that led up to it. In the past we had pretty much seen eye to eye on how things were going but [recently] we just weren't seeing eye to eye on drum parts. We've just grown different ways musically, and it was time for us to go our separate ways. Both parties felt it was the best thing to do."

He was replaced by Randy Carr, who served as the band's drummer for a handful of shows. Reece's departure began a seeming revolving door of the band rotating through drummers that would mark the better part of their next era.

After years of recording and relentless touring, Social Distortion took a hiatus. With Ness in total control of the songwriting and recording process, Danell became frustrated that the front man wasn't as open to his ideas as he was in the past. Unwilling to wait to have his ideas turn into songs, Danell formed Fuel, a side project with Social Distortion bandmate John Maurer. Danell also started producing bands, like Rockstar Barbeque.

During the hiatus, Ness wasn't concerned about filling the position behind the kit. Instead, he was focused on writing the band's best album.

"The priority is to get the writing finished," Ness said. "Right now we're writing like crazy. I've written about thirty songs in the last year. I really want to dig deep. I don't want this to be just another Social D record—I want it to be *the* Social D record."

In their time making that album, the landscape of the Orange County music scene would change in a major way.

14

THIS WASN'T SUPPOSED TO HAPPEN

I
n early 1994, the Offspring began work on their third studio album with Thom Wilson. The sessions were slated to take place in OC in order "to avoid the slog up to LA every day," Holland says. However, those best-laid plans went to waste as the studio the band looked at had technical issues they couldn't quite get past. So they headed up the freeway to Track Record in North Hollywood.

"I thought that studio was out of our league as far as what we could afford but we decided to just do it," Holland says.

"I think *Ignition*'s [sales] was at about forty thousand? Is that right?" Noodles added. "Still, that was punk rock standards. We weren't thinking about mainstream success at all when we went in to make *Smash*." (It was sixty thousand according to Epitaph.)

While at Track, the band's sessions went relatively smoothly outside of the infamous Northridge earthquake that left the room's ceiling drooping. Also at Track at the time? None other than Snoop Doggy Dogg. "It was actually pretty exciting," Holland says. "Because Snoop

Dogg was actually recording in the next room [at Track Records], and that was probably the biggest music act we had ever been that close to."

Up to that point, despite the rigorous tour schedule, *Ignition* sold about forty thousand copies. Not bad for a release by a relatively new regional band on an indie punk label, but not enough to light the lamp. Working with a budget of $20,000, expectations for the album weren't exactly high. Factor in the band having twenty days in total to record the whole thing, and pulling it off was akin to what their OC punk forefathers like the Adolescents and Social Distortion did in the early '80s. The Offspring had to call the studio to see if anyone was using it, and if not, they'd get the room for half price.

Holland started working on the album in late 1993. Some songs, like "Nitro" and "Genocide," came easy and were logical successors to what the band put forth on *Ignition*. Then, he started to expand his writing and thus, the band's sound. Knowing he wanted something mid-tempo, Holland wrote "Gotta Get Away," an aggressive song with elements of alternative rock weaved into it. Next came "Self Esteem."

"It was literally one of those moments where I woke up one morning with the melody in my head," Holland said of the song. "I had the bassline and the vocal melody for the verse. I just kept on thinking about it, and then a couple of weeks later, the chorus came and it was just lucky."

The album was nearly wrapped when Holland had an idea for a last song built around a Middle East–inspired surf rock riff. He had the "gotta keep 'em separated" line for the chorus swimming around in his head but decided to keep it a secret from the rest of the band until it was time to do overdubs.

"I didn't tell the other guys there was gonna be a Middle Eastern riff and a Mexican saying 'keep 'em separated' [sung by Blackball, who had the slang down since he was one of the only white guys in a Mexican neighborhood in Whittier] because I thought they'd say just forget it," Holland says. "So I was just gonna tell them, 'Don't worry, there's gonna be something cool in the spot, and after we record it you'll hear it then.' So they kinda went with it."

"Bryan was asking me, 'Jason, what can you do for us?'" Blackball said. "And I said, 'Man, I pretty much can't do shit.' But one day Bryan calls me up and says, 'Dude, come on down, I think we got a part for you.'"

Little did Blackball know what that would entail.

Heading up to Track, Blackball, who was also a big hip-hop fan just like the band, was excited to see Warren G and Snoop at the studio. Once being starstruck subsided (he asked and received a photo with the rappers), Blackball got to work.

In just five takes, he recorded his now iconic "You gotta keep 'em separated" line.

Even though it worked, they weren't sure it was going to.

After the session, Blackball and Dexter went to a nearby In-N-Out, and the singer tried to manage expectations.

"'I don't know if it's gonna be on the CD or not,'" Blackball remembers Holland telling him. "I said to him, 'I don't give a shit, it was just cool to do.'"

A month later, though, while at Iguana's, a bar in Tijuana, Dexter gave McLean a copy of their soon-to-be-released album. "He told me, 'Yeah, I don't think it made the cut,' and I was like, 'Ah, that's cool,'" Blackball said. After a slight pause, Holland told him the good news. "Dude, I'm kidding! They fucking love it and want to put it on the radio!"

"Come Out and Play" was the last song the Offspring recorded for the album, and it nearly didn't make the cut. The band is sure glad it did.

"It's a good thing we did it," Holland told *Us Weekly*. "It doesn't encourage the planning and preparation [we did]—'just go in off the seat of your pants and maybe it'll all turn out.' But it is funny how things work like that sometimes."

"Come Out and Play" was just one of the many songs from *Smash* that were inspired by things Holland saw in his daily life.

"Back then I was a grad student and I was commuting to school every day in a shitty car, driving through East LA Gangland central," Holland told *Rolling Stone* in 2014. "I was there the day of the LA riots. So I was very aware of that part of the world, and a lot of that gun stuff came out in songs like 'Come Out and Play.'"

"'Come Out and Play' was a sort of stunningly original track," Epitaph boss Brett Gurewitz told *Rolling Stone* in 2014. "It has that 'magic something' that hit songs sometimes have . . . it has this sexy darkness to it. It was very, very unique and extremely infectious."

"Really the only thing that seemed different to me about that one was the catchphrase," Noodles also told *Rolling Stone* in 2014. "'You gotta keep 'em separated.' When I heard that line it just made me laugh."

Holland also compared the song to the rap music that was popular at the time.

"There's kind of a rhythmic thing about the vocals; I talk instead of sing in a lot of parts," he said. "The whole beat of the song is kind of like the old War song 'Low Rider.'"

Other songs like the menacing "Bad Habit," which had an aggressive, buzzsaw sound to match Holland's derision of road rage, and "Gotta Get Away," were examples of the band's growing songwriting evolution.

Through *Smash*, the band didn't lose its sense of humor. Just like the Vandals before them, the Offspring incorporated humor into their songs. The album opener is "Time to Relax" (which nearly thirty years later is the name of the band's official podcast), a spoken-word track voiced by John Mayer (the actor, not the musician), which the band said would be a nice counterbalance to a punk album.

"I thought, 'Who's the most soothing guy you could imagine?' And in my head, it was going to be Bing Crosby," Holland said. "But Crosby was dead [he died in 1977], so we sent the copy to a voice-over agency in North Hollywood, and they couldn't get us a Bing Crosby impressionist, but they found someone with a soothing voice who was just a little bit off."

"It was over the top and certainly unique," Noodles added. "But he had this great voice for radio . . . and made us laugh."

Just ahead of *Smash*'s release, the Offspring brought Guerinot on board to manage them. They initially reached out to him at Wilson's recommendation around the time of *Ignition*'s release. However, with his job as the general manager of A&M Records and managing Social Distortion full-time, Guerinot didn't have the bandwidth to take them on. But he did help the band secure an opening slot for Fugazi when he told Holland to call Goldenvoice boss Paul Tollett, whom he gave a heads-up to about the young singer's impending phone call.

By early 1994, Guerinot was disenchanted with his work. One day, as he was pondering what to do, his assistant brought him a copy of *Smash* and told him that "Come Out and Play" was added to KROQ and that he thought the song was great.

"So I listened to the record and I was like, 'I know this guy! This guy called!'" he remembered. "I told him, 'This is great, but it isn't the best song on the record.' It was a good song, but I said 'Self Esteem' is the hit."

The common thread between these two songs and the rest of the Offspring's catalog? Catchy and memorable choruses. It's what differentiated the band from other punk bands. Having this element infused into their songs allowed the Offspring to stand out.

Guerinot was in the process of planning his exit from A&M and figured since he was into the music, he'd invite Holland to his office to chat. But before that happened, Guerinot called Kevin Weatherly, the program director at KROQ, to see how "Come Out and Play" was tracking.

"This thing's a fucking hit," Guerinot said of Weatherly's response. "He goes, 'I love this record. We put it on [the air] and it blew up right away. It's going off.'"

"My big advice for the Offspring was just listen to Jim," Joe Escalante said. "When Jim says do something, just do it. After a while you can fight with him, but for now just do this. And that worked out for them."

KROQ was instrumental in propelling the Offspring from playing in front of tens of people to thousands. With influential DJ Jed the Fish anointing "Come Out and Play" as his Catch of the Day, the song took off. "After he played it, we got on the phone and called the station," Noodles said. "We said, 'Play that one again, it was great!' The saying back then was 'As goes KROQ, so goes the country.'"

Before the days of social media, calling a station's request line was the only way for fans to register their opinion about a song. The band enlisted everyone they knew to call the station until the song organically took on a life of its own.

Guerinot left A&M in July 1994 with Social Distortion and the Offspring as his clients. Rebel Waltz, his management company, became his full-time job.

When *Smash* was released in April 1994, things didn't exactly take off. The band played at Goodies, a now-defunct club in Fullerton, and only about one hundred people showed up. In less than a month, things finally got rolling. A sold-out show at the Whisky a Go Go gave them confidence, and one moment from that show still stands out to

Holland. One fan in particular was calling for the band to perform "Self Esteem."

"I was amazed she was already calling out that," Holland marveled. "Then we played it and it went off and we were like wow, maybe there's something bigger going on with this record. It was a sign of what was gonna happen."

The moment was an early signifier of how the album would connect with audiences globally. Most importantly, *Smash* gained momentum in Southern California. After it was KROQ's Catch of the Day, "Come Out and Play" landed on the Furious 5, a segment where listeners voted for their five favorite songs of the day, which was put into heavy rotation. The song's video, shot for $1,500 in May 1994 by director Darren Lavett, captured the essence of the Offspring. The sepia-toned video featured the band performing the song in the garage of a house with tinfoil covering the walls. It also features footage of dogs fighting over a chew toy with a crowd watching, a horse race, a sword fight, and some clips of several snakes and snake charmers, not to mention fencing scenes.

"We all crammed into his garage and covered the walls with mylar, like what you see in helium balloons," Noodles told *Rolling Stone*. "It was a million degrees in there. Then we brought in a big fan. So this reflective plastic was kinda blowing around while we played. I think most of the budget was spent on beer and meat for the barbecue after the shoot."

McLean also remembers the video shoot fondly. He kept his experience with the shoot under wraps, at least publicly. When the video debuted on MTV's *120 Minutes*, Blackball finally let the cat out of the bag.

"I called my parents and told my mom to immediately put on MTV," he said. "She was like, 'Why?' and I told her to hurry and put it on." They couldn't believe what they saw: their son on MTV. "So they did and were like 'What the heck?'" he said. Due to his popular line and appearance in the clip, the band asked Blackball if he wanted to go on tour with them, which he politely declined, not loving the thought of playing that part as a full-time gig. "It's fun for like a week," he said. "You don't have to become a drunken idiot but that's what I chose, and I came out to the big shows."

As things blew up, Guerinot had a sharp vision of what the Off-spring should do.

"I loved that they were on Epitaph," he said. "I thought it was the greatest thing because I worked at a major and I loved that little Epi-taph Records was sticking it to the majors. I knew I could help with MTV, and there was nothing we couldn't do. And I meant that. Every-body was calling me wanting to sign the band and I would not let them take a meeting with anybody. Like not one."

Why? Guerinot has a simple explanation.

"I didn't want to send the wrong signal. What Brett and Andy were doing was exceptional."

Within months, "Come Out and Play" was in heavy rotation on MTV, which accelerated the Offspring's rise.

Powered by the album's first single, the rapid ascension was some-thing that the band's peers couldn't help but notice.

"I remember right around that time we were playing a snowboard-ing contest in Valdez, Alaska, opening for Pennywise," Noodles told *Rolling Stone*. "And all our friends were saying, 'The song is going off on KROQ!' I was with Byron [McMackin, drummer] from Pennywise and he said, 'Jeez, are we gonna have to open for you guys next time?'"

Jokes aside, McMackin wasn't wrong.

And the timing for *Smash* couldn't have been better. Earlier in the year, mainstream punk broke through in a way that was far different from its first era. Fellow Gilman Street alumni Green Day released their breakthrough album, *Dookie*, which set the stage for things to come. In 1994 alone, Bad Religion, Rancid, Jawbreaker, and NOFX released albums that reintroduced younger audiences to punk. Unlike the sloppiness of the recordings by the early punk bands, this polished, poppy version, along with infectious melodies and catchy hooks, inspired a new generation and ensured that the genre was here to stay. In just forty-six minutes (the band's longest album to date), the Offspring brought the Orange County sound to the mainstream.

"They were as important as Green Day's success was and Nirvana's success was because they were on Epitaph," Damian Abraham said. "No one else could have done that."

"It was life-changing, surreal, and extremely validating," Gurewitz said.

At the time, the label was really picking up momentum. First, Epitaph shipped one hundred thousand of Bad Religion's *Against the Grain*. Pennywise was starting to take off, and Rancid was doing well. "We used to think of punk rock gold as fifty thousand copies," Gurewitz said. *Smash* did that number many times over.

Despite Guerinot's hopes, the majors didn't back off from circling the band.

One day, Holland was approached at his Huntington Beach apartment by an overzealous major-label A&R rep. After declining to speak with him by saying that he was busy (he was taking out his trash), the rep followed him down to the street trying to pitch him on the laurels of their label.

As successful as "Come Out and Play" was in pushing the Offspring into the mainstream, the band's second single proved that Guerinot's instincts were correct. "Self Esteem" picked up where "Come Out and Play" left off. The song's angsty, self-pitying lyrics about a guy whose girlfriend sleeps with his friends and bosses him around coupled with the riff-heavy, thumping bass line caught on. As much as that helped propel the song, Holland's opening "La La La Las" differentiated the song from not just the rising popularity of punk songs infiltrating the mainstream, but rock as a whole.

"When I listened to 'Self Esteem' as a fourteen-year-old kid, it was like 'Wow this song hits,'" Abraham said. "It's like they were writing my thoughts. My favorite things about the Offspring when I was listening to them, they were emo way before I heard emo."

In his review of *Smash*, *Melody Maker*'s Andrew Mueller wrote, "The clear highlight here is 'Self Esteem,' a self-abasing, self-pitying slandering of some or other black-hearted wench set to a rocket as inventive as they get." European magazine *Music & Media* said that the band was "Nirvana's perfect replacement" and they delivered "the punky action so sadly missed on rock radio because of Seattlers who take themselves way too seriously."

"Well, I was wrong and right at the same time," Guerinot said. "They were both hits."

"I never knew so many people would relate to that," Holland said. "It's just kind of a turnaround. The girls are real cocky, and the guys are real passive."

Within four months of its release, *Smash* was certified Gold and Platinum by RIAA. By April 1995, *Smash* sold more than five million copies in the US and peaked at number four on the *Billboard* 200. It was the first album on Epitaph to achieve that status, and for years it was the best-selling independent album of all time until Adele's *21* was released in 2011.

"It was overwhelming and kind of scary," Gurewitz told *Rolling Stone*. "At the time Epitaph was a company of maybe five or six people, myself included. We had Offspring records filling my entire building on Santa Monica Boulevard, from the floor to the ceiling. The inside of the building looked like a Rubik's Cube of pallets of Offspring vinyl, cassettes, and CDs. Then we had another building downtown that was also filled, and rental space in external buildings. At one point the thing started selling so fast that we made an arrangement for the pressing plant to start shipping directly to the central warehouses of the major record chains, bypassing the distributors entirely."

The album's incredible success also forced Gurewitz into a decision he never thought he'd have to make.

"It also played into my decision to leave Bad Religion," he continued. "*Smash* was Gold or Platinum already, and I had just written what I felt was my best record ever [Bad Religion's Atlantic Records–released *Stranger Than Fiction*]. I was thirty-two years old, and it felt like the universe was telling me this was the optimal time to make a change."

Despite the deserved breakthrough after the long weekends heading up north and venturing out to the Inland Empire to play in front of minimal people and hunt for anyone who'd support them close to home, the Offspring still felt a sense of imposter syndrome about their sudden success. The band felt unsure about how they should feel when *Smash* did well. So much so that Noodles was uncomfortable leaving his job at Earl Warren Elementary School in Garden Grove, fearing losing his pension. He ended up taking a leave of absence in June 1994. As for Holland, he was working on his PhD in molecular biology at USC and had to put that on pause due to *Smash*'s success (he would eventually return to school and graduate in 2017). His professor tried to convince him to finish his degree, but Guerinot told him that if they didn't pursue the band full-time, they'd lose their opportunity to make a living playing music.

"We just started thinking there's no way that playing punk rock was a viable career path," Noodles said. "We might be able to do it for a couple of years while we're going back to school or whatever."

"We felt we were an amateur band up until this point," Holland said. "Then all of a sudden, now we have the chance to become a professional band. Let's take baby steps and learn how to do this."

The band's initial run of success after so many years of toiling anonymously was disorienting.

"There was a discomfort for the whole thing, for sure. Embarrassment," Holland told *Us Weekly*. "There's a perception when a band becomes well-known that it's not cool with some people anymore. We fought that in terms of trying to stick to what we thought was right."

The singer/guitarist was concerned that the band was being looked at differently, specifically by their friends, peers, and longtime fans. That led to the band retreating to the point where at the album's peak, they turned down an appearance on *Saturday Night Live*. Looking back, Holland regrets not performing in music's most prestigious slot.

"At the time, we really felt like we were just a garage band a few months before. We hadn't played a show bigger than 500 people. And to put us on a national live television show, we just thought it was probably going to be a disaster in terms of our performance. Maybe not? Maybe it would've been, and maybe it just would've captured the moment, but it just felt really uncomfortable to put ourselves up to that."

"For years, [*SNL* music booker] Marci Klein wouldn't talk to me," Guerinot said. "She was so angry about it, but not every artist does things like everyone else, and that wasn't what they wanted to do at that time."

But they never forgot where they came from.

In August 1994, Blackball turned twenty-one. To mark the occasion and to support their friend, the Offspring showed up and played a backyard birthday party at a rented house for their friend in Whittier. Once word spread, the riot police immediately arrived along with choppers in the sky.

As *Smash*'s album sales continued to soar, the band became the subject of some unwanted controversy. Through the Harry Fox Agency, a music publishing rights collector, Posh Boy submitted a claim that stated "Come Out and Play" lifted its solo from Agent Orange's 1981 song "Bloodstains." Posh Boy was the publisher and owned the copyright to "Bloodstains" and wanted Epitaph to pay a licensing fee for what it claimed was sampling the solo.

"Nobody wants to pillory anybody," Robbie Fields told the *Los Angeles Times* in 1995. "But I feel I have a fiduciary duty to represent Mike Palm's interests."

The label's claim was immediately refuted by the band. Posh Boy was seeking a penny for each Offspring album sold. At the time, since the album sold six million copies, by that math, Posh Boy believed it was entitled to $60,000. In turn, Guerinot hired musicologists to disprove what Posh Boy and Fields alleged.

"They're not even close to identical. They're both in the same scale, [and] there's no doubt there's an influence, [but] it doesn't mean that it's stolen," the manager told the *Los Angeles Times*. "If [Fields] feels he has something, he'll sue, and if we've done something that is proven wrong [by technical analysis of the two songs] we should be sued. But we don't feel there's any merit to it."

"I asked Dexter and he said, 'I had no idea,'" Guerinot said. "I love Agent Orange, but by any stretch of the imagination, wouldn't do that."

"That was really a shame because we were fans of Agent Orange," Holland told *Rolling Stone*. "And of course I was familiar with their music, but to say that we were stealing was just not true at all. We were talking about something that was really taken from surf music. Dick Dale or whatever. It really had nothing to do with that band."

"Anyone who listens will know what the issue is," Palm told the *Los Angeles Times* in 1995. "I'm not really going to state my opinion at this time, but I invite anyone to compare the songs."

As a bystander to the whole situation, Frank Agnew said that the notion that the Offspring ripped off Agent Orange was preposterous.

"I don't see how you can call that plagiarism; all it is is an Arabic scale," Agnew told the *Times*. "It just reeks to me [as if] people are after a piece of the pie. If the Offspring did a guitar solo that was reminiscent of one of my guitar solos, I'd be honored, not [antagonized]. I think it's real petty."

Despite the back-and-forth posturing and all of the noise, Posh Boy eventually did not file a suit. And ironically, the Offspring covered "Bloodstains" for the soundtrack to the 2000 film *Ready to Rumble*.

Of the situation, in 2008, Palm told *OC Weekly* that "they were saying that I was out to sue them. Some punk kid's perception of that is to think that I'm the bad guy. But they don't understand that the Offspring are millionaires, and I'm just trying to retain whatever little tiny thing is mine."

In addition to Agnew's comments to the *Times*, Posh Boy and Agent Orange were criticized by other bands in the scene. Specifically, the Vandals mocked the band with their "Aging Orange" song, released through Holland's Nitro Records in 1996. In response, Palm told the *Weekly*, "I thought the song was lame and out of line. You think there was some ass-licking going on there?"

It wasn't just in Southern California where the Offspring had radio support. After KROQ added "Come Out and Play" to its regular rotation, Las Vegas and Phoenix soon followed suit. As did the rest of the country, where Epitaph wasn't as recognized as it was on the West Coast. The Offspring changed that. The label became synonymous with genre-melding punk rock, which would help in the months to come with NOFX and Rancid releasing their breakthrough albums. The breakthrough was thanks to "Come Out and Play," which was bringing in a new audience.

"I knew it ['Come Out and Play'] was gonna be big because my brother who listened to Metallica and didn't like my weird punk rock took right to it," SiriusXM DJ Kat Corbett says. At the time, Corbett was spinning records at WFNX, an indie rock station in Boston. "And he loved it. I was like, 'Oh, this is gonna be big.'"

She was right. "Come Out and Play" caught on in Boston and had crossover appeal to fans of alt-rock, hard rock, and punk. Anything that could get bodies moving (and slamming), Corbett said, was going to appeal to the Boston music scene.

"Anything that was coming from the West Coast, I was in and was like give me more," she said. "Some bands, like Oingo Boingo, who were massive in Southern California, didn't translate in Boston. But the Offspring, the record blew up and could be played anywhere."

The hits kept coming.

"But the thing was like, OK, they had one song," Corbett added. "Then they had another single off this record with 'Self Esteem' and then 'Gotta Get Away' was another one! Then some other places would play 'Bad Habit,' which was a single. Four singles off a punk album was a pretty big feat."

As the band's profile soared after *Smash*, the Offspring's tour schedule was relentless. After "Come Out and Play" landed on MTV, the band quickly did as they planned. They took baby steps and rapidly graduated from playing in 500-seat rooms to 1,500-person small clubs to 5,000-person theaters.

"At one point, we were in Florida, and it [*Smash*] had gone to number twenty [on the *Billboard* 200]," Holland remembered. "And that's when I kind of thought, 'Wow, top twenty.' That feels pretty real."

The band's profile was so prominent that they were able to turn down arena-opening slots for Metallica and Stone Temple Pilots. It wasn't because of any sort of disrespect. Instead, it was all about the band's punk ethos.

"It just really didn't seem like the right thing to do," Holland said. "I still like the club thing, even if it's a big club. I like Stone Temple Pilots—it's not like we're saying we're too punk for that."

Along the way, they ran into an old friend in an unexpected place.

While the band was in Houston, somehow Holland randomly heard from James Lilja, who had just moved there for his residency and was literally unpacking his belongings.

"I was flipping through one of those city rags that shows you what shows were on," Lilja said on the band's *Time to Relax* podcast. "Then I ran across Offspring at Numbers, which was the place they were playing. At first, I thought, 'Oh my God! Someone stole the name!' Then I thought, 'Wait a minute, maybe it's them and maybe they need a place to crash.'"

Lilja was living in a house near the hospital and figured there could be a chance his former comrades needed a place to stay. He called the venue asking for Holland, who was practicing backstage, and was told he was unavailable. After a back-and-forth with the band's tour manager, Lilja was given backstage passes to the show. When he showed up, the band was "shell-shocked."

"I don't know who the tour manager was, but I remember one of them saying, 'I don't know how this [the band blowing up] happened and I don't know what's going on, but we gotta go right after this, we got no time.' It was crazy," Lilja said. "They had the 10,000-yard stare but it was a great show."

The year 1994 was a major breakthrough. Despite the fame, the band kept their hardworking punk rock ethos. At some junctures, they were playing five nights in a row. In that tour cycle for *Smash*, the band played over two hundred shows, including a run in Japan and Australia where they headlined the 1995 version of Big Day Out. On Guerinot's advice, the Offspring toured Europe four times, which laid the groundwork for the popularity the band still has overseas in the present day.

"It was exciting, but it was also like, 'Whoa, is this really happening?!'" Noodles told *Us Weekly*. The band ended up touring for nearly two years.

"I still love these songs," he continued. "'Come Out and Play' still sounds as fresh to me as it ever did. 'Self Esteem,' the same way."

"If there's any real legacy to *Smash* it's the independent spirit of that record," Noodles told *Rolling Stone*. "Because we took on Goliath with Epitaph. Hopefully, that has resonated."

Smash's sales helped Epitaph and some of the Offspring's peers. The label was able to reissue classic releases by earlier punk bands, primarily financed through the Offspring's earnings.

"I know a lot of people have sour grapes," Steve Soto told *Alternative Press* of the Offspring's popularity. "But [their success] has been good for me. They came up the same way everybody else did, playing the same crappy clubs. As far as everything goes with those guys, I think it's great."

If there was one night that crystallized the Offspring's decision to play in Europe, it was at a show in Milan, Italy. The Vandals opened for them, and from their vantage point, watching the Offspring play in front of ten thousand people in a country that barely spoke English was eye-opening.

"There were so many levels of inconceivable going on," the Vandals' Warren Fitzgerald said on the Offspring's *Time to Relax* podcast. "First of all, 10,000 Italians were at a punk show. When it came to the breakdown in 'Bad Habit,' they knew every fucking word—whether they even knew what it meant. At that point, it was like that was effervescent split with overspray. That was fucking bonkers!"

Looking back thirty years later, Noodles is still amazed by *Smash*'s unlikely success.

"The songs are every bit as [relevant] today as they were 30 years ago," he said. "But I feel that way about a lot of the music I've loved throughout my life, and especially all the music we've made. I can think back to when I first heard 'Come Out and Play' on the radio and just thinking, 'Whoa, what is this? This is mind-blowing. This doesn't happen to bands like us.' That was a very exciting thing."

15

PUNK MENTAL ATTITUDE

Somewhere between Bud Gaugh's departure and reemergence, Bradley Nowell started using heroin and meth.

"[Nowell's] eyes were a little more sunken in. He was a lot thinner than he was before," Gaugh said. "He was still fresh with it. At first, it seemed pretty harmless. He was just smoking and would do a little bit and wouldn't have to have it every day, like a weekend or recreational kind of thing. Then he started to really, really enjoy it and replaced drinking and smoking pot with it.

"Burroughs and all these other, you know, literary greats . . . everybody had their little closet full of secrets," he continued. "So it was well known that, you know, people would use."

In a half-baked effort to normalize the drug, he could often be spotted fixing heroin out in the open at parties and offering it around as if it was just an everyday hors d'oeuvre—but people generally weren't having it, least of all Gaugh.

After a few weeks, Gaugh got his life in order. He moved in with a friend of his and got a job. Then, seemingly out of the blue, he got a call from Nowell asking him if he wanted to jam again.

"That's when it started," he said. "That's when we started writing songs for *Robbin' the Hood*."

When Sublime's original members got back together and jammed, there was something markedly different about the songs they were playing. In the year Gaugh was away, Nowell's songwriting changed. The music got "harder" compared to *40oz. to Freedom*, and "the lyrics were a lot more streetwise" despite Sublime continuing to play sun-soaked anthems powered by the groove-laden rhythm section. In particular, on the hip-hop-infused "Badfish." The song opens with people talking, which Gaugh recorded at happy hour at the Bayshore Saloon. It captured what life in Long Beach and Sublime were like. Though its meaning would later be closely tied to Nowell's battle with addiction, the video captured the spirit of a band on the rise and looking to have a good time. Taking place on the beach, the band hosted a party with all of their friends, and it captured everything that went along with the Sublime lifestyle.

Nowell's drug of choice at the time was crystal meth. His songwriting process was comparable to a tweaked-out mad scientist, setting up eight-track recording units in his then-girlfriend Kathy Ramirez's living room, or writing lyrics in abandoned flophouses down in the San Juan Capistrano area in between waiting for his next score. He substituted live drums for rhythmic and spastic patterns from 808 drum machines that gave Nowell full creative control in his manic, genius state.

Sublime would go on to record seven songs.

The *Robbin' the Hood* sessions were funded by Brett Gurewitz and Epitaph, and Sublime recorded at Westbeach Recorders in Hollywood. The album featured No Doubt's Gwen Stefani trading vocals with Nowell on the up-tempo ska track "Saw Red." The demented lifeblood of the tracklist are the roughly tape recorded "soliloquies" of Raleigh Theodore Sakers, a mythical and disturbed mental patient obsessed with cock sucking and science fiction. Despite the venerable LA label being behind them, Sublime ultimately didn't sign with them and self-released the album in 1994.

"I was on the road at the time and I called my partner to ask how the Sublime stuff was going," Gurewitz said. "He's like, 'It's killer. But they're just like drinking 40s and smoking crack the whole time.' I had just gotten clean from my crack addiction and I couldn't be around it. So that's why I decided, 'OK, you guys keep the tapes.' Otherwise, history would have been different."

Following those sessions, Nowell's songwriting and confidence grew, and so did the crowds.

The relationship and push-and-pull between the band and the audience was symbiotic. The wilder the crowds would get, the more turbocharged Sublime's set would become. Mosh pits would swirl, and they'd feed off it. Freestyling (something they'd do when a show was going well) would become more common and was their favorite part of a show. Though the locals may not have realized it, Nowell was drawing on the dancehall/reggae influences that he picked up while watching bands in the Caribbean perform on family vacations. Honoring the legends he saw onstage, Nowell would serve as emcee for the band, poking and prodding the crowd to go along with his improvs. To his bandmates, Nowell would serve as the conductor, telling them when to stop and segue into a new song. The smoothness would depend on how hard Sublime partied before any given show.

"We were always one beer away from total disaster," Gaugh said.

When they crossed that line, chaos would ensue. Nowell would sling his guitar around his back and attempt to sing. Other times, he'd hold on to the microphone stand to keep from falling over while

Gaugh and Wilson kept the rhythm section steady . . . most of the time. "Sometimes it was me falling off of my stool," Gaugh admits.

Just as the music became amorphous and tonally agnostic, so was the crowd that showed up in the sweaty pits at Long Beach clubs to see the band perform. Hardcore punks, blonde beach bunnies, hip-hop heads, metal revelers, and wasteoids flocked to the sound, each eclectic note from the stage speaking to different pockets of buzzed and bleary-eyed youth.

As Sublime started to gain a foothold outside of playing the Long Beach party circuit, they began to cross paths with an upstart band from Anaheim who started gaining steam.

Despite building up a strong local following, Sublime found it difficult to be booked without being signed to a label. Happoldt, who served as the band's manager, would work the phones, but no one would call him back. Happoldt and the band came up with the idea to create their own record label. And that's how Skunk Records began. It wasn't a tribute to the stink-spraying animal. Instead, it paid tribute to the dankest Humboldt Skunk marijuana strain.

Once armed with the Skunk record label name, Happoldt suddenly had his calls returned. Little did the club owners know that literally nothing had changed.

"'Skunk recording artist? Of course, we've heard of you!'" Gaugh says. "It was that stupid."

As for the band's live show, things started to really take off. They were getting bigger, wilder crowds, and the energy was like those early punk shows Gaugh went to as a teen. Nowell learned how to work a crowd and used his background in dancehall to his advantage. He would stop playing guitar, sling it around his back, hold the microphone stand, and keep looking forward.

"It was symbiotic," Gaugh said. "The wilder the crowd would get, the wilder we would get. It was our fuel."

Yet Nowell's addiction yo-yoed. He'd remain clean for three to seven months, and then he'd relapse and be worse than before. It got to the point where the band was worried about touring because the singer was carrying heroin with him. They warned him not to be strung out on the road, concerned that he'd try to score and not know where and what type of drugs he was getting and from whom.

⌗⌗⌗⌗⌗

At the time, the new "label" was a major win for the band, who continued beating down doors through guerrilla marketing, including putting their first stack of albums up for consignment at legendary VIP Records in Long Beach—the store that helped spawn rap icons like Snoop, Nate Dogg, and Warren G.

By 1994, Sublime signed with Gasoline Alley, a subsidiary of MCA run by a young upstart executive named Jon Phillips, whose uncle, Randy Phillips, owned the label. He first heard Sublime when he received a cassette copy of *40oz. to Freedom* and procured a demo of *Robbin' the Hood* from a label colleague nicknamed Groovy Greg. He knew right away that the music was fresh and different from anything that was out there, specifically the grunge and alt-rock that ruled the airwaves. With the label's resources, Phillips felt like Sublime could transcend punk because their style was so multidimensional.

Phillips first saw them play at a UCLA fraternity party and knew right away that they were the real deal.

"I remember Bradley Nowell was sweating his balls and face off in the middle of this frat house living room," Phillips said. "He was singing 'Pool Shark,' basically prophesizing his own demise in front of my face and a frat house at UCLA. He had the punk rock spirit and didn't care if that room had 10 people or 100 people or 1,000 people. I knew there was something about this that's different."

Before they signed, in classic Sublime fashion, a prank almost kiboshed the deal. The band thought it would be funny to put their logo sticker on the older Phillips's brand-new, special-edition BMW. Needless to say, he didn't find it as funny as Sublime did.

Six months later, Sublime signed with Gasoline Alley, and Jon Phillips would leave the label to manage them.

There was some brushback from locals who said they sold out by signing with a major label, but the band saw it differently.

"Some people called us sellouts for a little bit," Gaugh said. "But really, is it selling out or just funding our fucking dream?"

✕✕✕✕✕

While the punk scene in OC was on life support in the mid- to late '80s, there was a group of youngsters in Anaheim who were just getting started. John Spence and Eric Stefani cofounded a new band after meeting at a Dairy Queen in Anaheim in 1986. Powered by blending punk and ska, with Spence on vocals and Stefani on keyboards, they started adding members. Those members included Stefani's sister Gwen on backing vocals, guitarist Jerry McMahon, the rhythm section Chris Leal (bass) and Chris Webb (drums), trumpet players Gabriel Gonzalez and Alan Meade, and saxophonist Tony Meade.

Their name? No Doubt, which happened to be one of Spence's favorite phrases.

"Everywhere John went, everything John said, it was always 'no doubt, man,' 'no doubt,' 'no doubt,'" Gonzalez told *SPIN* in 2024. "He's like, 'Let's just call the band No Doubt,' and we're like, 'Nah, dude, that's stupid,' but he was so convincing."

From the beginning, Spence's character stood out above the band's music. After one of the band's early shows in 1986 in which they played a backyard gig in front of a diverse crowd of punks, mods, skinheads, and other Anaheim outcasts, one of the band's friends was jumped by members of the notorious punk gang the Los Angeles Death Squad.

"They started to beat the living crap out of [him]," the band's former trombone player Kevin Wells told *SPIN*. Without thinking twice, Spence sprang into action.

"John Spence literally grabbed [our friend], pulled him away from the LADS, pulled him into the house, closed the door, saved his ass, and ran out the front door and got on his scooter and took off," Wells continued, describing Spence's courageous actions of his courageous actions.

No Doubt's foundation was in ska and punk. Spence was a fan of British ska forefathers the Specials and the Selecter, so much so that he replicated their fashion. The teenager was seen around Anaheim often rocking Fred Perry gear, penny loafers, and bomber jackets. Despite his reserved personality, when Spence went onstage and hopped on the mic, he transformed into a magnetic front man whose energy was impossible to resist.

"I'd look at John and be like, 'Wow, I could never see myself or anyone in the band doing what this guy did.' He brought a whole different energy. He had no fear," Gonzalez told *SPIN*.

"He started doing backflips—and then boom, mosh pit, boom, people are dancing, boom," No Doubt's then–trombone player Kevin Wells told *SPIN*.

The band's mix of ska, punk, and pop was to No Doubt's advantage. That amalgamation of sounds helped the band get booked on a variety of bills with bands in genres within their Venn diagram. The scene was more regional than Orange County–specific. Colleagues included the Skeletones from Riverside and the Donkey Show from San Diego rather than the punk bands in Anaheim and the rest of Orange County. That made them a target. In the 1980s, two-tone ska wasn't very popular. "It felt like this underground thing that only a few of us knew about," future No Doubt drummer Adrian Young said. "It's a highly driven, passionate way to play music."

No Doubt instantly had to fight off the naysayers at shows who thought they were too much of one genre versus too much of another. Specifically, at a 1987 show at Fender's Ballroom, No Doubt were slated to go on second on a bill of ten bands. The first band mocked No Doubt throughout much of their set, but their antics received little response.

When Spence led No Doubt onstage, things changed.

"John was a hype man, he was a phenomenal front person, he controlled the crowds," Gonzalez told *SPIN*.

As great of a front man as Spence was, not everything was well. During his sophomore year of high school, he was hospitalized at a psychiatric ward, and to this day, few details are known about why he ended up there. Additionally, few if any of Spence's friends knew much about his personal life.

"John was just trying to reassure us that everything's gonna be okay, and he didn't seem different," Johnson told *SPIN*. "When we were walking back, [my friend] was like, 'Why is he in there?' and I was like, 'Didn't you see the bandages on him? I think he tried to commit suicide,' but that's how shocking it was . . . even in the psych ward, he didn't seem like he was struggling."

After attending several of the band's shows, Tony Kanal joined the band as their bassist. To that point, Kanal's experience was playing saxophone in the jazz band at Anaheim High School.

"When I was going from ninth grade into tenth grade, the bass player in jazz band, Dave Carpenter, was graduating, and Mr. Stouffer said, 'Who wants to audition to be the bass player?'" Kanal recalled. "I looked up to Dave, he was a friend, and he was the coolest guy in the room. So I raised my hand and between the summer of ninth grade and tenth grade, I started learning how to play bass."

By eleventh grade he was adept enough to capture the attention of Chris Webb, a fellow Anaheim High student who was a year older . . . and a member of No Doubt.

"He had seen me playing bass in like the pep band at basketball games," Kanal said. "He came up to me through a mutual friend, Andy Stanley, and said, 'We just started a band. We've played some backyard parties, we're about to play our first club show. And we wanted to know if you would come down and check it out.'"

Webb also told Kanal that they were looking at their options on bass and wanted to gauge his interest in potentially joining the new outfit.

Kanal went to Fender's Ballroom on that March 14, 1987, night to check out the band's show, which featured eight bands and was headlined by the Untouchables. He was blown away. Spence's energy was unmatched, and he knew instantly that they were incredible. At this point, Kanal had yet to listen to ska.

By the time the band played next on April 19, Kanal had auditioned and joined the band. Through Eric Stefani, Kanal was introduced to the music of the Specials, the Selecter, Madness, Bad Brains, and the English Beat. It was life-changing.

Things were moving quickly for No Doubt. Although they were getting flack from other bands for not being pure enough, their live show won over the naysayers. Spence and Gwen Stefani leading the charge as the band's vocalists gave them a duality unlike any other band in the region . . . and genre. There was an unspoken kind of competitiveness between all the bands in the emerging ska world, but in the sense that everyone wanted to play their best and outshine their peers.

Even beyond the regional ska scene, there was interest in the band outside of Orange County, and things were starting to buzz.

Then tragedy struck.

On December 21, 1987, Spence shot himself in the head and died at the age of eighteen.

"I only knew John for nine months of my life when I was sixteen years old, but I have wonderful, indelible memories of those formative years," Kanal told *SPIN*. "I am forever grateful that I got to share the stage with him for a brief period of time. John was a kinetic ball of incessant energy who pushed us all to up our stage game."

Kanal, who was at this point the band's bassist, learned of the front man's death from Eric Stefani. Spence's death came just days ahead of the band's show playing with ska band the Untouchables at the Roxy in LA. Reeling, the band had little time to decide on their future. Onstage at the Roxy, Spence's friend Jason LaComb told the crowd that the band was done.

"All of us have dealt with this tragedy in our own way, but perhaps the hardest barrier to face is what No Doubt will do tonight," LaComb said. "Let us all experience a tribute to John Spence, a truly good person. This is for you, John, the last No Doubt performance."

However, after thinking it was over, No Doubt decided to continue and honor what Spence started.

"No Doubt decided to keep the band going because they knew that's what John would have wanted them to do," Eric Keyes, the band's archivist and friend, said.

And Alan Meade took over for Spence on vocals.

Soon, shows at local colleges, Fender's, and the Whisky a Go Go became commonplace. As were opening slots for ska-punk veterans Fishbone.

"[Fishbone singer] Angelo [Moore] was very aware of No Doubt," Fishbone bassist Norwood Fisher said. "He had a friendship with Eric Stefani."

"I would go over to Gwen and Eric's house and hang out," Moore said. "Before that, we hung out at the same clubs, and that's how we met."

Soon they'd become such good friends that the Fishbone guys would be at the Stefani house hanging out and watching TV.

Above all, No Doubt aspired to have a dynamic stage presence that could compare to Fishbone's. They wanted to evoke the same feeling in people who saw them to feel how they felt when they saw Fishbone.

"Those guys set the bar with live shows," Kanal said.

Slowly, the band's lineup went from revolving to fermenting. In 1988, guitarist Tom Dumont, who was a music major at Cal State Fullerton, replaced Jerry McMahon after leaving heavy metal band Rising.

"It was a different age, and those bands weren't about music," he said. "They were into drinking, wearing spandex. I was into music, and being a part of No Doubt, that was the first time people actually came to see the band."

A year later, Adrian Young took over for Webb on drums. A music fan since his father bought him Journey's *Escape* and the Ramones' *Road to Ruin*, once he discovered punk, Young quickly became a fan of the Vandals and T.S.O.L.

He started going to punk shows at Fender's Ballroom when he was a teenager, seeing bands like 7 Seconds and ska-punk bands like Fishbone and . . . No Doubt.

"I was like, 'This band is awesome,'" Young said of seeing No Doubt for the first time when he was seventeen. The first time he saw them was when they opened for Fishbone. "I got it instantly. I went to multiple shows of theirs before I joined."

When he joined No Doubt, the self-taught Young was still new to playing drums. "I told them some number that was a lie," he said. "It was like a year or a year and a half." Despite being the new guy, Young and his rhythm section battery mate Kanal clicked immediately, sharing a similar vision and vibe. Though he was new to it, the drummer was forced to elevate his playing to a gear he didn't know he had. For the next two to three years, all Young did in his spare time was practice so he didn't feel like he was playing catch-up to his bandmates' more advanced musical skills. An athlete in his younger years, Young's competitive fire burned to the point where he didn't want to be seen as No Doubt's weak link.

"I am of the opinion that a band is only as good as its drummer," Young said. "We're the ones driving the train onstage."

Still, the dark cloud of Spence's death loomed over the band as No Doubt did their best to move on from the loss. In time, though they never truly recovered, they were able to push ahead by making music that was true to themselves and his spirit.

"It was just fun," Young said of his early years in the band. "It felt like a fire drill at first, but it set the tone of how I was going to approach things as a professional. I looked forward to rehearsal every Thursday and every Sunday at the Stompbox [in Anaheim]."

"We put in our ten thousand hours," Kanal said. "We put in all those early hours of rehearsal to get ourselves tight. After every show, we would go back and watch the video of the show we just played and to revel that we've just done a fun show, but also to critique ourselves. We had a great feedback loop for ourselves."

Although they leaned heavily into ska, No Doubt landed choice spots with bigger punk bands. That cross-pollination was encouraged by Goldenvoice, which would book them with Bad Religion, Social Distortion, and the Untouchables. Sometimes that didn't work out too well, at least initially.

"I remember we opened up for Bad Religion up in Berkeley," Young said. "The first song we played was 'In the Dark.' All the punk Bad Religion fans said, 'Fuck you guys. You guys are fags.' But by the third or fourth song, we had 'em. We had enough fast songs back then and the pit was going. That was usually the case. We didn't have a hard time having punk fans get into it."

Soon, Meade would leave the band. Replacing him was backing vocalist Gwen Stefani.

Eric Stefani wrote the band's songs. Lyrically, the songs' perspectives were autobiographical, yet his sister would sing. Slowly, Gwen was building a magnetic stage presence. At a time when female-fronted male bands were a rarity, the musicians' ability to confidently support Stefani as she evolved into a front woman was imperative in their growth. The band grew tighter.

"They came up with a new brand of ska," Moore said. "We were all part of the new wave of ska that evolved from the original Jamaican style and what was going on in the UK. They had their own style of that too."

By 1990, No Doubt had buzz, even if they were continuously receiving rejection letters from record labels (which they kept). They went into Jim Dotson's South Coast Recording Studios and recorded a demo of what they thought would be their first record. It would soon not be needed. In 1991, the band signed a multi-album deal with producer Jimmy Iovine's newly created Interscope Records, despite interest from Island at the time. Even though his label signed the band, Iovine wasn't initially blown away by No Doubt's songs. However, for a guy who worked with Bruce Springsteen, Patti Smith, Tom Petty, and Stevie Nicks, among many other rock legends, Iovine knew a star when he saw one. He had that feeling about Gwen.

"You're gonna be a star in six years," Stefani recalled Iovine saying to her.

But No Doubt kept their DIY work ethic. Unlike other emerging bands, they were incredibly organized. No Doubt kept a physical mailing list on which they compiled thousands of names of fans. The members had mailing list parties where they would write back to every fan letter. And it's hard to imagine these days, but it allowed them to target fans *without* utilizing social media.

"If we were going to go to Northern California, we could just send it out to our mailing list," Kanal said. "Having those parties . . . we really enjoyed that camaraderie between us and our extended family of friends."

As they steadily built up a following, the Anaheim-based band started to take off. But to some, being based in Orange County didn't help their cause.

"People used to say, 'You guys are behind the curtain, right?'" Young said of the geographical prejudices the band faced. "Almost in a mocking way. We always thought it was so fucking stupid. I heard that so many times not just from punk guys, but rock guys too."

"It was us against the world," Kanal said. "We wanted people to hear our music, and we want to play for as many people as possible."

What couldn't be misconstrued was No Doubt's passion for their craft. As the band started to hit their stride, everyone's position within the band's structure was clear, including Kanal acting as the de facto manager.

"That was something that came naturally for me," Kanal said of handling the band's business. "In addition to being the bass player, and writing songs, I really enjoyed that part of it."

A year later, they were tapped to open for Fishbone during the ska-punk band's three-night stand at the Roxy in support of *The Reality of My Surroundings*.

At the moment, though, not everything was great. At a 1992 show in Oxford, Mississippi, there were only five paid customers to see them. Another in San Diego saw them play for Australian exchange students in a convention room. Usually, No Doubt's live show convinced even the hardest of skeptics of their legitimacy. Not at this gig. Of the 150 people in attendance, when the band started playing, some came forward and instantly turned and went the other way to socialize.

Even at home, things weren't easy for No Doubt. Too poppy for ska and not hard enough for punk, people outside of the band's fan base had a hard time pegging what exactly No Doubt was.

"There was a guy at KROQ that was talking about our first album and told the Interscope rep that it would take an act of God for No Doubt to get on KROQ," Young said. "I'm not a religious guy, but I find that really funny."

Around this time, a demo tape from a band from Long Beach landed in Kanal's hand. That tape? *Jah Won't Pay the Bills*.

In this case, that literally meant he caught it in his hand.

"The way No Doubt and Sublime got hooked up was, the guy who directed the 'Date Rape' video threw a tape—our first demo tape, *Jah Won't Pay the Bills*—at Tony Kanal onstage," Miguel Happoldt said. "And Tony was blown away by it and he tracked us down and we started playing shows. That was a huge break for us because No Doubt was already well-known and sort of professional. They were like, Fishbone-good, and Sublime was still kind of garage-y."

"I would listen to that thing in my car, and we wore that thing out," Kanal said of *Jah Won't Pay the Bills*. "We were so inspired and moved by that original demo tape."

No Doubt would see Sublime perform when they could before, inevitably, they started playing shows together. Eventually, Gwen Stefani would sing on Sublime's "Saw Red," and Bradley Nowell returned the favor on "Total Hate."

"You could tell the crowd liked that," Young said. "There was definitely a vibe, even though our sounds were quite different. It just categorically worked."

The two bands became colleagues . . . and fast friends. They played shows together at the Kono Hawaii club in Anaheim and at parties in Long Beach.

But you couldn't find two bands, though sonically similar, so far apart lifestyle-wise.

"There was no competition—there was no chance," Happoldt told *OC Weekly* in 2012. "They [No Doubt] were always rehearsed, all the songs arranged, they looked good, you know what I mean? Sublime showed up in the van half-drunk and played whatever they wanted to. Sublime loved that about No Doubt and No Doubt loved that about Sublime. No Doubt was like Richie Cunningham and Sublime was like Fonzie. Brad admired the professionalism. He said, 'One day we're going to have to be like that.'"

As aspirational as Nowell's idea was, Sublime was never going to match No Doubt's ability in that regard. Their friendship transcended music. They'd hang out together, and Nowell played with No Doubt at Kanal's surprise birthday party in 1993.

No Doubt's self-titled debut was released on St. Patrick's Day 1992. Some of the songs from the demos at South Coast were on the album, but they were recorded after No Doubt signed to Interscope, along with a batch of new songs. Produced by Dito Godwin, it was a commercial flop, selling only thirty thousand copies and making zero inroads on the radio. The timing wasn't right for the band, given that heavy guitar-driven songs permeating from Seattle ruled the cultural landscape. The world wasn't ready for sunny Orange County ska-punk, at least not yet.

In those formative years, No Doubt played shows with several other up-and-coming bands in the area, including the Cadillac Tramps, Guttermouth, and a group of guys who recently relocated from Bakersfield: Korn.

"It seemed like they never had a song to get the attention of the bigger labels," Young said of the Tramps. "They had the sound, they had the players and the live show. Everything was rockin' and sounded super bitchin' and I liked it a lot."

The Cadillac Tramps never drove on Easy Street. The band cared little for shiny finishes, sleek lines, or a smooth, quiet ride. Its rough-hewn style was forged through a fusion of hammering aggression and a swampy rhythmic crunch of dirty blues and R&B.

Fronted by Michael "Gabby" Gaborno—a bulky, bouncing energy source with a growling vocal delivery and the stage persona of a vato loco court jester from the depths of hell—and including members Jonny "Two Bags" Wickersham, bassist Warren Renfrow, and drummer Jamie Reidling, the Tramps generated a cultlike following in the early '90s that made them both a feared and respected local entity. They were heirs to the throne in a new era of Orange County punk.

With songs that sketched hilarious and heartbreaking slices of street life, the band pointed to such ideals as self-reliance, pride, and a rejection of drugs as an escape.

A Cadillac Tramp "means somebody who's down and out, but they still have their inner class. It's a dignity type thing," guitarist Brian Coakley told the *Los Angeles Times* in 1991.

Sporting '50s-style slicked hair, assorted goatees, dark shades, and flamboyant tattoos, they looked like the seedier version of the Sharks and Jets in *West Side Story*.

Wickersham, who named the band when it began in late 1987, interpreted the name of Cadillac Tramps to describe pride in persistence: "The world might crumble around your feet, but you still keep trudging," he said.

It's an ethos the wiry guitarist lived firsthand. At one point during his teen years, Wickersham was homeless, all his stuff packed into a couple of Safeway bags. Even after he got off the streets, Wickersham's shopping-bag luggage left him with a nickname that stuck.

The members of the band found their entry to the gritty side of life in the punk rock movement that swept Orange County when they were growing up in the late '70s and early '80s.

"For me, it wasn't just a [style of] music. It should've been called 'punk life' instead of punk rock," Gaborno told the *Times*. "I decided, 'I'm sick of being the quiet little kid in a houseful of loudmouths,' and [punk] gave me the excuse."

Though they'd been raised on punk, members of the band felt the music had lost its way over the years, turning into more of a look and a sound than a genuine rebellion. "I got fed up with punk for a while, not wanting to hear so much whining, but concrete ideas and statements," Coakley told the *Times*. "It got to be a fashion bazaar."

In 1987, Wickersham, who had turned to the blues for inspiration, began playing in earnest after only dabbling for years. He approached Gaborno about starting a band. When it was launched, Coakley was on hand too, folding his love for Motown, Aretha Franklin, and James Brown into the band's gradually evolving sonic stew.

It was, Gaborno recalled, as ground-level a beginning as a band could have: "We started writing songs on a beat-up old acoustic guitar with holes in it, and a paper plate [for a lyric sheet]," he told the *Times*.

Luckily, between the popularity of the young band's individual members in the music scene and the contacts that came with them, they were able to move fairly quickly into playing coveted gigs. "The whole cast of bands in Orange County helped us out," Coakley said, mentioning Joe Wood, Big Drill Car, and Jack Grisham's new project at the time, Tender Fury, among the Tramps' early cosigns. "They knew us from around. We said, 'We've got this band together,' and they basically gave us a shot" as opening acts.

Toward the tail end of 1989, Jack Grisham and Ron Emory invited the Cadillac Tramps to open for them at a highly anticipated T.S.O.L. reunion show at the Celebrity Theatre in Anaheim. That's when the Tramps knew they were gaining momentum.

"I didn't realize we had a draw, but when we walked onstage to play that night, the crowd started going nuts," Wickersham said. "We looked at each other like, 'Wow, they know who we are.'" In the past eighteen months, the band had emerged as an Orange County favorite, and they felt they had established a following in Los Angeles as well.

In late March 1991, the band released their debut album, *Cadillac Tramps*, on Doctor Dream Records. The album represented a clean and forceful rendering of the Tramps' high-impact live sound. Lyrically, it ranged from humorous street vignettes to topical broadsides against lying politicians and South African racism—a subject he says he addressed partly to vent his anguish over racism closer to home.

An anti-drug perspective also runs through several songs—put there, members say, by their own past bouts with abuse.

During the period between 1986 and 1988, punk and its offshoots in OC continued to change shape again to include sounds and bands that were more in line with the genre now dubbed "alternative." Bands like Grisham's next band, Cathedral of Tears, meshed with other acts of the time like Children's Day, Psychobud, and Exobiota. It was an era that overlapped with the metal-leaning punk bands and the acts that were the alternative to the Poisons and Guns N' Roses of the world.

Rynda Laurel worked for a booking agent in that scene at the time in OC and LA before moving to New York briefly. When she returned in 1992, she had been focused on getting sober. OC did and still does have a very large sober community in the punk world, and at the time, the Tramps were on the wagon as well, struggling to get clean from a life of addiction that gripped all of them, especially Gaborno. Laurel actually first met the band in recovery meetings at a time when many of OC punk's stalwarts like Ness and Grisham were also getting clean and becoming beacons of sobriety for those who'd been weathered and worn yet somehow managed to survive the wild lifestyle of the '80s. They had set out on the path to a healthier life with punk still at their core.

"That's what brought me into the community," she said. "All of these people, and that's why we rebounded. What bonded us then was we would all as a group go to see the Cadillac Tramps because it was an opportunity for a lot of us that were in, especially in the music business, to figure out 'How do I learn how to have fun again without drinking and doing drugs?'"

The Cadillac Tramps had become almost like missionaries in that period of time, giving many punks who followed them their first entry back into the music scene in Orange County. Their amazing, high-voltage live show showed the energy of a wild party band, but the scene around them was focused on sobriety—at least at the time, Laurel remembers. Back in California, her new role as A&R at Charisma Records allowed her to try to help get the band noticed by the industry. "Why aren't presidents of labels like, 'Why is nobody paying attention to this fucking band?'" she asked. "A major label needs to come in and make them huge. And that's what I set about to do."

The problem was that their powerful live show never properly translated onto their records. Laurel enlisted rock producer Howard Benson, who at the time had just previously worked with the second incarnation of T.S.O.L. on the albums *Revenge* and *Hit and Run*, to produce a project for the Tramps. Like the Tramps, Benson was also stuck in a bit of a rut when it came to only producing hair metal bands. The prospect of working with a fresh, talented band like the Tramps inspired him to agree to work on the record for a mere $3,000, which included him driving from Calabasas to work with the band on the song "It's Allright" at Doctor Dream Records—a label he would ultimately buy from David Hayes in 1990.

The second thing Laurel was committed to trying to pull off was getting the band in front of a major act who could see their potential live—for the Tramps, that band was Pearl Jam.

For the Cadillac Tramps, August 1993 was a saga of Shakespearean proportions: first a comedy of errors, then all's well that ends well.

At some point in the middle of it, the road-weary band must have thought about trading its kingdom—or at least its battered 1985 Dodge Ram touring van—for a Lear jet.

The unlikely series of events began on August 6 in Seattle, when Pearl Jam saw the Tramps' gig at the Crocodile Cafe. In an era where grunge was beginning to rule the world, the Tramps' moxie and bluesy punk fusion set them apart.

Sufficiently impressed with what he saw, Pearl Jam bassist Jeff Ament told his bandmates, and the group recommended the Tramps as the opening act for two sold-out concerts on August 11 and 12 in the Canadian cities of Calgary and Edmonton.

"I remember seeing Jonny Two Bags back then and thinking he was cool as shit," Pearl Jam guitarist Mike McCready said. "He had his double cutaway Gibson and I just thought it was cool."

What stood out to McCready and his bandmates was the Tramps' authenticity.

"It was the realness of it . . . the punk ethos," he said. "But they looked cool, they had their hats, and they cared about how they looked, and they just rocked! Gabby had this hell of a crazy energy. We're always looking for someone different to open up, and do to this day. And we knew our audience would be blown away by the Cadillac Tramps because they were so different from us. We were super serious back then and they had that Southern California attitude and just brought this chaos to the stage."

But nothing was certain.

The Tramps played August 7 in Portland, Oregon, on the last night of their five-week national tour and then headed for home. Coakley said it was his assignment to call in from the road to see whether the talked-about opportunity with Pearl Jam had panned out. The band wasn't banking on it.

"We've heard this before," Coakley told the *Los Angeles Times* in 1993. "'The Chili Peppers are going to take you on tour'; 'Nirvana likes you.'" So Coakley got some much-needed sleep in the van, and by the time he awoke, he'd forgotten about calling in for instructions concerning possible dates with Pearl Jam.

"It completely slipped my mind. When I walked in the door [back home in Cypress], my dad said, 'You [screwed] up.' We had to turn around the next day and drive back. We had driven 24 hours straight down the West Coast. We slept at home, then drove all the way back to Calgary, which was like a 39-hour drive."

Things were made even more hectic due to the fact that Gabby and at least one member of the band's crew had criminal records, which would've blocked them from getting past Canada's uber-strict border authorities. Pearl Jam sidestepped this by slipping them in through the Vancouver border, where they allegedly had friends in the border authority who could usher them in quietly, Laurel said.

At the end of it, the Tramps got to Calgary and still had enough gas left in the band's tank to impress the audience and make some new friends in high places.

"The crowd received us really well," Coakley told the *Los Angeles Times*. "I look over to the side, and there's [Pearl Jam singer] Eddie Vedder filming us with a Super 8 camera, laughing and waving at me and just really enjoying it."

For the Edmonton show, Coakley said, Vedder came out and introduced the Tramps before their set. "He said, 'This band drove thirty-nine hours to get here,' and that we were the best band that ever opened for them. It was one of those trips where it's like, 'Wow, is this real?'"

After the amazing reception from the Edmonton crowd, the band was on a high, which immediately got smashed back to reality after their van following Pearl Jam's tour bus broke down after the show. "After the show we're behind this big huge stadium, and underneath the van is Eddie Vedder and Gabby trying to fucking fix the van so we can get to the next show," Laurel said with a laugh, shaking her head.

"That's hardcore," McCready said. "That's something that would break lesser bands."

Not only did Pearl Jam love the Tramps enough to help with their van, at the Calgary show they did what they could to make sure their crowd saw them perform, starting the show notably later and waiting till the arena was fairly full to get them onstage, Laurel said. Back in LA weeks after the Canada run, Pearl Jam invited the Tramps to be their guests at the MTV Video Music Awards where they were the night's biggest victors, scoring four Moonmen in top categories for their groundbreaking video for the song "Jeremy." Photos from backstage show the bands partying and laughing and getting crazy together to celebrate Pearl Jam's success. All signs pointed to the Tramps being successful by association.

Doctor Dream's president, David Hayes, knew that the band was always just on the brink of success. Prior to their Pearl Jam gigs, bigger labels tended to regard the Tramps as an exciting live band whose appeal might not translate well on record. After they all but stole the show in Canada, he said A&R people (from big labels) "might think twice about the Tramps because they're getting the endorsement of bands that sell millions of records," he told the *Los Angeles Times*.

Suddenly, music biz types from record companies and big enter-tainment law firms came calling Laurel trying to get their hands on the Tramps. "What's up with this band? Who is this band? What are we doing? Why didn't we sign them?" Sadly, the sparkle on the Tramps wasn't destined to materialize. Despite the interest, no major label ever fully committed to signing the band. When things didn't happen fast enough after all that big buzz, it died back down and never revived. "Ultimately, no one was really willing to step into that spot that needed to level them up," said Laurel, who soon parted ways with the band after they expressed more of a desire for a tour manager than a band manager. Two years after the band's near miss at stardom, internal ten-sions forced the band to abruptly call it quits in 1995. Just prior to that, the band put out what would be their final album in 1994 on Doctor Dream, ironically titled *It's Allright*. This misspelling, intentional or not, was an indicator that things were definitely not alright.

Between frustration that a record deal hadn't panned out and the financial tensions facing all the members of the band who still worked day jobs, mostly involving manual labor, a seething tension was bub-bling between Gaborno and Coakley, who seemed to be at opposite ends of the Earth when it came to their ideas on how to manage the band. Locally, they were still looked up to and played big shows like the one they headlined over their punk idols D.O.A. at the Whisky a Go Go in January 1994. They'd packed the place to the point where people were passing out as the show raged like an exploding powder keg. But the success on a hometown stage wasn't enough to pay the bills. Coakley had already started a side project called Rule 62 with him as lead vocalist and guitar player, and that band would go on to be signed to a lucrative deal on Madonna's label, Maverick Records. Gabby started Manic Hispanic with Steve Soto, a wildly popular punk cover band that still plays shows to this day.

Though the goal had been to get the band signed, Gaborno and Coakley could never see eye to eye and often sabotaged each other's efforts to get the band a deal. As tensions boiled over, they hit a breaking point in a shouting match that ended with both members quitting the band along with Wickersham, who also couldn't take it anymore.

After the split, Coakley went off and did Rule 62 and Gaborno started a band called the X-Members. Both bands got deals but ultimately went nowhere and eventually broke up.

A band that two years earlier seemed to have the sky as their limit came crashing down between the Offspring becoming rock stars with *Smash* and No Doubt reaching even higher heights with *Tragic Kingdom*. Though both had opened for the Tramps in many shows, they surpassed them by developing a rock sound with a more high-gloss, palatable take on OC punk and ska, melding it with pop and slick production in a way that captivated audiences who'd never even seen them play live. It was something the Tramps, for all their live magic, were never able to conjure up.

"I'm not gonna lie, in the Tramps we developed a chip on our shoulder after a while because we just didn't fit in," Wickersham said. "That's not to say we didn't love these bands—when it came to No Doubt, we were supportive. That band was fucking great."

Wickersham remembers he and Adrian Young driving home from a gig they'd played together filling in for Gaborno's side project, Manic Hispanic, and Young playing him demos of *Tragic Kingdom* in the cassette player of his beat-up white pickup truck.

"And at that point, a lot of ska punk was popular and I wasn't hearing ska punk on their album. I was hearing like, new wave," Wickersham remembers. Prior to this, No Doubt was mostly known for that bright, brassy sound popular at the time. Confused by what he heard, Wickersham asked, "Why are you guys not capitalizing on what you already do?" Young replied, "No, no, we just want to do this, man. This is what we want to do." His guitarist friend replied, "Fair enough."

Of course, a new sound didn't mean an easy path forward. Despite the growing number of naysayers prior to their supernova success, No Doubt kept plugging away. They realized quickly that they had to be willing to try new things and experiment with their sound. No Doubt gradually deviated from playing ska shows, even if there was some backlash for that.

"The ska thing was a bit territorial," Young said. "Especially with that third generation. We got a lot of flack for that, but it wouldn't stop us because we didn't want to be a ska band forever."

No Doubt continued to play shows in Southern California and became known as a must-see live act. Considering they had no mainstream radio play, playing shows at colleges (UCI was a popular stop, as were noon shows at Cal State Fullerton) helped them gain a following.

The odyssey of getting *Tragic Kingdom* into the world nearly broke them up. But with hindsight being 20/20, it sure didn't hurt that they had something supernaturally good, and for that, Wickersham couldn't fault his friend for doing something different. They were playing by their own rules, the same way the Tramps had done, but with one minor detail, Wickersham noted—"they made the record they wanted to make and it's fucking full of hits, man."

16

TOTAL LOVE

erhaps the biggest win in Sublime's guerrilla marketing mission that remains a bit murky is how their first hit, "Date Rape," a song they released in 1991, made it onto the airwaves at 106.7 KROQ. The song was originally written by Nowell when he was in Santa Cruz. While there, campus date rape was a major problem and Norwell decided to write about the issue. The group didn't have an intro and happened to be listening to Fishbone, who Sublime considered the "masters of the segue." That inspired Wilson to ask his bandmates if a "bum, bum, bum, bum, bum, bum, bum" worked. It caught Gaugh's attention, who asked him to play it again. Sublime wasn't a ska band, yet "Date Rape," with Wilson's bass line and the incorporation of horns, would make people think otherwise.

At the time, KUCI DJ Tazy Phyllipz, who was an intern at KROQ when he first heard of Sublime, had them on his popular UCI radio show, *Ska Parade*. He remembers hearing the horn-powered earworm "Date Rape" and being instantly mesmerized by how fresh, crass, and unconventional it sounded compared to what was going on at the time.

According to Phyllipz, after seeing Sublime perform, he used his connections at KROQ to get the band's single in the hands of veteran DJ Jed the Fish. It instantly became a fan favorite, with calls lighting up the request line every hour, and a runaway hit.

The irresistibly catchy tune fused ska and punk and was a sardonic look at the bad things that happen when someone commits date rape.

Yet Jed the Fish wasn't pleased to play the song on the air.

"I have never been clear on the song's motivation and point of view," he said. "It claims to have a moral but I can't discern it."

"We were at a party a long time ago and we were all talking about how much date rape sucked," Nowell said in 1995. "This guy named Stanley was like, 'Date rape isn't so bad; if it wasn't for date rape I'd never get laid.' Everyone at the party was bummed out about it, but I was cracking up and I wrote a funny song about it."

To that point, Jed the Fish points to the last line of the song, which is "neither point of view nor justification. On the whole, I'm ashamed of KROQ's rabid support of a morally ambiguous and controversial song. The lyrics—despite their length—could have been more sensitively written instead of whipped out like they obviously were. Play it on the radio, sure, but play it ten thousand times, come ON!"

"I ended up being the middleman working the single and promoting it," Phyllipz says. "And I didn't get paid for it. I'm happy that my efforts have, literally, been able to change the musical sounds of the world. People didn't know what ska was. You had to say dumb things like, 'It's faster reggae.' *Ska Parade* got the message out there. My show was the springboard. I was the eye of the storm."

After KROQ started playing "Date Rape," Nowell returned the favor to Phyllipz by playing *Ska Parade*'s release party, with Sublime appearing as the night's surprise guest. It was the first time Sublime performed since "Date Rape" was taking over the airwaves. "We had mutual respect for one another, and I still miss my friend [Brad] to this day," Phyllipz said.

But that didn't mean they were psyched that *that* song was on the radio, nevertheless breaking. They would have liked it if a "better" song that represented who they were then, not three years ago, was on the radio.

That's not to discount the song's success. Sublime was excited about "Date Rape" breaking through on the airwaves. After it blew up on KROQ, Sublime shot a video featuring now-disgraced porn star Ron Jeremy featured as the judge at the rape trial and the "large inmate" referred to in the song who rapes the man who committed the crime.

"Date Rape" had long been retired from their live shows, and now due to its unexpected success, it had to be reincorporated. With only sixty to seventy minutes onstage as opposed to the party circuit they started on, Sublime preferred to play their newer material.

"It was the opposite of N.W.A.," Gaugh said of the rappers who would get arrested onstage for playing "Fuck Tha Police." Fans wanted to hear the controversial, catchy song. And their thoughts on the people who didn't like the song or its message? "Suck ass!" Nowell and Gaugh said at the time.

Based on the strength of the unexpected success of their single, Sublime found themselves on the most prestigious lineup of the spring Southern California concert calendar. Flanked by Jeremy and Lou Dog, Nowell's beloved dalmatian who appeared almost everywhere with him as the band's unofficial mascot (including on tour, in album art, and in interviews), Sublime was ready to kick ass . . . and party.

At the time, the Weenie Roast was the legendary station's annual kickoff to the summer concert season. In 1995, the show was notable for Sublime's inclusion, which for those inside the mainstream felt like it was out of nowhere.

And party they did. The backstage interview with KROQ that was aired showed a band that was ready to throw down. Before heading down to Irvine Meadows Amphitheatre for the show, the band was miffed that they didn't receive enough passes for their crew. They ended up making fake passes so everyone could get in.

Anyone who'd seen Sublime at that time wasn't surprised by their behavior, especially the members of No Doubt.

"I used to love to go see them because—and I mean this really affectionately—two out of three gigs, they'd be a total mess," Tom Dumont told the *Los Angeles Times* in 2024. "But then that one out of three, they were just transcendent."

This show, which featured a guest appearance by Stefani on "Saw Red," was better known for Sublime's backstage antics. On top of their wild on-air interview, Lou Dog bit an executive's kid, and they stole beer from alt-rockers Bush.

As the band's partying and behavior got more out of control, KROQ turned elsewhere for another rising band that was more professional: No Doubt.

When Sublime took off, there was already cause for concern. Nowell's drug use would worsen. While recording *Robbin' the Hood*, Nowell's bandmates noticed that he'd dabble in drugs. At this point, he replaced drinking and smoking pot with heroin. It got to the point where Nowell tried to socialize using heroin.

"It was his guilt that drove that," Gaugh said. "He wanted it to be OK. He'd sit there and start fixing dope in front of a roomful of people. Like, dude, that ain't cool. He wanted to pass it around like it was a joint."

"It seemed to me that he didn't know that much about it," said

Troy Dendekker, Nowell's girlfriend and future wife. "He was so ready to tell me that he was on it, and he wasn't ashamed that his audience knew if he was in the bathroom doing it."

Things got so out of control that Nowell and Gaugh would have heated arguments that devolved into fistfights. One incident took place when Gaugh said that Nowell OD'd a girl he was seeing at the time. Another incident took place in Las Vegas when according to Gaugh, Nowell introduced someone to heroin, and they ended up OD'ing and nearly dying.

"It was like, 'Dude, you don't fucking do this,'" Gaugh said. "It's not fucking pot. It's not fucking booze. You're not passing a bottle around. You're passing a fucking revolver."

Gaugh confronted Nowell and said if he sent another person to the hospital from using heroin, he'd beat the shit out of him. Then the Vegas incident happened, and Gaugh "beat the fucking snot out of him." "It fucking hurt," Gaugh said. "I saw him the next day. I was like, fuck, dude. I'm sorry. I didn't mean to fuck you up like that. But fuck you made me mad." He closed by telling Nowell if he continued to shoot people up, eventually he'd go to prison for a long time . . . if he even made it that far.

WARPED

With "Date Rape" propelling the band locally, Sublime, through its long-running relationship with Kevin Lyman, a former Goldenvoice executive, was asked to perform at a new festival that kicked off in 1995. The Southern California promotion and booking company Goldenvoice was formed in 1981 by Gary Tovar, and by the early '90s, the company was striving to be *the* tastemaker in the punk and alternative music scenes. Lyman was an integral part of that. By his own account, during his twelve years at Goldenvoice, Lyman would attend 320 shows per year. He'd book shows at UCI and Orange Coast College, including a memorable Vandals one where the crowd nearly tore the gym apart while rocking out to the band.

Lyman had been familiar with the trio since their nascent days, having procured a copy of their original 1991 demo tape, *Jah Won't Pay the Bills.*

"I'll never forget listening to it and being like, 'Wow, this is something,'" Lyman said. After hearing the cassette, he went to see Sublime at a bunch of house parties and shows and was impressed. He started booking them at ska shows across LA.

On the strength of that experience, Lyman brought a lineup consisting of Sublime, No Doubt, and the Offspring to the Rocky Mountain states, hitting college ski trips during spring break.

"They [Sublime] were always that band that were willing to do anything," he said.

"It's so funny to look at that bill and be like, 'What a monster bill,'" Holland said. "That's a stadium lineup now."

Having booked the band throughout SoCal, Lyman was familiar with Sublime: their rise, their rowdiness, and their magnetic live show. Most importantly, the booker knew how well the trio would translate if they were able to harness that backyard energy in front of tens of thousands of new fans.

In March 1995, Lyman cooked up a concept for a festival that was like none other. It would combine skate and surf culture and punk rock. Christened the Warped Tour, Lyman aimed to have it ready to go that August.

"When Warped Tour started, I had to go to people who knew me, trusted me," he remembers. "No Doubt and Sublime are naturally people for me to go to for this concept."

On the heels of the roaring success of "Date Rape," Lyman booked Sublime in the second slot on the Warped Tour. The group was only slotted underneath New York hardcore heroes Quicksand.

Lasting a month between August and September, the Warped Tour would become Southern California's answer to Lollapalooza with numerous stages, a half-pipe for the skaters and bikers, and a climbing wall. Its roots were based on what Lyman saw happening in Orange County.

"OC was always this place for action sports and music," Lyman said. "That was where it all came from. Bands like Sublime were at the center of it."

All of the bands on that first Warped Tour shared buses. Unfortunately for New York post-hardcore band Orange 9mm, it meant shacking up with the rowdy Long Beach troublemakers. The combination of vegan Buddhists with crack-smoking pirates made for a wild inter-bus dynamic.

As much fun as the band had playing in front of the largest audiences of their career, they ran into a problem with their four-legged friend, Lou Dog. Though the feisty dalmatian was the official mascot of Sublime and the unofficial fourth member, he managed to piss off (and on) the skaters. After a week of nonstop complaints from everyone on the tour, Lyman had enough.

"Skaters were getting bit," Gaugh said of the two board riders who Lou snacked on at the Buffalo show. "They were breaking their arms on half-pipes but if they got bit by a dog they threatened to sue." Eventually, Lyman told the band they had to go, though not for long.

"It was only for a week, it was the Kevin Lyman probationary period," the promoter said with a chuckle. "But I had one rule on Warped Tour: No dogs and no friends. I'll never forget when Louie bit those two people, I went, 'Brad! That dog!' And he said, 'Well, he hates skateboarders . . .' I go, 'Well you're on a *fucking* skateboard tour!'"

The penalty was missing the one show between New York and Seattle. "I let them come back and play the last few shows, but they were on probation," Lyman said.

That New York show, in particular, is what got Sublime in hot water with the promoter. There wasn't a lot of food to go around on that first tour, and at Long Island's Nassau Coliseum, Lyman discovered two boxes of gold: in this case, that was cereal and milk. As pleased as he was with that discovery, he was just as appalled when he saw Lou Dog gobbling the contents of one box out of a bowl and Sublime's friends eating the other, which caused him to "lose my shit."

When they were ultimately too big to not be on the tour, Sublime would find themselves in hairy situations. Gaugh was arrested twice on that tour within a span of a few days—caught once in Florida for possession of drugs while driving, causing him to miss a show, and again in South Carolina for misdemeanor simple possession—but that time he didn't miss the gig.

"Even today, Brad Nowell is the guy who would still be in the Warped Tour parking lot," Lyman said. "That's where he was most at home, being natural."

For the West Coast leg, old friends No Doubt would join Sublime onstage. At some shows, Stefani would combine with Nowell on vocals for "Total Hate" or "Saw Red," which was a crowd-pleaser. The mosh pit and chaos of the crowd would slow down. At the time, there weren't many collaborations or duets at punk shows. Seeing Stefani and Nowell was an instant showstopper. "It was when you saw the softer side of Brad," Lyman said of the collaboration. "But a lot of times their shows were such trainwrecks it was hard to see. When Gwen and he would do a song together, you saw that side of Brad that all of us knew—the *real* songwriter who wrote with a lot of emotion that was different than other punk bands."

Of course, being the mid-1990s, the national media kicked up a storm over these bands competing against each other when the truth was far from that. Even today, when twenty-two thousand people will go to the Queen Mary for a reggae-inspired festival, that couldn't have happened without what Sublime did on the first Warped Tour. The group laid the foundation for helping launch the festival from a regionally inspired event to a cultural phenomenon. It's helped Lyman build an empire and is something he's incredibly grateful for.

"I love that band," Lyman said. "And you know, they're still my favorite band."

At that time, the thing that had eluded Sublime was recording an album that captured the true essence of their sound. While *40oz.* and *Robbin' the Hood* pushed them beyond Long Beach, something was *slightly* off with what the trio wanted. Now, armed with a major label deal and even more momentum, they sought to make the album that had sonically eluded them. It became more essential to capture their sound, that unique vibe of OC punk and Long Beach swagger, which initially stole the hearts of a generation and now a sect of a subculture.

As they geared up to record their third album, Sublime was ready to show the world what Long Beach already knew. Pulling together reggae kids, tattooed punk rockers, surfers, skaters, Chicanos, hip-hop fans, and many more, this trio of miscreants managed to meld the sound of the city they were from.

"Sublime could have only existed in Long Beach," Jonny Wickersham said.

Things were blowing up for Sublime externally, and they were about to live a dream that seemed so far away just seven years earlier. That success came at a very steep price.

⁂

When they weren't touring or working, No Doubt steadily built a studio at the Stefanis' grandparents' garage, with some of the members moving into the house when the grandparents died. They used the space to their advantage, writing and working out songs at their own pace.

Tragic Kingdom, the band's second album, took two and a half years to make, which for a band of No Doubt's size at the time was a massive gap. So much so that the band was able to release its B-sides, titled *The Beacon Street Collection*, in March 1995, seven months before *Tragic Kingdom* was released in October 1995. Despite being a compilation of outtakes, the album did well. It sold over a hundred thousand copies, which convinced Interscope that No Doubt had a future.

"We had so many songs that we knew wouldn't be on *Tragic Kingdom*," Young said. "We got so sick of the label holding off putting out our record that we said 'Fuck it.' We had all the other songs and we figured they wouldn't give a shit if we put it out ourselves . . . and we did."

So much time had gone by that the band's thought process in releasing *The Beacon Street Collection* was to give fans something new, and they weren't 100 percent sure that Interscope would even release *Tragic Kingdom*, which was a nickname Dumont's seventh-grade teacher had for Disneyland.

"It felt *that* uncertain," Young said. "So we put out a couple of seven-inches and *The Beacon Street Collection* that we paid for ourselves."

Interscope got them time at a cheap studio once a month and "staved them off." The band wasn't feeling love and support from the label at the time. So much so that they found an affordable rate on a studio in Santa Monica and had to take advantage of it. That was just one example of No Doubt having to scrape and claw to find time to record. The album was recorded in eleven different studios of their choosing in those two and a half years. In that time, No Doubt worked with several different producers because the label wasn't satisfied with where the band's sound was. The work ethic behind *Tragic Kingdom*, even though they were signed to one of the biggest emerging labels at that time, was no different than the DIY world of Orange County.

Ultimately, after all that trial and error, No Doubt ended up having Matthew Wilder produce it.

As the recording process lumbered on, the band tinkered with their sound. Songs like "Different People," "Sixteen," and "Sunday

Morning" had fused elements of ska-punk, while "The Climb" clocked in at a shade over six and a half minutes. "Don't Speak" was the band's epic breakup song power ballad.

In 1994, the band suffered a major blow. Eric Stefani, who was the band's chief songwriter at the time, left the band to become an animator on *The Simpsons*. His departure left an opening for Gwen, Kanal, and Dumont to write. That allowed the band to lean more into rock and away from ska, leaving just four members of No Doubt. His departure had a major effect on the rest of the band.

"It wasn't easy, but for her, it was especially tough," Young said. "But one thing about our band is that up until we had kids, our band was our number one priority. It was everything. Not just for a couple of years here. I'm talking about the whole way through. Hurdles and dramatic things were not going to stop the band."

More specifically, the three cataclysmic events in seven years that could have derailed No Doubt—Spence's suicide, Eric Stefani's departure, and the breakup of Gwen and Kanal, who had dated for years—didn't. Those were big moments that might have given some members a reason to pause, but they didn't deter them from continuing.

"It was so scattered that we didn't feel like that record was going to get finished," Young recalled. "We didn't feel like the label believed in the band."

And he was right. James Saez, a second engineer on the album, said that the label didn't know quite what to do with the band. He could see that No Doubt was onto something. The buzz around the band would soon transfer to the masses, and Stefani was on the cusp of being a superstar.

"I thought she was amazing," Saez said. "She had a quality that was interesting, which I often force people to pay attention to, which is that she didn't sound like anybody else. Mike Ness is the same thing.

You don't hear him on a record and go, 'I wonder who that is.' And the way Gwen sang and her style was not something you could correlate to a bunch of other singers. I think that was a huge strength and they used it well. When she got onstage and she sang, she was one of those people you couldn't keep your eyes off of. When she was singing, she really was passionate."

An outsider who was working with No Doubt, Saez saw a plucky band of upstarts fighting for their recording careers and trying their best to make things work.

Stunningly enough, *Tragic Kingdom*'s release came six years to the day after Iovine said Gwen would be a star.

"We weren't supposed to be a big band," Young said. "And if you listen to *Tragic Kingdom*, it wasn't a cohesive record and I liked that. We sounded like a lot of different bands at different times but on the same record."

The album's eclectic vibe was all a matter of timing. If the band rushed to put out another album after their self-titled debut, they likely wouldn't have been able to develop in the way they did.

Unlike other bands from the area, No Doubt wasn't afraid to embrace where they were from. On the album's cover, Stefani is seen holding a rotten orange with the members standing in the background in a field. They weren't trying to prove that they were cool.

"We were this awkward ska, funky rock band," Young said. "Some people would have been like, 'Oh, that's a freaking pop band.' That's OK if that's how you see it, that's fine. We were comfortable in our skin . . . for better or for worse."

The album's first single was "Just a Girl." The song, cowritten by Gwen Stefani and Dumont with production handled by Matthew Wilder, was the first written by the band without Eric Stefani. Powered by Dumont's bouncy lightning bolt of distorted flange, Stefani's defiant lyrics pertained to her annoyance with her father after he admonished her for driving home from Kanal's house late at night.

"I just wanted to write a song to express how I was feeling in that moment and I never in my wildest dreams thought that anyone would hear it," Stefani told *People* in 2017. "I remember coming up with every single line [and] I have a really bad memory but I really, really remember that moment and feeling I could really relate to myself and this song . . . I felt like it really echoed exactly how I felt."

"So much of that material was about our personal relationship and what we were going through at the time," Kanal said. "As tough as that time was for both of us, the sincerity and the raw emotion that she was expressing, people could relate to that. There were real feelings, sincere emotions that everyone at some point in their life has experienced. Those songs that we did together transcended what we were doing, and connected on a much bigger level."

"[This] was Gwen's first time really writing all the lyrics herself so to me, it went the opposite from selling out," Dumont told *Backstage Online* in 1996. "We have done something that is even more personal. Now we have Gwen singing and writing about her own experiences. It makes it more natural. She's a singer, she should sing about herself or sing what she wants to sing."

At the time of the album's release, KROQ's airwaves were dominated by the Offspring, Green Day, Alice in Chains, and Nirvana (even though Kurt Cobain had died a year earlier). Sunny ska-punk wasn't on many people's radar, which made it hard for No Doubt's members to envision a path forward. "The whole thing didn't seem real," Young said. "Then when it started to happen, it was very, very surprising."

Tragic Kingdom was released to positive reviews. Despite expressing his disdain for "Don't Speak," *Rolling Stone*'s David Fricke described No Doubt's sound as "ear candy with good beats, not just bludgeon-by-numbers guitars" and as "a spry, white-suburban take on ska and Blondieesque pop."

"The band is bright, hard-hitting and kinetic, as sharp production captures the core, four-man instrumental team and adjunct horn section at their best," Mike Boehm of the *Los Angeles Times* wrote in his review.

The *Village Voice* critic Chuck Eddy wrote, "No Doubt resurrects the exuberance new-wave guys lost when '80s indie labels and college radio conned them into settling for slam-pit fits and wallflower wallpaper."

When "Just a Girl" was released as the album's first single, there was nothing like it on alternative radio, let alone top-forty radio. The song wasn't an inescapable radio classic at the beginning and took a while to catch fire. Once the song took off, it went from being played on a couple of stations to being unavoidable.

"Just that alone was such a shocker," Young said of hearing "Just a Girl" on the radio. "So it was a big thing to watch it keep climbing, like, 'Wow, this is really happening.'"

The album's second single, "Spiderwebs," sounded familiar to longtime fans. Unlike their earlier material, "Spiderwebs" was a commercial blast of ska-punk and quite the earworm. Stefani wrote it after one of her admirers recited poetry outside her window, describing her angst at the situation and the need to screen her phone calls to avoid the caller.

In a flash, Stefani shot up into the rock *and* pop stratosphere. She became a role model for women's empowerment, and soon young girls all over the world replicated Stefani's sense of glamorous tomboy style favoring crop tops, low-slung jeans, chunky chain wallets, bright blonde Bettie Bangs, and a sparkling bindi in the center or her forehead. Soon, Gwen was known on a first-name basis and was the It Girl of the moment. She was as popular and known as Madonna, Mariah

Carey, and Alanis Morissette. The band's high-energy performance on *The Late Show with David Letterman* saw Stefani leave the stage and end up on top of the host's desk and guest chairs before finding her way back to the stage.

"It didn't feel real because it wasn't expected," Young said of No Doubt's meteoric rise after *Tragic Kingdom*. "Our first record at Interscope didn't have any kind of national traction and we didn't get any radio play. We were very skeptical that this would amount to much of anything."

Unlike a lot of bands of that time, No Doubt was very aware of their aesthetic. At the time of *Tragic Kingdom*, it was easy to tell what the band's sense of style was. It stood out, and the band's look would be rocked by fans who saw them perform.

Once afterthoughts, No Doubt's music videos were in heavy rotation on MTV. *The* coolest tastemaker at the time was befitting of a band confident in their own skin.

The biggest was still to come.

"Don't Speak" was recorded a year and a half before *Tragic Kingdom* was released. Composed by Eric Stefani, the song's lyrics were famously written by Gwen on Kanal's computer after he broke up with her, ending their seven-year relationship. Following their split, Stefani rewrote the song's lyrics.

"It used to be more upbeat, more of a '70s rock-type thing," Stefani told the *Independent*. "[When] Tony and I broke up . . . it turned into a sad song."

The song catapulted No Doubt to pop stardom. "Don't Speak" hit number one on the *Billboard* Hot 100 chart, a position where it would remain for the next sixteen weeks, and was named the number one song of 1997 on that chart. The song's lengthy standing was a new record for the chart.

"Don't Speak" was a crossover hit. It also topped the adult top-forty chart for fifteen consecutive weeks. It landed at number six on the Adult Contemporary and number nine on the Rhythmic charts, and it peaked at number two on the Modern Rock Tracks chart, where it remained for five consecutive weeks. It was also the number one song in the UK, Ireland, Belgium, the Netherlands, Norway, Sweden, Switzerland, and Australia.

✖✖✖✖✖

Just a few months before No Doubt's explosion, the Warped Tour provided a platform to introduce them to the world. Just like their album, before the festival found its groove, it had to ride through a wave of chaos.

"We evolved in a way that we always stuck to—look to the future, pay homage to the past, never judge what was going on now," Kevin Lyman said. "We had bands from the old school complaining about these young bands that were on the tour. I said, 'Look at those kids' faces in the barricade. They're singing their brains out the same way people were singing to you at Fender's Ballroom.'"

Kevin Lyman was born in 1961 and grew up in the sleepy LA suburban college town of Claremont. Though it wasn't home to a huge punk scene outside of hyperlocal bands like the Unforgiven and the Stepmothers, it was a short jaunt from Orange County just down the 57 freeway through Brea Canyon or a ride down the 10 freeway to LA to see shows—either way, punk kids in Claremont had to travel to be in the punk scene. Lyman, who discovered the sound and the subculture at the tail end of high school around 1978, was instantly hooked on the melodic aggression, the style, and the characters who swarmed the pit on Saturday nights or stuck out like sore thumbs among the lockers in the general population of high school kids. The first punk he remembers crossing paths with in 1978 was a newly transferred high school classmate who went by the name of Xerox Clone.

"He had dyed hair, safety pins, the whole look," Lyman said. "And, you know, we're talking suburban LA school. We're out in the suburbs, similar to what Orange County really kind of was, a tough place to be a punk, because at the time the groups were simple, it was the jocks, and preps and that kind of thing. But, you know, they just tortured the guy Xerox. One day I just talked to him and said, 'Hey, not everyone out here is like this.'" Xerox started telling his new ally, Lyman, about punk rock and what was going on in the scene. Lyman started going to see T.S.O.L., the Adolescents, and Social Distortion, and he immersed himself in show culture around SoCal.

Fancying himself more of a person behind the scenes, Lyman's fast addiction to punk led him to start throwing shows of his own. After enrolling at Citrus College, where he studied recreational administration, he quickly got a job at the student union doing just that. His first foray in the promotional world was a fun, but not very lucrative, "$2 Tuesdays."

"It was two bands for two bucks, which shows just how bad at business I was," Lyman said. His coup de grace was getting T.S.O.L. booked for a lunchtime gig at the college. In the early to mid-'80s, colleges in OC were beginning to become a hotbed for punk. Cal State Fullerton started to have a reputation for its raucous punk shows at lunch.

Robbin Brandley was someone Lyman came up with in the world of OC college show promotion. As a Saddleback College journalism student, she worked with him on a number of college shows on different campuses, including her own. Tragedy struck when Brandley was stabbed to death in an unlit campus parking lot on January 18, 1986. Before her grisly murder at the hands of a former Camp Pendleton marine-turned-serial-killer named Andrew Urdiales sent shockwaves through Orange County, Lyman knew her as a kind and passionate music fan and one of the early people who got him started in the world of event promotion.

"[Robbin] was like a catalyst for me," Lyman said. "I was doing shows with her at her school at Saddleback College, you know, we would bring in bands from the Inland Empire, and we were doing them in her college gym. She was murdered in the parking lot. It's kind of a crazy OC story."

Pressing on in the business of live music, Lyman got good at getting away with crazy shows "because no one knew anything about the punk rock scene at that point," he said. After bringing up bands like Social Distortion and T.S.O.L., a lot of college show promoters started to book bands from OC's straight-edge punk scene—including raucous hardcore bands like Uniform Choice and Vision. "These types of bands were always the biggest pains in the ass—they would cause the most trouble at all shows," Lyman said. "Because they said they were straight edge and I go, 'Give me a drunk fucking punk, they're easy to deal with, you're under the guise of being a straight edge, you're causing more trouble than anything.'"

Regardless of what punk subsects were coming to the stage to get their artistic aggression out (sometimes it was just regular ol' aggression too), promoters like Lyman saw the bands tapping into something primal yet evolutionary about the local crowds. These were OC kids who already felt disillusioned or repulsed by the promise of prim and proper suburban life that described the '80s version of the American dream.

"I think living behind the orange curtain at that point, you know, was a struggle for some people, and you had an element that was leaning probably a little to the far-right side and included some white supremacy mentality down in Orange County with some of the punks down there that we had to deal with," Lyman said.

When he wasn't throwing shows at school, he was doing them in people's backyards. This time the stakes were a bit more lucrative. "It was five bucks, five bands, all the beer you can drink. And when the beer ran out, we'd call the cops on our own show," Lyman said.

Lyman was working with punk bands from all over Orange County as well as LA, with a mix of ska that included Fishbone and others. In addition to backyards, Lyman's early gigs happened in venues from airport hangars to fraternity houses. "It was just such a rad music scene. And I was trying to blend it all together, even back then." After college, Lyman went away to live in Hawaii for a little bit to run a weight-loss camp for girls in Hawaii, as he told *Billboard* magazine. "It wasn't that serious, the motto was, 'lose weight, get a date, get a tan, get a man.' It wasn't too politically correct, we'd get in trouble for saying that today," Lyman admitted. But then he came home in 1985 not really knowing what to do. He quickly reunited with Paul Tollett, who was already working for Goldenvoice. At this point, Lyman credits OC as one of the best local scenes around. Shows at Fender's Ballroom in nearby Long Beach introduced him to bands in the Orange County scene.

Long before multibillion-dollar promotional companies, talent agencies, and tour managers came into play, punk rock was mostly ruled by the fist. The people running the shows were tough, the people in the bands were tough, the fans were tough. "Really the qualification I brought to the table was I knew how to read," Lyman said. "Goldenvoice was transferring into this concept of really booking shows, not just calling people and going, 'Hey, do you wanna come up and play?' Because that's how guys like Gary Tovar booked bands: 'Hey, I got some money for you' . . . just these handshake deals. So all of a sudden, there started to be contracts."

At that point Lyman was working with a more seasoned promoter, a woman named Marcel Brumos. She owned a company called High

Times Events that was booking the first wave of Americana rock bands like Lone Justice and the Blasters, the style of music that later crossed over into Social Distortion and bands from Orange County. High Times and Goldenvoice co-promoted a show together with Motörhead—a real, legit band with real contracts and tour riders.

After seeing how it was being done at the next level, Lyman started working with Goldenvoice on more shows. He saw the methods behind Tovar's madness—one of which was always finding a student to get involved with who usually happened to hold a position with whatever student activities program a school had. That was who could open the door to getting Tovar's bands booked. Using local universities like Cal State Fullerton and UC Irvine as conduits to bring in young bands and bigger marquee talent like Iggy Pop and PiL was the next step in blowing down the doors for punk culture in OC. For Lyman, the formula allowed him to flourish as a booker working on Goldenvoice shows for about thirteen years. The experience of cutting his teeth in the live music scene led to Lyman's first major gig as the stage manager at a brand-new festival conceived by Jane's Addiction front man Perry Farrell in 1991—he was calling it Lollapalooza. It was billed as a traveling Woodstock that allowed fans from across the country to experience an equal parts eclectic and electric lineup of bands ranging from Siouxsie and the Banshees to the Butthole Surfers.

By this point, Lyman was seasoned and well-connected to all the bands. He went on to work on the first three Lollas, gaining the tour experience and know-how to manage a massive production.

"It was easy to be innovative when none of us knew what we were doing," Lyman told *Billboard*. "We really did change the way the business worked, because we didn't know better. I didn't know you couldn't move gear around on a union stage in Chicago or New York, I had a job to do. They didn't know what to do with me, beat my ass or what. I was breaking every rule, but I didn't care, I just wanted the work done. Now, many years later, they look forward to our tour coming through, they bring their kids down."

By 1991, Lyman was a one-man production management army for Lollapalooza. In 1992, he was stage managing and took on some of the assistant production manager roles, and by 1993, because some of the people at the top of Lollapalooza didn't really want to deal with the artists, they hired Lyman to be the artist liaison. "I was paid way more money to teach the Buddhist monks that were out with us with the Beastie Boys how to play basketball," Lyman told *Billboard*.

As time went on, Lyman saw that Lolla was starting to lose its charm. "They thought they could run it part-time, shut down from September to January, then pick up and book a lineup and put the tour together," he said. "You have to work on these things year-round."

It was only a matter of time before he decided to leave his post and start his own company, the Kevin Lyman Group. It was the first major step he took toward founding what would become the Warped Tour.

One thing Lyman took from Lollapalooza for the purposes of running his own festival was how to showcase different sides of the same culture—namely, music and action sports. For over a decade at that point, punk had been the soundtrack to skateboarders who thrived on adrenaline and bone-breaking reckless abandon, similar to surfers. And both groups lived by similar codes and loved the same music. "Really what we saw with Orange County was that it was the first real market where music and sports came together," Lyman said.

He'd seen the combination work firsthand in a festival setting. Prior to Lollapalooza, Lyman launched a pair of events in 1987 called the Vision Skate Escape and the Holiday Havoc. For the former event, Lyman said he paid the Red Hot Chili Peppers, an emerging buzz band at the time, $250 to play on top of a ramp at the end of the skate contest inside UCI's gymnasium. By defying gravity, skateboarding and punk were being pulled together through events like these. Soon Social Distortion was playing Lyman's other show, Holiday Havoc, and Lyman had started working on other skateboarding events—Board Aid, Board in the OC, Boarding for Breast Cancer, and others—all with the not-so-subtle tie-in of a punk rock soundtrack. "It was constant, this kind of action sports thing. And that really emanated out of Orange County that blended this music," Lyman said. At a certain point, things got so big with tens of thousands of people attending that one of the events Lyman planned, Board in the South Bay, got canceled because it was too big for local authorities or venue owners to contain. Even at UCI, where the show was supposed to be moved for a larger capacity, the crowds were too much.

Though the Board in the OC franchise had run its course after brushing up against the mainstream and getting its feathers ruffled, Lyman conceived of a new idea that would become the Warped Tour.

On paper, the timing for this new festival concept couldn't have been more perfect. The bands that had been fostered by the SoCal punk, hardcore, and metal scenes who'd managed to peek their head above the scrum of their aggressive-but-less-popular counterparts were suddenly becoming hot targets for agents and record companies. These A&R types were reaching out to the underground and signing bands left and right in the wake of hits like the Offspring's diamond-selling debut *Smash* on Epitaph Records, Green Day hitting the motherload with *Dookie* landing on Reprise Records (and selling over twenty million albums to date), and several others like Bad Religion making a major label debut on Atlantic after leaving Epitaph. Punk bands were suddenly in high commercial demand. But there was also a major fervor around the alternative music scene—which brought together music from disparate parts of the underground from hardcore to pop-rock, ska, and indie—that found a home on KROQ FM, championed by the likes of Jed the Fish and Rodney Bingenheimer.

As a promoter at shows in LA and OC, Lyman would work with bands like Sublime, Orange 9mm, and Quicksand—bands that would not so coincidentally wind up on the first Warped Tour bill on a nightly basis. Yet none of these bands that were packing the pit and raging on sweat-soaked stages had ever played together. In 1994, Lyman had an idea: "If we can get them all together, 1 plus 1 might equal 3. All these bands I was listening to and watching had something relevant to say, we just needed to get more kids to hear it. And I thought if we pulled them together, they would be able to hear that."

In a time before punk rock and its various offshoots became a chart-topping phenomenon, American punk was mostly surviving in pockets on the coasts, whether it was East or West, or in big cities where underground scenes were able to grow roots with venues and labels as conduits for the sound. Without the support of major radio and MTV just prior to the boom of Green Day and the Offspring in 1994, there wasn't commercial support. Certainly not on a large enough scale for kids in rural and suburban areas to hear it and be affected by it.

"We weren't getting the support of [national] radio, we weren't getting the support of anything, we had to go make that ourselves," Lyman said. "For me, it was just also doing the shows and seeing all these kids coming out and figuring out a way to bring this together with the action sports world and putting our resources together as a scene to take this music nationwide."

From the start, Lyman had the perfect lineup forming in his head for the first Warped Tour: Quicksand headlining the show with L7, Sublime, Orange 9mm, and No Use for a Name topping the bill along with Deftones, Guttermouth, Face to Face, No Doubt, CIV, Seaweed, Fluf, Into Another, Swingin' Utters, the Grabbers, Good Riddance,

Dimestore Hoods, Supernova, and WIZO. On the action sports side, he'd bring together a list of heavy hitters in skateboarding, rollerblading, and BMX, including Remy Stratton, Steve Alba, Angie Walton, Neal Hendrix, Tom Fry, Rene Hulgreen, Keith Treanor, Arlo Eisenberg, Jaya Bonderov, and Mike Frazier.

Meanwhile, Bingenheimer championed OC punk on the airwaves, Gary Tovar was using his money from the drug trade and other ventures to fund the shows, and there was a great crop of over twenty bands that Lyman had stockpiled for the Warped Tour along with some of the top names in action sports. Then there was a hunger from fans looking to take the music further, and the budding festival circuit was a by-product of these factors that brought the Warped Tour into the world before it even had a name. In fact, the first name for the Warped Tour wasn't even "the Warped Tour."

"The original name of the tour was gonna be 'The Bomb,'" Lyman said.

The scrappy promoter said he couldn't afford name searches back then. "At the time, you had to go hire a lawyer, it was like $400 per name search," he said. "And I've been through like four names and that was the term that people were using, like, 'that's the bomb.' I'd hear that a lot, so I said let's name the tour 'The Bomb.' And it was clear the name was okay for touring."

On the day Lyman planned to announce the tour, April 19, 1995, the Oklahoma City bombing horrified America and dominated the headlines. Immediately, Lyman knew he had to scrap the name of his festival if he wanted to avoid incurring the backlash of the entire country. And he had to move fast. Luckily, he got inspiration from *Warp* magazine, a publication put out by TransWorld that, much like its parent outlet, focused on the worlds of surfing and skating. Lyman immediately called the magazine's editor, Fran Richards, and asked if he could borrow the name. Prior to that, both men had worked together on a number of events for the magazine, so Richards was willing to cut Lyman a break to save his hide.

Richards's response was, "Don't put out a magazine called *Warp*, and I won't put out a tour, and you can use the name."

In hindsight, the ability to use extreme sports media in a collaborative way with a festival was groundbreaking. Not only did it give both the festival and the publication a profile boost due to name recognition and the bands and athletes on the bill, but it showcased the lifestyle that the festival was about—one that would soon come to circle the globe. Incidentally the magazine ended up being short-lived in the States, though *Warp* still survives in Japan.

The first year of the Warped Tour leaned heavily on SoCal bands who shared the stage with Quicksand, already a major headlining staple in the New York hardcore scene by the mid-'90s, alongside the eclectic, hard-thrashing outfit Orange 9mm. Though the band, who had put out two seminal post-hardcore albums by 1995, broke up just months after their headlining slot at the Warped Tour, the merging of big-name aggressive alt, punk rock, and indie bands of East and West came with extra cache behind a rising act like Quicksand. The fact that it came together at all was kind of a miracle.

"Really, that first year kind of came together because it was people that knew me," Lyman said.

While in hindsight it may seem like perfect timing to have capitalized on two acts like Sublime and No Doubt who were on the brink of stardom, putting two untested bands on the road was a risky bet for Lyman, who was sweating the ticket sales.

"It was a little early for me," Lyman said. "They didn't move any tickets across the nation. You know, they were strong in certain markets but especially when we went out to like Milwaukee and even Chicago, I didn't realize how they had not gotten exposure."

The tour took place three to four times per week and grossed roughly $25,000 per night, and out of that organizers had to pay for the skate ramp and production and stage crews. At that point the highest-paid band, Quicksand, was getting around $1,000 per show, Lyman estimates. "We didn't have any food, no one knew what we were doing. We were out there just making it happen."

Though the tour was brutal financially, there was a certain buzz around it that surged on the energy of the unknown and up-and-coming acts that teens in cities and, more importantly, suburbs around the country were becoming aware of or were already fully obsessed with.

The tour officially kicked off on June 21, 1995. The night before was a cramped one in the Lyman household. A group of festival musicians, including the band Fluf from San Diego, and some skateboarders on the tour slept on their floor. "We were living in the hills in this funky house. And then literally we were going down in the morning," Lyman said. "And I just remember standing there with a clipboard and everyone's names because we shared buses that first year." As he made his way through the checklist of bus-riding festival participants, each of them was directed to a specific bus until he finally got to Sublime, who would be sharing a bus with L7, Orange 9mm, and No Use for a Name. At the very end of the roll call, he realized he had two extra people ready to board who were not on the call sheet—a pair of skateboarders who stowed away looking for a good time. Though Lyman might've been annoyed, he allowed the skaters to stay on, and the caravan rode out to the first destination, Salt Lake City.

On the way there, the crew stopped in Las Vegas and parked at the Rio Hotel to chow down on the all-you-can-eat buffet, the last real meal the crew ate for about twenty-five cities. Even on this pit stop before the tour kicked off, the excitement of this new rolling punk rock summer camp felt electric. The prospect of dozens of bands, skaters, bladers, and BMXers spending days doing what they loved in good company, traveling the country and building new fan bases everywhere they went, was intoxicating. So much so that some members of the crew who'd stopped in Vegas forgot to get back on the bus.

At one point, Lyman remembered the buses preparing to leave Sin City and sailing slowly through the pantheon of lights on the Vegas Strip, unaware that some passengers were frantically skateboarding behind trying to get his attention as they raised their arms. "And then the driver looks back and notices them and goes, 'I think we left a couple of people behind.'" The buses stopped and they got on, and the posse drove overnight to Salt Lake, arriving at sunrise around 5:30 a.m. the next morning to set up for the first show.

That initial show took place at Saltair, a historic Mormon amusement park and space that provided a safe environment for Mormon patrons—probably not the first place you'd think of to host a pack of ramp-riding, punk, and post-hardcore miscreants and their ilk. But there they were. The first Warped Tour show drew about eight hundred people. Tickets were a whopping fifteen dollars.

In addition to the ramps and the amps, Lyman brought along a big surprise he'd hoped would become a Warped Tour staple—a climbing wall made to look like the front of a house. "I thought it would be fun to have something at a punk rock show that no one had ever seen," Lyman said.

It took every person on the tour to help erect this giant wall.

The first kid to try it, an excited young teenage boy sporting a mohawk, looked up with amazement. So far, Lyman's desired "wow" effect had been attained. "How much to climb the wall?" the kid asked. The question baffled Lyman, who had no intention of charging extra.

"I thought, 'Is that what the world is coming to? How much . . .' Look, you paid fifteen dollars to come to the show, go climb the wall!"

The kid was equally baffled. "It's free?" He wasted no time getting his grips and climbing up there. No one questioned how the attraction was going to make money, and yet everyone on tour who could help dutifully worked to load the giant wall off and on the freight truck that carried it into town behind the buses—though sometimes it took a few tries to get it on.

From there, the crew of six buses hit their next stop at the Inaugural Fields in Boulder, Colorado. Things on the tour were already shaky, or shakier than they had been. The tour wasn't selling well. On top of it, the promoters at the venue hadn't bothered to set up any concessions for the show—try having a festival with nothing to eat or drink. Having to think fast, Lyman came up with the cheapest alternative possible.

"I sent someone to Walmart and bought a little bar with a barbecue. And we sold hot dogs for a dollar and sodas for a dollar. We actually made some money on that—everyone had to eat," Lyman said.

The next day the show promoter called Lyman yelling about how he'd lost money on the show. "And I didn't know what to tell him, like, 'Hey, thanks for the bonus though.' The promoter got even more pissed, screaming his head off: 'Fuck you and your fucking bonus!'" "Whaddaya mean bonus?" Lyman said, "Oh, yeah, you give us a bonus because you forgot to bring a food stand. We sold our own food. I think we cleared like $2,000 on the thing. You know, we bought $500 in hot dogs and sodas and sold $2,500 or something throughout the day."

For their third show, the tour moved on to Texas, and the first place they stopped to rest on their way to Dallas was a cheap hotel in Amarillo next to a big steakhouse. Since the tour couldn't afford hotel rooms on days off, they pulled into parking lots, and people used the amenities at the hotels and slept on the buses. There was a little swimming pool at the hotel next to where they'd parked in Amarillo that their crowd commandeered and turned into a beer-soaked party. Then they drove on to Dallas, where Lollapalooza took place just a few miles away—a slight oversight that pretty much ensured the Warped Tour would sell even fewer tickets than it did at its previous two shows. It was to the point that the promoter in Deep Ellum at the show's location, the Bomb Factory, thought they had canceled. The show wasn't even advertised, Lyman said.

When the Warped Tour crew arrived at the venue, they decided to go through with the show and set everything up themselves. They allowed the homeless and skater kids into the show for free. Things only went downhill from there.

"When we got to San Antonio, we were struggling. We cut shows or they were being moved to smaller venues," Lyman said.

"Finally the tour made it to the Stone Pony, in Asbury Park, NJ, where we actually drew like two thousand people. We thought, 'Oh my gosh, this is turning around,'" Lyman said. "We made it. . . . In so many other years you would have never gotten past those shows, but we had no option. That's why I think at work everyone knew this was the only option, this is our chance. So as chaotic as it was, all the bands and everyone who showed up helped make it happen."

The jerry-rigged nature of the show was no indicator of the talent onstage, which was all top-notch. Even on the nights when the bands partied a little too hard, they always found a way to bring it during the show. From the lead act, Quicksand, with its deft flurry of crunchy guitars and sternum-punching breakdowns, to the melodic four-chord fury of No Use for a Name and the cool, catchy alt-rock power of Fluf, a band fronted by the late Otis Barthoulameu, a.k.a. "O." He played in several other highly regarded bands like the Makeup Sex, Systems Officer, Olivelawn, Harshmellow, Octagrape, Reeve Oliver, and Woofer.

Lyman understood how good all the bands were because he'd been working with them at club shows and knew they could light up a crowd. "It was like these kids got turned on to music in a different way," Lyman said. "It wasn't a little pocketed part of a scene, it was like being part of an overall culture."

As the Warped Tour continued on its maiden voyage, it left traces of that culture scattered across the country. What appeared to be a single-day showcase of bands from the coastal cities was actually a process that included young local bookers in every town the tour visited who were indoctrinated and inspired to promote the shows and the bands themselves. They were the foot soldiers who made sure that the crowd in front of the stage knew where to find the Warped Tour and its bands after they left town through mailing lists, archaic websites, or merch and music the bands put out that continued to spread like punk rock dandelion seeds floating, landing, and growing roots of their own. The fandom blossomed at record stores and high schools and backyard parties, everywhere kids went to get hyped on new sounds. Local record labels and radio stations were always invited down free of charge to participate and see the scene that was slowly being built around them.

The most fervent response to the music came from New Jersey. Much like how OC is often compared to LA, Jersey kids grew up in the shadow of the Big Apple as the redheaded stepchild of America's preeminent cultural metropolis. Even many of the punks from the gutters of the Bowery thought of themselves as superior to their suburban counterparts in Asbury Park.

"Those suburban kids, we're not going to be as welcome or feel welcomed coming to the rescue. So they had to create their own space and their own places," Lyman said.

But New Jersey's punk roots included iconic bands from all areas of the punk spectrum—the zany, jet-propelled anthems of the Bouncing Souls; the artistic weirdness of Electric Frankenstein; the tough-guy felon core of the Fury of Five; the unabashedly catchy pop-punk of Midtown; and spanning all the way back to the granddaddy of them all, the Misfits. Each had something specific to contribute that felt akin to what OC was all about in terms of its place in the West Coast punk scene.

If there's one thing the Warped Tour helped give a platform to, it was the suburban frustration that fomented in the punk scene in the '80s and morphed into something that was also potent in the '90s, and every town in America has some version of that.

"We tapped into it in weird places like Boise, Idaho, and gave kids a place to go and then encouraged those kids to start their own little scenes of music," Lyman said.

The pocket of bands that started with the Warped Tour in '95 didn't remain stagnant either. This was mostly thanks to Vans shoes stepping in to sponsor them during their second year.

Soon, with a legacy SoCal shoe company behind them, it was just a matter of time before bigger bands started finding their way onto the lineup, adding a stamp of legitimacy to the festival in the process.

Much of Lyman's early career in event promotions had already laid the groundwork for what he went on to do with the Warped Tour, blending bands, bikes, skateboarding, and in-line skating—he just didn't know it at the time. He had gained experience working on action sports events like the Swatch Impact Tour, an early action sports extravaganza that traveled around the US, which Lyman worked on for veteran concert promoter Bill Silva.

The show featured a portable show stage that was made of steel and measured fifty-five feet wide and thirty feet deep with a weight of thirteen tons. Riders swooshed by on their boards and bikes from end to end, doing choreographed routines together as well as solo-ramp acts while a disc jockey spun records with music video segments blaring on a large screen.

Riders at the time included skateboarders "Gator" Mark Anthony, Joe Johnson, Chris Miller, Jeff Phillips, and Kevin Staab, and bikers included Ron Wilkerson, Mat Hoffman, and Brian Blyther. Jimi Scott joined as the sole in-line skater.

Add in his role developing and producing similar events like Vision Skate Escape, Board Aid, and Boarding for Breast Cancer, and there was an inherent recipe for success that Lyman was building through merging the cultures of action sports and live music. It started with the X Games, founded a year earlier in 1994 with the first summer competition taking place in Rhode Island.

"The reason the Warped Tour kinda happened was that I was in the snow at one of these events and heard two people talking about the X Games. They were saying, 'Oh, now it's gonna be on TV.' But I thought, 'Wouldn't it be better if we did it ourselves and brought this music we have in Southern California?' So the timing was very important with that," Lyman said.

The concept sounded nice at the time, but Lyman was broke. The first year of the Warped Tour was financially disastrous. The promoter was back to working the club circuit trying to make ends meet. But he still held out hope of seeing a future with his half-pipe dream, which was not connecting all the way with his desired audience of teenagers and twentysomethings.

"Warped really wasn't punk in the first year, and when I look back at it now, that's probably why it wasn't successful," Lyman admitted to *Billboard* in 2015. "It was almost too eclectic for the audience I was trying to appeal to. At first, it was more my sound, from working in the clubs every night. I liked indie, Seaweed; I liked L7, a grungy punk sound; I liked Sublime, a surf reggae sound; I liked No Doubt, a ska sound. So putting it all on one bill the first year, I think now, was too confusing for people."

Despite having managed to book two well-established bands—NOFX and Pennywise—for the next year's installment of the fest, venue promoters didn't want to pay Lyman any money to host or market the wandering festival.

"They were literally saying, like, 'You can come here, we'll give you some door money if you can draw people. But if all bands don't play I'm not paying you,'" Lyman said. "I remember in Chicago promoters told me, 'If all the bands don't play, I'm not giving you money.'"

At one point, one of Lyman's former partners with the Warped Tour convinced him that he had a friend at Calvin Klein in New York City who would sponsor the event. Yes, at one point the nation's longest-running punk rock and skateboarding festival could have been called the "Calvin Klein Warped Tour." Lyman recalled, "My wife actually drew a skateboard ramp that said Calvin Klein Warped Tour at one point. I wish I still had that. It would've been the biggest branding mistake, it would've never worked."

Luckily, thanks to a record-setting blizzard in January 1996, that didn't happen. Executives at Vans shoe company in New York City were stuck at home because all planes were grounded for a whole day. During that twenty-four hours, Lyman got a call from Vans asking him to come out there. "I thought they wanted to be involved with amateur skate programming," Lyman told *Billboard*. "I had fifteen minutes with Walter Schoenfeld, Vans' CEO at the time, and I just had to go for it, it was this fine line of nothing to lose."

A little bit cocky and a little bit scared, Lyman met with Schoenfeld in New York and told him no one would ever go watch amateur skating unless it was attached to his successful music festival because that was what really drew people to these events. With a bit of charm and convincing, Lyman had a sponsorship deal within fifteen minutes that saved the tour.

Surprisingly, not only did the CEO seem to agree during the conversation, he also wrote a check. "I saw him writing a '3' down, I thought $30,000, and he gave me $300,000," Lyman said. On top of that, when he found out Lyman and his company had sold the merch rights for the tour for $100,000 to Sony Signatures, the legitimate old-school T-shirt company who had no idea how to sell to this crowd, he gave him an extra $100,000 to buy the merch rights back.

"Basically, they helped us survive the second year. I had bought the talent, but I hadn't paid for it. We came home that summer and paid everyone back from the first year," Lyman said.

Looking back, the thought of a snowstorm in New York leading to a partnership that would launch the longest-running festival in SoCal history is hard to fathom. Yet for the Warped Tour, it almost seemed like a case of Goliath helping David. From the perspective of Vans, however, it was a bit of the opposite. At the time, the Orange County shoe company was crawling out of bankruptcy, one of several instances in the company's history when the financial situation was looking as checkered as the iconic slip-ons made famous by Jeff Spicoli in *Fast Times at Ridgemont High*. In 1982, the company, then known as the Van Doren Rubber Company, had gotten a big boost when the aforementioned Jeff Spicoli wore their black-and-white checkered slip-ons in Amy Heckerling's classic '80s teen flick (written by Cameron Crowe). The surfer dude almost single-footedly spawned a Vans shoe renaissance.

In an industry based on teenage trends, Vans had mostly clung to a shoe design that was two decades old. The company still manufactured its kicks in the United States, despite the fact that virtually all of its rivals had shifted production overseas.

But even with its ups and downs, Vans' strategy was mostly a success for years.

The company geared up for more production, but the fad passed, and the sneaker maker quickly fell into Chapter 11 bankruptcy. When private investors pulled the company back from the brink of insolvency and took over in 1988, earnings rose. But the company continued to have problems.

In the early to mid-'90s, Vans was helped by a booming market for athletic footwear. By the end of its 1992 fiscal year, the company's profit peaked at $6.5 million.

However, soon after this, Vans' fortunes hit a downward spiral as the company faced mounting pressure due to slumping sales in the athletic footwear market and a California recession, another symptom of the 1992 California budget crisis. On July 1, 1992, the California state legislature and then-Governor Pete Wilson failed to pass a state budget by the constitutional deadline. This created a financial panic when the state government ran out of cash reserves on July 2 and began paying employees and contractors with IOUs, which major banks agreed to honor for the time being until a budget was officially signed sixty-three days later.

This brought the Teamsters Union pounding at Vans' door, trying to organize workers in the city of Orange. Meanwhile, Vans was facing increased scrutiny from immigration officials who were cracking down on illegal workers.

Teamsters officials accused Vans of closing the plant to skirt the union's organizing effort.

"The image of the company has changed," a Vans executive who requested anonymity told the *Los Angeles Times* in 1995. "People are looking for new things, and they're taking to international shoes. The basic, traditional Vans shoes aren't as popular as in the past."

In an attempt to put more of an emphasis on fashion, Vans turned to South Korea to produce a new line of skater-friendly shoes. Vans called it its international collection, and it was designed for teenage boys and others who were skateboarders or who possessed a "skater attitude," company reports said.

Sales of those shoes boosted the company's ailing revenue figures by 10 percent, to $63.5 million, in the nine-month period. Earnings more than tripled in that period, to $1.8 million, compared with a year earlier.

But increased overseas production that stemmed from the popularity of shoes made in Korea would come at the expense of factory workers in Orange. As sales of the Korean-made shoes increased, production requirements in SoCal dissipated. By early '95, Vans laid off several hundred workers in Orange and later closed its manufacturing plant in the city in June of that year. It was in this climate that the shoe company made a deal with Lyman in their first big foray into the public since declaring and working their way out of bankruptcy a year prior.

Compared to the first year, when Lyman would take anyone who would join on tour, 1996 was a major step up, at least in perception. With Vans on board and with the bit of buzz they generated throughout the punk circuit, the tour was able to land esteemed punk bands NOFX, Blink-182, and Pennywise on top of the bill. Even though he'd always strived to create an eclectic festival, the punk ethos and sound were at the heart of what started the Warped Tour, and from that year on, the tent just got wider and incorporated more genres. Imagine a festival before this one where rap-rockers 311, West Coast hip-hop legends Tha Alkaholiks, alternative metal fixtures Deftones, and surf-rocker Dick Dale all shared the same bill—it would have been considered impossible.

In 1997, Lyman tapped Social Distortion to coheadline with the

Ramones, a dream scenario for punk fans, many of whom were too young to have ever seen the OC and New York godfathers of their respective scenes during their early days on opposite coasts. At the time, Ness and company were still touring on 1996's *White Light, White Heat, White Trash*. They had a reputation for being hard to work with, especially Ness. Early on, Lyman said that the venerated front man would need to check his ego on this tour with no place for rock stars. "People are like, you're gonna have Social D, Mike's hard to deal with, and I go, 'That's gonna be his problem, not my problem,'" Lyman said. "Because everyone's having a great time out here. And if he decides to be hard to deal with, no one's gonna deal with him." Fortunately, according to Lyman, the band saved most of their rock-star swagger for the stage. "He was just fine. He had a good time I think. I don't know if he'd say it now. But he handled it really well," Lyman said.

Despite the band's well-mannered demeanor, the sheer brutality of the tour resulted in the band vowing never to do it again by the end of the 1997 run.

"It's a hard tour," said Eileen Mercolino, one of the sponsorship managers on the Warped Tour who started working part-time for Lyman in 1996 and went full-time organizing the show throughout the year in '99. "Especially those first years because catering was like a chow wagon," Mercolino said. "The early artist diet on Warped consisted of chili, sub sandwiches, and cereal—that was about it. Three squares a day. They were still out there with the bare necessities until Kevin brought out real catering in '98. We were in a lot of fields, and then you have to go get shower rooms, and just, like, basic human comfort is difficult in those kinds of situations. It got a little better as the years went on because we started playing in more parking lots of amphitheaters and other kinds of arenas, which had facilities for everybody's locker rooms and whatnot, but dressing rooms in those early years were pretty sparse."

Early into Social Distortion's Thursday night Warped Tour set in 1997 at the Olympic Velodrome in Carson, Ness offered a brief history lesson for young punks in the crowd.

"Society wasn't always that friendly to punk," he told a sold-out crowd, going on to describe the music's outlaw existence before being embraced by the mainstream in recent years.

Roughly sixteen years after Ness started the band, the relatively newfound acceptance threw punk into an identity crisis. In an effort to redefine itself, various subsects of the genre solidified into their own scenes—from hardcore to power-pop punk. It may not have been obvious to the eleven thousand fans in attendance that Thursday, but the Warped Tour itself symbolized many of those changes.

The few ska-punk hybrids on the bill still proved popular, from the smooth, percolating approach of LA's Hepcat to the Mighty Mighty Bosstones' brass-heavy Bostonian bravado. Outside of the punk realm, LA rappers Tha Alkaholiks turned in a boisterous set, and Royal Crown Revue whipped up a scintillating stretch of vintage swing. Much of the eight-hour event, though, was dedicated to a spectrum of straight-ahead punk that included Blink-182, the Vandals, Descendents, and Pennywise.

While the crowds were fierce, some reviews were skeptical of the staying power of SoCal punk. The *Los Angeles Times* wrote in its review that "Mainstream acceptance of such stylings has forced punk adherents to find more emphatic ways of expressing their defiance. The problem is, when the struggle to rebel overshadows the substance of rebellion, it's reduced to a mere pose. Despite its scope and a few inspired performances, too much of Warped '97 felt like punk huckstering."

During a far less sunny stop in Chicago, critics called the fest a "wet and wild party."

"As a steady, if no longer torrential, rain fell on the parking lot of the United Center Friday afternoon and the Mighty Mighty Bosstones roared through 'Numbered Days,' one could see steam rising from the mosh pit of exuberant teenagers," wrote the *Chicago Tribune.*

"The image captured the mix of chaos, jubilation and precipitation—lots and lots of precipitation—that marked the Chicago stop of the Vans Warped Tour '97. In the end, there were some silver linings in the third annual installment of the punk music and outdoor recreation festival, even if dark clouds derailed many promising aspects of the outdoor event."

Though the festival crowds were often content to keep their rambunctious antics mostly harmless, an exercise in caution was almost always needed. Ness traveled with his bodyguard 24/7, especially at a stop in Salt Lake City. At the time and years before, the area of Salt Lake where the tour performed was a hotspot for skinheads looking to meet someone they thought was a like-minded musician, but who in reality couldn't stand them.

"We had to be very careful because of the skinheads," Mercolino said. "There's a lot of skinheads and violent ones in Utah, which was really weird. We had to have extra security that I do remember. I also remember he had a bodyguard with him 24/7 because people would try and get in fights with them all over the place. Just so they could say that they got in a fight with Mike Ness."

From then on, the Warped Tour seemed to get bigger and bigger every year. Shows grew from five thousand to ten thousand attendees to routinely topping twenty-five thousand. "I remember one show where there wasn't enough local security and the kids were waiting to get in and they knocked down a chain link fence and just started streaming in," Mercolino remembers. "And I just remember standing there just freaking out. Kevin was there, everybody was just like, 'Oh my god, you kids get back! You gotta stand in line. You got to get your tickets.'

They just started stampeding in. So that was kind of crazy. We weren't used to that."

In 1998, Garden Grove's Save Ferris appeared alongside the likes of MxPx, Reel Big Fish, Mad Caddies, No Use for a Name, Reverend Horton Heat, Royal Crown Revue, Staind, Unwritten Law, the Vandals, and the Specials.

Initially, the ska-punk band was apprehensive about joining summer's hottest ensemble tour.

"Of course, when we were offered this tour, my perception was, 'We can't do this tour,'" Save Ferris singer Monique Powell said. "They're going to eat us alive. Fucking eat us alive."

Powell's fears proved to be wrong. The band elicited positive reactions, and the crowd bounced up and down to their hit cover of Dexys Midnight Runners' "Come On Eileen."

One of Powell's favorite moments from the tour didn't take place onstage, but it was just as vindicating as earning the respect of a rowdy festival crowd that was mostly there to see harder bands whip up a mosh pit.

"One day during the tour, a woman walks up to me, very beautiful," Powell said. "And there's a little tiny boy with her and he's wearing a Save Ferris shirt. And she goes, 'Monique, I wanted to introduce you to my son. He will not take the shirt off.' It was the son of [Chino Moreno], the singer of Deftones. He was literally four years old and he was wearing a Save Ferris shirt like it was his favorite."

With Vans' sponsorship also came a mega skate ramp that often took center stage at the festival. Every year it was summoned out of Lyman's warehouse in Montclair and loaded onto a truck that followed behind the tour buses. Skaters like Neal Hendrix took advantage of it every day possible, busting out high-flying, board-flipping contortionist moves in front of roaring crowds.

"They were a huge part of the tour," Mercolino said. "The motocross guys were absolutely nuts, and they would get in trouble constantly. You never want to go on their bus because you never knew what was going on there. But that was always very exciting." Mercolino remembers one day at Warped's show at Irvine Meadows when Lyman had things set up so that when Rancid was playing, the motocross ramp appeared behind them, and it looked as if motorcycles were soaring over the band.

When the stunts didn't involve skateboards or motocross, the BMX street course was on fire with riders grinding and flipping their bikes like acrobats in the street skate competition. It all coalesced with the soundtrack of throttling guitars, raw power vocals, and pounding drums that had been the sonic backdrop of SoCal punk culture for years. It was a vibe that helped to once again launch clothing lines deeply tied to Orange County in a newer era.

In 1999, Lyman signed a partnership with the brand-new surf label Hurley and got Blink-182 to wear the brand's clothes onstage. The trade-off was for the band to get free seats on one of the Warped Tour's buses since they couldn't yet afford their own transportation. The move signaled a turning point for both band and brand: Blink had just replaced its former drummer Scott Raynor with Travis Barker, and Hurley's founder, Bob Hurley, had left a successful career with Billabong to start his namesake clothing line earlier that year. Four years later, Blink was selling out arenas and topping *Billboard* charts, and Hurley had grown into a $70 million business, which Nike acquired in 2002.

"We launched Hurley during the Warped Tour in 1999," Mercolino said. "Bob Hurley had been at O'Neill before [getting let go from that company] and deciding to start his own company. He bought a full-page ad in a surf magazine for the Warped Tour and just put 'Hurley' at the bottom of it."

At the time, Mercolino ran all the sponsorships for the festival, and they would literally bring her gigantic bags of clothes for all the girls on the tour. Lyman had mostly women running his production while the largely male crew was running the stages. "So they just gave me these giant bags of clothes, and they would just outfit us for the whole tour the whole time every year," Mercolino said. "And that's literally like people would just see us and then the guys, you know, they got their own bags, clothes. So all they were wearing was Hurley and Volcom, Electric sunglasses. All the Orange County companies were launching off of the Warped Tour."

18

WON'T DRAG THEM DOWN

By the time Social Distortion were ready to get to work on their fifth studio album, an influx of previously rarely heard material had already been released. Through Guerinot's new label, Time Bomb Recordings, Social Distortion put out *Mainliner (Wreckage from the Past)*, which was a singles and rarities compilation of material from the early '80s, and they reissued *Mommy's Little Monster* and *Prison Bound* on CD.

By the end of 1995, Ness was writing and ready to record. However, the band's process was upended. The group worked with producer Michael Beinhorn at the label's behest. It immediately took him and the band out of their respective routines.

"He was a ballbuster," Ness said of the producer. "In the past, whenever we had twelve songs, we went in and recorded them. I gave him the twelve songs, and we met at this park in New York City, and he's telling me I have to keep writing. He used past songs as an example. It's not something as an artist, if you knew what it was, you'd bottle it up and sell it. It's one out of twenty songs you achieve that."

Despite that, Ness acknowledged that the recording of this album was a critical point in the band's career.

"I needed pushing," Ness said. "You can rest on your laurels after a couple of successful records, and he was pushing me. That was one of the most valuable lessons of my career—he saw something in me that I didn't see."

While living in New York City during this time, Ness wrote "When the Angels Sing," a song about his late grandmother, and "I Was Wrong," which ended up being the album's first single. "I wrote several songs there by being fucking agitated," Ness said of his time on the East Coast.

Before he headed to New York, though, Ness met one of his heroes: Johnny Cash. Having referenced him on *Prison Bound* and covered "Ring of Fire," it was a thrill for the meeting to finally happen. Cash was sitting in a room at a studio next door watching religious programming, and Ness went over to him . . . although he was a bit uneasy at first.

"I saw him and it was like, 'Fuck, he's eating dinner,'" Ness said. "Then, I grabbed my guitar and walked in and said, 'Hey, man, I'm Mike. I covered 'Ring of Fire' and can you sign this real quick?' And he did. That was epic."

Unlike the blend of punk, rockabilly, and blues that marked the band's previous three albums, *White Light, White Heat, White Trash* had a markedly harder sound. Deen Castronovo played drums on the album, and Social Distortion later added Chuck Biscuits of Black Flag, D.O.A., and Circle Jerks fame to the lineup.

"Everybody was very serious on that record, in the studio, like there wasn't much fooling around," said James Saez, who would go on to work with the band in the late '90s. "They were committed, and the album came out great."

Lyrically, Ness looked back on ten years of sobriety and realized that not all of his problems were due to drugs and alcohol. Many songs were about self-improvement, while a couple were political and addressed social issues, like how "Don't Drag Me Down" was Ness ruminating about witnessing racism at concerts.

The album was met with mixed reviews, and it ultimately peaked at number twenty-seven on the *Billboard* 200 when it was released in September 1996. Yet later, it landed at number 171 on *Rolling Stone*'s 500 Greatest Albums of All Time list in 2004.

"What's really ironic about this record is that it probably has more similarities to our first album, from 1983, than any of them," Ness said at the time. "And that was purely unconscious. A lot of those emotions resurfaced. Or I just got in touch with them. I don't think they ever go away.

"The last thing we wanted to make was a cute alternative record, you know what I mean? In so many ways we wanted to move forward. But I feel like in more ways we reverted backwards. Replanting the roots. Back to basics."

Social Distortion spent the better part of the next year on the road. Things were clicking with Biscuits in the fold. By the time the band toured Europe, Danell returned to Orange County for a few weeks to witness the birth of his first child, Duke.

With the Cadillac Tramps done, Social Distortion called upon Jonny Wickersham to step in for Danell. The two bore an uncanny resemblance to each other. At the time, Wickersham was playing with U.S. Bombs, the outfit led by Duane Peters.

Missing part of the tour, returning, and then missing his family would have a profound impact on Danell, leaving him to wonder what his next steps were.

⬛⬛⬛⬛

As the Offspring became big shots in Orange County, they'd often run into bands who were orbiting the same sonic stratosphere. No Doubt and the Offspring recorded their demos at Jim Dotson's South Coast Recording Studios. So why there? It cost ten dollars per hour to record. Having access to the studio for an inexpensive fee taught the bands how to properly record and develop their songwriting process. For No Doubt, though, it is where they recorded their first album when they were unsigned around 1990 to 1991. They weren't unsigned for long. After No Doubt did that, they were snatched up by Interscope later in 1991, and the material recorded at South Coast Recording Studios was never released.

"We were pretty green and young at it," No Doubt's Adrian Young said. Unlike the Offspring, who were pros inside the studio, No Doubt were better live, mainly because they had more opportunities to perform live because they weren't straightforward punk.

That didn't mean they were slouches.

"I remember Jim playing some for me one time and going, 'Wow, these guys are going to be huge,'" Holland said.

"We didn't think that," Young said in response with a laugh.

One time, the pair rehearsed at the same space in Fullerton, where the bands got a bird's-eye view of what the other was doing.

With the success of *Smash*, Holland used some of his newfound funds to start his own label. Formed in 1994, the label, called Nitro Records, was based in Garden Grove after initially starting at Holland's Huntington Beach apartment. Like any new label, Nitro started humbly.

"I get this call on my answering machine saying, 'Hey, this is Bryan Holland, and my manager Jim Guerinot said you were looking for a job,'" said Ernest Kemeny, a longtime product manager who previously worked at Sony. He knew that there was a new label in town, but that was it. "'So I thought I'd give you a call. Call me back.' And I was like, 'Who is this Bryan Holland guy that he knew Jim Guerinot?'"

He found out quickly.

When he went to the Nitro HQ, which was off Valley View on the 22 freeway, it wasn't quite what he expected. It was buried in a nondescript industrial complex with no sign. Finally, after walking around, Kemeny saw a big pistol that said "Nitro" pointing down the hallway.

"Then I knock on the door and it's Dexter from the Offspring with his hair," he said incredulously. "And I'm just like, 'You're Bryan?' And he said, 'Well, yeah, that's my real name, Bryan, but everybody calls me Dexter.'"

Over the next thirteen years, Nitro served as the home to artists like the Vandals and Guttermouth and reissued albums by T.S.O.L. and the Damned. In the label's early years, Dexter hired Blackball away from his job at the box manufacturing company to serve as a jack-of-all-trades. He'd pick up the mail at the label's PO box, handle merch, and serve as the head of A&R. After hearing an emerging band called AFI, Blackball urged Holland to sign the Northern California band to Nitro. The label's vibe was familial, with Holland often hosting backyard parties (the Halloween ones were most memorable) with the In-N-Out truck catering. When not touring, Holland was in the office working on his various endeavors. But this was no vanity project: Holland made sure that the bands signed to Nitro reflected his ethos.

Nitro wasn't the only OC-based label to emerge. After Rebel Waltz took off, Guerinot founded Time Bomb Recordings in 1995, a joint venture with Clive Davis's Arista Records. Vowing to change the music business, Guerinot boldly saw his new venture as a way to shake up how labels were operating at the time, which did not go over well with his contemporaries. His pronouncement put a bull's-eye on the company, pressuring everyone to succeed immediately. "People had very high expectations of Guerinot because of his success as the head of marketing for A&M, and being such a big manager," said Emily Kaye, who was one of the first Time Bomb employees.

Time Bomb's ethos was simple: find the bands they loved.

Guerinot brought Social Distortion, and later Mike Ness as a solo artist, to Time Bomb after the completion of the band's contract with Epic. The label wasn't confined to punk. Other artists signed to Time Bomb were Death in Vegas, Wellwater Conspiracy, and eventually Sunny Day Real Estate. Old friends like the Vandals and the Offspring also had material released through the label.

Guerinot, who by now had become established as a talented and intense executive—so much so that he was nicknamed "the Colonel"— was on his own.

"He was the most intense person I've ever worked with in my life," Kaye said. "And I felt like I had a lot to prove."

Coming with Guerinot from A&M Records where she worked in A&R, Kaye shared a passion for music. They started at an office on Main Street in Laguna Beach that looked over an ice cream shop. Guerinot's fire to succeed grew as his management company flourished.

"He spent the majority of his time fighting for his artists . . . he was relentless," Kaye said. Now, that group included Rancid in addition to Social Distortion and the Offspring. "I learned so much. And I realized at that point that there was nothing more important than making sure that the artists you work with are taken care of. . . . He was very well respected and feared."

With that fire came some initial misses. Kaye was hunting for new young bands to sign to Time Bomb. On a tip from a music journalist at *OC Weekly*, she ended up meeting Tony Kanal. At that time, she was told that No Doubt was dormant (though most importantly, still on Interscope), but that he was sitting on the demos for what would become *Tragic Kingdom*. After a lunch meeting, she brought the No Doubt bassist by the Time Bomb offices, and as he was leaving, Kaye told Kanal if things didn't work out with Interscope that they should talk.

"Guerinot said, 'Who was that?'" Kaye said. "'Oh, this is Tony from this band called No Doubt.' He goes, 'I know No Doubt because aren't they on Interscope?' And I said, 'Yeah. But they're not doing anything.' And he goes, 'Stop. Don't ever talk to him again. Don't ever bring him by the office. Just stop, we're not fucking with Interscope.'"

19

RIGHT SOUND, WRONG WAY

fter headlining the SnoCore tour in February 1996, Sublime were ready to record their third full-length album. The trio hunkered down with David Kahne, best known for his Grammy-winning work with Tony Bennett the year before and for producing Fishbone, Paul McCartney, and the Bangles. There, they knocked out four songs that would land on the new album: "What I Got," "April 29, 1992 (Miami)," "Caress Me Down," and the George Gershwin–sampled "Doin' Time."

Although the band was productive, Nowell's out-of-control partying and socializing derailed those sessions. Kahne ended up quitting.

"It didn't bother me in the sense that, 'Oh my God, he's sticking a needle in his arm,'" Gaugh said. "I understood that part of it. But it was just always just disgusting to see it."

Enter Paul Leary.

The Butthole Surfers guitarist may have seemed like an odd fit for the Long Beach bros, but sonically, there was mutual admiration.

Sublime were on a West Coast tour when they first heard the Meat Puppets' *Too High to Die* album. The sound, songs, and production knocked them off their feet. Then they grabbed a copy of the Butt-hole Surfers' *Independent Worm Saloon* and were impressed that they worked with Led Zeppelin's John Paul Jones and loved their recording style, in particular their psychedelic sound.

In Tempe, Arizona, to produce a Meat Puppets album at the time, Leary first heard "Date Rape" when he stumbled upon an AM radio station playing the song while scanning for punk. Whenever he'd tune in to the station, the song was being played. It was inescapable.

"It always cracked me up that they played it so much," Leary said. "After about two weeks of that I was back to the hotel, and the phone rings. It's my agent asking if I'd be interested in working with a band called Sublime, and I was just like, 'Whoa, abso-freakin-lutely!'"

After he listened to a cassette of the four songs Sublime recorded with Kahne, Leary instantly knew Sublime had something big on their hands. At the time, he was confused as to why they wanted to work with him. Soon, he'd find out.

"I got back to them and said, 'You need to stick with this guy. I mean, this stuff is great. And I don't know why you're talking to me,'" he said.

From the beginning, Gaugh wanted to use Leary instead of Kahne, but he said that the label was insistent they use Kahne because he was the hitmaker. Also, Kahne preferred drum loops and samples rather than Gaugh's raw energy. They went back and forth, and then when Kahne quit, the opportunity to use Leary presented itself.

"David doesn't like us," Gaugh said. "He's pretty upset with us and thinks we're just a bunch of fuckups. Paul gets it, and can we just cut this David guy loose? Although, he's turned out some pretty quality recordings. But we really just wanted Paul to be the producer."

When Leary went to Long Beach for preproduction, Nowell

disappeared for a few days. By the time he finally reemerged, Gaugh and Wilson wanted to go surfing in Mexico, leaving the producer stranded and with nothing to do—except to hopefully hang out with a front man who may or may not be present. When they did hang, there was an instant connection. Leary went to Nowell's house and met Troy Dendekker and their son, Jakob. They'd hang and go get tacos, with Leary amazed that Nowell could order in fluent Spanish. During his time in Long Beach, he didn't hear a single note of music, but he got to know Nowell, which would help in the studio.

Despite the topsy-turvy nature of his visit, Leary saw Sublime perform at a local dive.

"It was like being inside a volcano," Leary said. "I sat at the back of the soundboard with Miguel and I could see Bradley's head bobbing around every once in a while, but man, they had the place pumping."

Being in Austin nearly 1,400 miles from Long Beach allowed the band to lock in as much as possible to create something they knew was great. Jon Phillips knew the band had to get out of Long Beach to avoid the distractions. Leary enabled Sublime to succeed by letting them be themselves. He got them to the point where they were comfortable playing, then he'd hit the record button and let them rip.

"The trick was to just wait for the good stuff to flow by and grab it," Leary said. "They deserve all the credit. They have their own sound, their own guitars. Bud was the most unique drummer I'd heard in forever and Eric on the bass is an animal."

"It was the greatest recording experience that I've ever been in," Gaugh said. "Still to this day."

When they got to Austin, and after a day playing at South by Southwest, Leary worked his magic. On "Pawn Shop," Gaugh attributes the drums' fat sound to Leary's direction. The same for the scratches on "Doin' Time."

"I liked watching them go through all their different styles of music, you know, from the punk rock to the reggae and whatever," Leary said. "They just were all over the place and that's what made it so much fun."

Not everything that the band did went smoothly. "Pawn Shop" was a slightly reworked version of the Wailing Souls' "War Deh Round a John Shop."

"All these songs were borrowed. No wonder [our songs] are so good," Gaugh said. "I'd heard that shit before somewhere. They were fucking super pissed. Honestly, we were like, 'We loved your guys' music, and what do they say about flattery? Sorry man.' We gave you the publishing they deserve and told them that we'll record a song for you—Eric and I would put a song together for them."

That was enough to persuade Barrington Levy, Tippa Irie, and Half Pint to jam with the duo. Later, their promise would be honored on a Long Beach Dub Allstars album when they enlisted Irie to perform on "Sensi" and brought him out on a subsequent tour.

Yet, as always with Sublime, the wild card was Nowell. His behavior was increasingly erratic, and his drug use worsened. Having Lou Dog around didn't help.

"I begged them not to bring their dog because the studio said no dogs, the condominium they were staying at said no dogs, and they showed up with all their dogs," Leary said. "Lou Dog completely destroyed one of the studio doors. He just clawed at it until it was pretty shredded up. They crashed the studio car. There was a sauna and one of the guys put the towel over a light bulb and then the next thing you know, the studio is on fire. Then they borrowed a truck from the studio, proceeded to wreck it, and got kicked out of four sets of condominiums they were staying at because of the dog."

That was just the tip of the iceberg.

"There was no reining in Lou Dog," Leary said. "That dog had his own agenda and didn't listen to anybody except for Brad. At the end of the night, there was this almost ritual where Brad would grab Lou Dog by the tail and he plopped his thumb right in the dog's butt and smile at me. He must have done that ten times over the course of the recording. When we were wrapping it up and got to go home, Bradley was sitting on the sofa with Lou Dog sitting next to him, and Brad was jacking him off. I acted like nothing was going on until finally I was like, 'Tell me you're not jacking off Lou Dog,' and he looks at me and goes, 'He really likes it.'" "It may have happened once or twice," Gaugh said with a laugh.

While Gaugh and Wilson drank beer and smoked weed, Nowell took it to another level with his heroin use. Trips to the bathroom were longer and longer, sometimes up to forty-five minutes. Tension was building, with his actions starting to impact the session. It was nerve-wracking for people in the studio and led to fights over concerns for his well-being, including having it out with Leary. Nowell fired Leary and then Phillips for supporting the producer, and then he relented a day later.

"I just couldn't take watching him killing himself anymore," Leary said. "So I sent him home, and he was not happy."

With Happoldt by his side, Nowell left the sessions and headed back to Long Beach. Getting on the flight would prove to be another challenge. Nowell couldn't hide his track marks from flight attendants before Happoldt alertly told them they were from a bad bee sting.

Despite all of the band's external struggles, by the end of the session, Sublime and Leary knew they had created something special. All of the songs hit exactly how they wanted them to, and they saw how far they'd come since sneaking into Cal State Dominguez Hills.

"The songs are jamming," Gaugh said. "And *this* is the sound that we were striving for from the get-go and now finally, we got it."

"One hundred percent of the credit goes to the band," Leary said. "I think anybody could have produced that record. It was extremely fortunate for me, life-changing to get to work with them . . . and what a difference it has made in my life."

By the time Nowell married Troy Dendekker in May 1996, they had already had their son, Jakob, nearly a year earlier. Jakob's birth was the motivation for Nowell to get his using under control.

"I think he was scared for a while and especially after Jakob came along," Gaugh said. "He was more concerned about it."

That worked for a while. After he returned home from Texas, Nowell was drug-sick for several days, and it got to the point where Troy and Jakob went to stay at her family's house. Then was an intervention with his father.

"I couldn't be prouder of your music and all the things that you've done, but at the same time, I'm definitely afraid you're going to kill yourself," Jim Nowell told his son. He knew that no matter what happened when he was performing, the one place his son wasn't safe from drugs was at a music venue.

"I asked him, 'Why the drugs, especially the heroin, why the heroin?'" Jim said. "And he said, 'Well, they expect me to be larger than life and they expect me to do things that they wouldn't necessarily do. I can handle it.' Of course, he couldn't handle it."

Nowell went to rehab and cleaned up for a bit, but the temptation was still very strong. Yet as he got clean, it was the happiest he'd been in some time, and it showed in his performing. Sublime played a show at the House of Blues in Los Angeles, and Jim said it was the best he'd ever heard his son perform.

Sublime had big plans for the rest of 1996. There was a show at the House of Blues on Sunset Boulevard, along with a short West Coast run scheduled in May and June before heading to Europe right after to promote their new album, which was to be self-titled and slated to be released in July.

"I remember he was so proud that he had cleaned up on his own and was doing really good," Gaugh said. "I remember on that last tour, he was like, 'Man, I just want to get high one more time.' He was like, 'We're going to Europe, dude! The fucking album, it's hitting, bro. This is fucking it. We're going to have the fucking time of our lives! Let's fucking go get high one more time. Come on, Bud. Let's go get loaded.' I said, 'Dude, no, no, you know what happens? Three days from now you're going to be fucking buying it every day.'"

Wilson and Gaugh knew it was their time, and they needed Nowell to not just be aware of that, but to stay clean. Initially, he did. They were excited that he was clean because *he* wanted to be clean as opposed to being forced.

The first date of their May 1996 West Coast warm-up run went great. Nearly two thousand people showed up in Chico to see the band play. It was a rowdy, excitable crowd that tore down the fence and overwhelmed the venue's security.

That night at the after-party, Nowell relapsed.

And a few nights later, he was dead.

⁂

Following their show in Petaluma, Sublime had no intention of staying in Sonoma County when San Francisco was about an hour's drive away. By the time they got to town and their crummy room at the Ocean View Motel at 2:00 a.m., everyone was ready to call it, except for Nowell. Sharing a room with Gaugh, Nowell asked him if he was interested in taking a walk on the adjacent beach with him and Lou Dog. Gaugh declined, tired from the evening.

When he woke up the next morning, he found a blue Nowell unconscious and Lou whimpering. He attempted to resuscitate his friend, the same guy who he beat up in a fit of rage out of concern, the same guy who was his musical brother. It didn't work.

By the time the paramedics got there, it was too late. On May 25, 1996, Bradley Nowell died at the age of twenty-eight from a heroin overdose. He and Dendekker had finally tied the knot only a week earlier.

"He had plenty of dope in his backpack," Gaugh said. "He had fuckin' I don't know five, six, seven, eight needles filled up with dope that he got from the promoter. I remember when the police came, they're like, 'Are you sure none of this is yours?'"

Livid at their best friend's death, they considered heading back to find the promoter who gave Nowell the drugs. Knowing that they could have killed him, they didn't go.

After Nowell was laid to rest in Tustin, Gaugh and Wilson knew they had an incredible album they couldn't do anything with. The band's label, Gasoline Alley/MCA, initially wanted Gaugh and Wilson to find a new singer. They immediately shut that notion down.

Sublime was released on July 30, 1996. To their surprise, the album not only did what they expected, it blew up.

"Tragedy sells," Jim Nowell said. "In a lot of ways, that was it. That opened up his music to a lot of people who wouldn't normally be listening to it."

"What I Got" was a massive success. Using Half Pint's "Loving," with the song's blending of Beatles-tinged melody, reggae, and alt-rock, the song hit number one on *Billboard*'s Modern Rock Tracks chart and number twenty-nine on the *Billboard* Hot 100 Airplay chart.

The album's second single, "Santeria," was a smattering of loose grooves and reggae rock. To this day, the song is in rarified air. Regardless of its fairly moderate chart success (top five on *Billboard*'s Modern Rock Tracks chart, number forty-three on the Hot 100 Airplay chart), the song is Sublime's most streamed song. As of spring 2024, it had over 750 million streams, outpacing its closest competitor in the catalog ("What I Got") by 275 million. Turn on alt-rock radio any-where, and the song is likely playing or will soon.

"I don't listen to a lot of radio when driving around," Leary said. "But when I do, 'Santeria' still gets played quite a bit, and it never gets old."

"The fact they made that timeless music in a situation that was less than desirable because of substance abuse and got it done was a mira-cle," Phillips said. "It was a race against the clock. Your superstar has a monkey on his back, and no one knows how to deal with that."

"That was such a masterpiece, man," Brett Gurewitz said. "Bradley really came into his own as a singer and player. Then the guys in the rhythm section are just so heavy in their groove. People don't realize how fucking great that record is. I put it on a level with [Rancid's] . . . *And Out Come the Wolves*, [the Rolling Stones'] *Sticky Fingers*, and [Bruce Springsteen's] *Born to Run*."

Sublime's success remains bittersweet. Nowell wasn't around to see the album take off, and the rhythm section couldn't tour without the singer/guitarist.

"It's impossible to forget him when practically every time I turn on the radio, I hear Sublime," Dendekker said. "So I never want it to be a painful thing."

"My biggest regret is that Jakob will never know him," she contin-ued. "He's turning into a young man, and he'll never know what his dad was like."

PRETTY FLY

By 1996, the Offspring were flying high, literally. Dexter Holland got his pilot's license and bought a plane. After painting the anarchy A on the twin-engine Cessna Citation's tail, he aptly called it Anarchy Airlines.

"I've always wanted to do it. I just like flying airplanes," Holland said. "Some people are into golf, some people are into shooting deer. I'm into flying."

What also happened in 1996 was that the Offspring were starting to have their heads turned by major labels. Despite the initial resistance, majors were knocking on the band's door. In time, the band and Epitaph would hit an impasse on how to move forward.

Epitaph was insistent that the band owed it one more album. The Offspring thought otherwise. In March 1996, the label filed a declaratory relief complaint, which aimed to keep potential major label pursuers at bay.

When the spat went public, the band felt little choice but to defend themselves.

In a letter sent to the Offspring's mailing list, Holland outlined what exactly was going on between the band and the label. The tension between the band and Epitaph came to a head when the band learned that Gurewitz was allegedly seeking suitors to buy Epitaph.

We tried to renegotiate with Brett to do more records on Epitaph starting last March, because we wanted to stay on the label. We had been trying to stay on Epitaph all along, actually. When *Smash* first started getting big in May of '94, Brett approached us and said he wanted to sell the record to a major label in return for a royalty override on it. We convinced him not to do it. In July of '94, when the record started taking off in Europe, he approached us again about selling the record to a major label in Europe. Again, we had to beg him not to. We wanted to stay on Epitaph because they gave us our start, and we like to keep the same people. We have the same booking agent, the same crew, etc.

So we didn't meet with any major labels—not one. Meanwhile, Brett met with all of them. Geffen, Capitol, Sony, you name it, and he met with them. They wanted to buy Epitaph, and he was listening. He told people that he wanted to be the next Richard Branson. Oh yeah, he met with Richard Branson too.

It's important to a lot of the Epitaph bands to be on a label not associated with a major. When we confronted him about selling, he denied it. Finally though, last December, he admitted that he wanted to sell part of the company to "raise capital."

After laying out the things the band didn't do, like *SNL*, *120 Minutes*, and *The Late Show with David Letterman*, Holland said that the band's disagreement was with what Gurewitz did, including him conducting interviews with *Forbes* and *Newsweek*, before outlining the band's negotiation with the label.

> We negotiated for about a year, but couldn't get everything ironed out. It's true that he offered us a great advance and a great royalty rate. But the last contract he sent had some big problems for us. It said we couldn't do cover songs. It said Ron couldn't play in his other band. It said he could use our music on as many compilations as he wanted to. One version of the contract had a clause in it that allowed Brett to take out a life insurance policy on me, so that if I died, he would profit. That's when we realized that this was just about money for him.
>
> He refused to negotiate any more last January, and a week later, he decided to pull the whole offer. To keep it short, he eventually sold our contract to Columbia.
>
> We believed in sticking up for the indie label, and we shouldn't have. We stayed true to Epitaph while Brett met with every major label. Brett says publicly that major labels are bad but, of course, he was in Bad Religion when they signed to Atlantic. He wrote a lot of the songs on Stranger than Fiction that came out on Atlantic. Also, Brett sued us. And, he tried to force us to stay on his label. There was no indie spirit there anymore.

"I think that this sudden success went to my head, I didn't handle it super well," Gurewitz said. "And a lot of stuff happened in that era for me, culminating in a relapse. So I had seven and a half years clean and sober from heroin and crack addiction. I wasn't ready for that level of success."

With the Offspring's runaway success, the label head grew concerned about keeping the entire roster happy.

"I was worried that my other bands like Pennywise and Rancid would feel like they weren't important to me, because the Offspring were so important to me," he said. "We had a tradition at Epitaph of celebrating one hundred thousand record sales with an ice cream cake. A special achievement at our level, right? So I remember we had a party for Pennywise because one of their records hit one hundred thousand when *Smash* was having its astronomical ascent. I remember the Offspring saying, 'Oh, you never got us an ice cream cake' and feeling like I didn't care about them, and they even talked about it in an interview at the time. I'm just trying to make Pennywise not feel like the redheaded stepchild. Of course I loved those guys. They changed my life."

So when the Offspring made the accusations, it hurt Gurewitz, who called them "patently false."

"I never had any intention of selling the company. Ever," he told *Alternative Press* in 1997. "I've been saying that now for nine years.

"I won't ever sell," he continued at the time. "I'm going to run my company until I'm done, then I'm going to turn it off. I might be the first person to do that. If [the Offspring's] excuse for selling out to the man is that they thought I was going to do it first, well, that's pretty silly."

Nearly thirty years later, Gurewitz's stance hasn't changed, but he would have done some things differently.

"I regret that I engaged in the press and we went back and forth," Gurewitz said. "I didn't want much. I just wanted them to do the third record with me. And I think it would have been huge. I think they wanted to have their cake and eat it too. They wanted to go to a major and blame me for it.

"I am grateful for knowing the Offspring and how life-changing our connection to each other has been," Gurewitz said. "It's benefited my life knowing them."

Once they parted ways with Epitaph and joined Columbia Records, the Offspring continued to work on their fourth studio album. Based on the strength of *Smash*, expectations for said album were extraordinarily high.

"Yeah I felt the pressure," Holland told *Alternative Press* in 1997. "I'd write a line and say, 'Does this hold up to the eight-million test?' It can be really overwhelming when you think about it like that, so you just have to try and put it aside. There's a certain point where you have to say, 'This is what we do, and we tried. It's probably not 100 percent brilliant. But this is what we're about, where we are right now.'"

"Lightning struck last time," he continued. "I'm not going to expect to live our lives that way. When we used to play at Greg's house, he used to say, 'Maybe someday we'll get big like the Adolescents.' We said that like it was an unattainable dream. Now we're talking about whether we'll jump off a cliff if we only sell three million records."

As *Maximum Rocknroll* rose to prominence in the late '80s and early '90s, its ultimate punk attitude toward major labels endured. If a band was on a major label, *Maximum Rocknroll* would cease coverage. Famously, the publication (and 924 Gilman Street) turned its back on Green Day and Jawbreaker when they signed with majors. Anything remotely seen as "selling out" within that community damaged a band's reputation among diehards. To that point, when it was first released, *Maximum Rocknroll* gave *Smash* a positive review, something that wasn't lost on the band when the publication eventually turned on them as they started selling millions of albums.

"I'd like to ask *Maximum Rocknroll*: What if their magazine started selling a lot?" drummer Ron Welty said in 1997. "What if their magazine started selling eight million copies without doing anything different? What are they going to do, stop making the magazine? Are they assholes or sellouts? It's the exact same situation."

That stigma of leaving the indie world behind was something that weighed on the Offspring.

"That was a difficult time, for sure," Holland said. "It was weird as far as changing labels. At that time, it was a big deal when you went to a major label. It was kind of like, 'Are those guys sell outs?' There was a real stigma attached to it. We were genuinely concerned about it because we tried to stay true to the indie spirit. The fact is no matter what we did, it was probably going to be perceived as a sophomore slump. At the time though, it was like 'Gosh, I hope it goes over.'"

Internally, the Offspring tempered expectations for their fourth album. They knew they struck platinum with *Smash*, and by breaking every possible indie sales record, the guys were aware lightning wasn't likely to strike twice. That said, they also wanted this album to be its own body of work and not *Smash: The Sequel*. They wanted to expand the Offspring sound, and every album since their self-titled debut did just that. Self-released, indie, or major label wouldn't derail the trajectory of album four.

"I'm really glad we did because we set the stage to do lots of stuff later on," Holland said. "Now, it's sort of become a fan favorite since then, and I mean this in a positive way, but we [want] to do our *Pinkerton* now."

By *Pinkerton*, he's referring to Weezer's 1996 sophomore album that was maligned when it was initially released. In fact, it was so derided that Weezer went on hiatus for four years, and singer Rivers Cuomo ended up leaving LA to attend Harvard.

The Offspring had no such tough luck. Released on February 4, 1997, *Ixnay on the Hombre* was a success—just not to *Smash* levels. The album was recorded between June and October 1996 in

Hollywood with Dave Jerden producing. The album was not close to *Smash* in sound or album sales. It sold a million copies in the initial run, which paled in comparison.

When the tour began, the Offspring finally came to terms with the fact that this punk rock thing might just work out for them.

The album's first single, "All I Want," was a straight-ahead punk ripper. The song clocked in at just under two minutes and peaked at number thirteen on *Billboard*'s Modern Rock Tracks chart. The next single, "Gone Away," had a different fate. The song was heavier both lyrically and instrumentally. It stems from an incident that took place at a Baskin-Robbins in Huntington Beach where Holland and his then-wife were getting ice cream. Then, several shots were fired at the shop, causing patrons to take cover.

"The idea that we came so close to death was a real life-changing moment," Holland said on *The Bob Lefsetz Podcast* in 2021. "It was right when we were recording *Ixnay*, and I was coming up with the idea. I knew I wanted it to be heavy, but I didn't know what it was going to be about yet. I know it's not a direct connection, but it made you think about dying and about grief and about what that would feel like, and what if my wife would have been the one?"

"Gone Away" was a hit. It was the band's first number-one single, topping *Billboard*'s Hot Mainstream Rock Tracks, and peaked at number four on the Hot Modern Rock Tracks chart. The song remains a staple in the band's setlist, with Holland performing the song solo in a pensive manner.

The album did well enough, and more importantly to the band, it didn't tank. The reviews were lukewarm, but the Offspring spent most of 1997 on the road in support of *Ixnay*, which served as a solid transitional album. More importantly, though, it showed the band that they had a sustainable future in music and there was no turning back.

"I realized, OK, it's been three years since I left, and I can't go back to being a janitor," Noodles explained. "If I did, I'd have to start at the bottom rung."

Little did they know what was to happen next.

✕✕✕✕✕✕

After wrapping the *Ixnay* tour in December 1997, the Offspring got back to work almost immediately. The band was back in the studio with Dave Jerden in July 1998 and stayed there through September.

As Holland composed the lyrics, he noticed that things were darker in America than it may have seemed. On the surface, everything was flying high. The economy was booming, and things seemed generally okay. But as the idea for the album coalesced, Holland took a look around and didn't necessarily like what he saw. In this case, that meant a satirical look at posers, wannabes, a seemingly aimless generation drifting along, cultural touchstones like the wildly popular daytime tabloid talk show *The Jerry Springer Show*, and political correctness. The theme of discontent was present in Holland's lyrics.

The band went on to title the album *Americana*.

"The songs on *Americana* aren't condemnations, they're short stories about the state of things and what we see going on around us," Holland told *SFGate* around the time of the album's release. "We want to expose the darker side of our culture. It may look like an episode of *Happy Days* out there in America, but it feels more like *Twin Peaks*."

His discontent was present throughout the album's thirteen tracks. Some songs, like "Pay the Man," had origins in the *Ixnay* sessions. As they experimented with *Ixnay*'s "Mota," the Offspring incorporated Latin sounds on *Americana*.

The band's biggest hit was a novelty song, or at least that was the intent.

"It's really inspired by wannabe gangsters," Holland said. "Guys who go to malls and get the gangsta rap clothes. Guys on *Ricki Lake* who won't listen to their moms."

"Pretty Fly (For a White Guy)" was *Americana*'s first single. It was unlike anything the Offspring had released. Holland's work and time hanging out with the Vandals during *Hitler Bad, Vandals Good* was evident. Opening with the German gibberish that Def Leppard used on "Rock of Ages," which cost the band $10,000 to use, the song ridiculed wannabes who became immersed in hip-hop culture not because of serious engagement with the music but because it made them seem tough and attracted women.

The types Holland is taking aim at, he told *SPIN* in 1998, "are from, like, Omaha, Nebraska, regular white-bread boys, but who act like they're from Compton. It's so fake and obvious that they're trying to have an identity."

Much of Holland's scorn wasn't at hip-hop and rap. Instead, he targeted the rising tide of boy bands that were ascending. It was obvious in the band's music video for the song.

The video—starring Israeli actor Guy Cohen, who beat out Seth Green for the main role, and directed by rising director McG—sees the main character cruising around town in a lowrider before trying to impress Black and Latino people who shake their heads at him. He then ends up breakdancing and gets tossed in the pool at a party. The video concludes with Cohen's character scaring his fairy costume–wearing sister with his appearance.

"I'm sure lots of people see the video and go, 'Dang, that guy's cool.' I was watching MTV, and one of the NSYNC guys had the same Fubu jersey I wore in the video," Cohen said. "The Offspring didn't even realize it, but we were making fun of the biggest teeny-bopper group there is."

"That's kind of the beauty: making fun of people who don't know they're being made fun of," Holland said.

The band was criticized in some quarters for their rockist stance. *SPIN* called "Pretty Fly (For a White Guy)" the "great premillennial Disco Sucks song."

In Orange County, the song was instantly ubiquitous and caught on in high schools.

"Every year they had a talent show where people did dances and skits to like popular songs," singer/songwriter Andrew McMahon said of his band's performance at Dana Hills High School in South County. "We did 'Pretty Fly (For a White Guy)' with my math teacher. It was part of what you would consider a quintessential sort of Orange County late '90s playlist."

As for the album itself, the reviews weren't great.

The A.V. Club said *Americana* was "a record bad enough to create a backlash against not only pop-punk, but also novelty songs, guitars, smug thirtysomethings, and the human race." *NME* called it "straight-forward, brainless thug-punk," while the *Los Angeles Times* criticized the lyrics, saying, "Creeping suburban ennui, adolescent angst and girl trouble remain familiar targets for the Orange County outfit's heavy-duty sarcasm," and the band couldn't "match its inciteful musical attack with a more insightful sense of purpose."

In one of the few positive reviews, *Entertainment Weekly* wrote that the Offspring "sound as volatile as ever, spewing riffs on complicated '90s chicks ("She's Got Issues") and pathetic wannabes ("Pretty Fly [For a White Guy])." Robert Christgau of the *Village Voice* wrote in his favorable review that "while keeping it light keeps them on the right side of their frat-boy base, it also makes the fuckups they mock and mourn seem all the more hurtful."

Not that audiences cared. The album peaked at number two on the *Billboard* 200 and sold nearly two hundred thousand copies in its first week. *Americana* remains the Offspring's highest charting album.

In addition to "Pretty Fly (For a White Guy)," the album spawned two additional monster singles with the Beatles-tinged "Why Don't You Get a Job?" that tackled a couple arguing over employment and "The Kids Aren't Alright," a song inspired by Holland driving around Garden Grove and seeing people he knew had lives that didn't turn out so great. Featuring a driving guitar riff, the song is widely considered one of the band's best.

When "Weird Al" Yankovic released his version of "Pretty Fly (For a White Guy)" called "Pretty Fly (For a Rabbi)," it earned the band respect in surprising quarters.

"All of a sudden my daughter was like, 'Wow, Dad! You're in a real band!'" Noodles said.

"'Weird Al' put us over the edge," Holland said. "Isn't life weird?"

Even with their fame and cultural relevance as influential as ever, the Offspring never lost track of who they were.

"As far as the bands who got big, they're just top dudes," Fat Mike said.

In the '90s ska had become ubiquitous—from the radio, to record sales, moves, and TV. But it wasn't the two-tone sound emanating from the music of mods from working-class England. Refracted through the prism of SoCal, the color of the genre exploded from black-and-white checkers, shades, and skinny ties into a full-blown candy-colored rainbow of horns, spiky hair, and outlandish outfits. The fast chords and DIY ethos of punk combined with brass into something positively infectious that would eventually be labeled as ska-punk or third-wave ska.

Just like their punk predecessors before them, the kids of the '90s OC ska scene were in the crosshairs of a movement that kicked off in the right place at the right time.

To this day, most people refer to ska music as "fast reggae"—but in reality the sound of ska predates reggae music, though both originate from the same place, and ska is undoubtedly the grandfather of the music most often assigned to Jamaica. It's the sound that slowed down and became labeled as rock steady, which slowed down into reggae.

Ska began in Kingston, Jamaica, at the end of the 1950s when the sound of Mento, the homegrown music of the island, comingled with jazz and American R&B to create a gumbo of syncopated "riddims" and bright tempos that made it stand out. The new sounds brought waves of joy and danceable vibes to Jamaican clubs like Foresters Hall, Chocomo Lawn, and Jubilee Tile Gardens. Whether they were outdoors or on hot, shabby dance floors, Kingston DJs, called sound operators, hosted parties for a few shillings with bass pumping from handmade speaker boxes that rattled with sound and could be heard from miles around. The vibrations wafted through the hot island air, mixing with the smell of brown stew chicken, ackee, and saltfish.

Early Jamaican bands like the Skatalites idolized the jazz legends of their day such as Lester Young, John Coltrane, and Charlie Parker. The song structure merged with tempos that landed on the second and fourth beat to bring together a bubbling, infectious groove.

The dancehall gatherings attracted packed crowds of young lovers and friends who danced all night to the music of Laurel Aitken, Derrick Morgan, Prince Buster, Desmond Dekker, Jimmy Cliff, and Bob Marley. Behind the scenes, sound system operators recorded these upcoming artists with house bands full of horn players and rhythm sections who would sweat and play all day inside ramshackle studios to earn a living. With the music they recorded, operators would use the taped recordings in their live sets to spark movement on the dance floor at nightclubs where they would preside over the party. A lot of operators would battle each other in the clubs for the biggest crowds in sonic skirmishes called "clashes."

Competition was often fierce between sound systems—the groups and recording engineers who made the music crowds loved. The shade-wearing, sharply dressed crews that did the battling were known as "rude boys," who often flexed their power by breaking needles from the turntables of rival sound systems and starting fights that could clear out a party in minutes.

But how did this music and culture make its way to America? It arrived via an indirect route, mostly through the migration of Jamaican people who took their music with them to the UK when they came searching for work and opportunity, landing in places like Brixton, Notting Hill, and Coventry. Ska became the soundtrack to parties all over England. It was only a matter of time before songs like "My Boy Lollipop," "007 (Shanty Town)," and "One Step Beyond" began to resonate with the white working-class youth. Gradually these kids combined their love of punk and soul with reggae and ska to create their own version of the music they called 2-Tone. The name was born from a label of the same name founded by Jerry Dammers of the Specials. From 1979 to 1984, this evolution of ska became one of the most popular sounds of England's youth. This ska movement sounded different from its Jamaican predecessor—it was fast, frenetic, and eclectic in a way no other music could quite capture. Bands like the Specials, the Selecter, the Beat, Madness, and Bad Manners soon topped the UK charts with songs that drove at the political climate and inequities of the time. The multiracial lineups were a physical manifestation of unity that expanded beyond England into America, taking hold in the cities first and then the suburbs—especially in Southern California.

For many, the zaniness of third-wave ska was the ideal pendulum swing away from the heavy melancholy of grunge that permeated the airwaves. The ska scene had a certain amount of angst merging with fun and irony. Many people were tired of the heavy drone of grunge or the hairspray and testosterone of arena rock. Finally, people were getting hip to the subculture of the ska scene.

In the mid-'90s the ska scene was largely a collage of DIY shows where bands would rent out halls or pop up in random places where a PA and stage could get quickly assembled and torn down. The scene thrived on all-ages shows pushing a youth-driven audience that was there for a shared energy that had nothing to do with the beer sales that made most traditional clubs their money.

Going to ska shows was a unique experience, and audiences dressed up for the shows just like in the UK and Jamaica with distinct old-school looks and band shirts. Bands dressed in three-piece suits and sweated through the fabric in the packed clubs.

The sound provided a place onstage for the once highly derided band geeks to suddenly fit into a scene that was bubbling up and gaining popularity. The eclectic mix of horns and distortion fostered countless talented bands with OC roots, including The O.C. Supertones, Jeffries Fan Club, and the Pharmaceutical Bandits (later known as the RX Bandits) to name a few. Places like Cloud 9 and Studio K at Knott's Berry Farm in Buena Park, the Galaxy Theater in Santa Ana, Music City in Westminster, and Side By Side skating rink in Huntington Beach were among the ska-friendly hubs.

You could wear whatever you wanted, and there were no rules—all outfits welcome, especially costumes. In Huntington Beach, a band called the Aquabats took the sentiment to new super heroic heights. Their spandex outfits were fashioned by a friend of the band's who worked at a wetsuit company.

Formed in 1994 by singer Christian Jacobs, bassist Chad Larson, and trumpeter Boyd Terry, who were in other bands at the time, the

Aquabats started as a joke, literally. With the scene taking off and being brought to the world, they thought everyone in the Orange County punk circles was taking themselves too seriously. Having grown up going to punk shows in LA and OC, Jacobs said that the band was inspired to do something different than what was going on, which was so regimented and structured. Also, seeing bands like Hepcat and their fans dancing, being friendly, and smiling showed him that punk didn't have to be aggressive as long as it went against the grain.

"We were influenced by bands like Devo and bands from the '60s that wore costumes," Jacobs said. "At the time when we came up with the costume idea, superheroes were super dorky. We were like, 'What could be the most kind of offensive thing to that?' The whole superhero costume thing was just kind of punk. We were trying to be punk *to* the punk scene. It was like what's the most nerdy thing we can be right now? Making fun of superheroes was like, our way of being punk."

And that it was.

They decided to use superhero monikers: Jacobs was The MC Bat Commander, Larson was Crash McLarson, and Terry was Catboy. They didn't give up their other bands. Instead, they viewed being in the Aquabats, now an eight-piece ska band, as a "weekend gig."

The group was on the receiving end of hecklers when they'd play at the Showcase Theatre, Cafe Obey in Yorba Linda, or the Ice House in Fullerton. "We could get shows going because the initial impression of us was that this wasn't threatening," Jacobs said. "But we were all misfits in our own way."

They'd play with "harder" bands like Sublime, HFL, WhiteKaps, and the Vandals, and their fans weren't feeling what the Aquabats were giving them, from the look to the sound.

"People were *mad*," Jacobs said. "We'd come out in our costumes and people would spit at us. I'm like, OK, right! This is what punk is supposed to be: eliciting a reaction. When you're in a room with every-one dressing the same way, you're supposed to flip it upside down."

Like their fellow Huntington Beach brethren the Vandals, the Aquabats were making fun of what they saw and were having fun doing so.

Within a year, Goldenvoice took notice of Orange County's superhe-roes. After a show, Paul Tollett approached the band and asked if they'd be interested in recording an album for Goldenvoice's new record label.

"To me, it was someone believing in us beyond being like, 'This is silly and stupid,'" Jacobs said. "He said, 'You guys have something and it's something special. And I want to put it out.' It was getting a bless-ing from the pope and gave us a purpose and we didn't want to let Paul down."

Over the years, the Aquabats achieved mild success among a core group of diehard fans. Famously, though, at the time of Tollett's inquiry in 1997, the band had just brought in a new drummer: Travis Barker. It was the budding musician's third band after playing in Snot and Feeble, the latter of which is how he connected with Larson. After playing with the Aquabats for a few years, Barker was tapped by Blink-182 to replace Scott Raynor in 1998. He's been in the same position ever since.

The Aquabats went on to play the Warped Tour and released their second album on Goldenvoice/Time Bomb Recordings.

As the years went on, respect for this cast of outsiders grew. In time, families would show up to their shows and let their kids crowd-surf on inflatable pizza slices, and they even won over other bands, like H2O, who understood what the Aquabats stood for.

"I hope that we could be inspirational to other people in the punk scene to be like, you don't have to wear a uniform," Jacobs said. "You don't have to be the cool guy. You don't have to be the toughest guy, do you know what I mean? Just be you and have fun."

It doesn't get more punk than that.

✖✖✖✖✖✖

Born to a Moroccan mother and Jewish father, Monique Powell had a love for music at a young age. When she was eleven, she knew she wanted to be a singer and already had a voice teacher. Her older sister was into bands like Devo, David Bowie, the Specials, Depeche Mode, and the Sex Pistols, and their sense of fashion stuck out.

As a student at Pacifica High School in Garden Grove, Powell's operatic leanings and her punk influences were often in conflict. "Being in the drug scene and yet being in musical theater, there was always a push and pull for me," she said.

Eventually, that would see her attend Cal State Fullerton and take opera classes. Yet to Powell, playing music always felt like a realistic path forward, and opera wasn't it. Her high school classmates were already out on the town playing shows and making waves in the scene. One such band? Reel Big Fish.

"I was already exposed to Reel Big Fish and I saw it at their first show," she said. "Aaron Barrett wasn't even singing, there was a female guitar player."

All of the bands in the emerging OC ska scene were very close. In particular, Powell was close with her high school classmate, Reel Big Fish's Scott Klopfenstein.

Reel Big Fish formed in 1991, initially as a cover band. By 1992, they shifted gears and released a demo of originals. Though the lineup was different, by the mid-'90s Barrett took over for Ben Guzman as the band's singer, and their sound leaned heavier into ska.

By 1995, things started to take off. That year, Reel Big Fish self-released their debut album, the twenty-one-track *Everything Sucks*. Through word of mouth and aided by their upbeat live show in which they treated performing for fourteen people as if it were fourteen thousand, the album took off. The band caught the attention of Mojo Records and inked a deal with the label.

They opened for Cherry Poppin' Daddies on their two-month US tour. It gave the band a tough portrait of what life on the road was like when they weren't playing for their audience.

"We were getting booed a lot," Klopfenstein said. "We weren't punk enough for the punk kids. We weren't ska enough for the ska kids."

Making $400 per month, the band had to learn the ins and outs of a national tour on a shoestring budget. Until the unexpected happened.

Everyone on the tour gathered in a hotel room while at Penn State University in August 1996, where they watched their first single off their second album, *Turn the Radio Off*, debut on MTV. It was "Sell Out," with its infectious blast of ska-punk.

"We were like, 'Did that really just happen?'" Klopfenstein said. "Like, that's weird. We're in a hotel room. It's a strange environment and a strange thing with kind of strange people."

What was weird turned surreal. A week later, their tour manager told them the order of the bill had to change, and now they were the headliner. To the band's surprise, on the strength of "Sell Out," which eventually peaked at number ten on *Billboard*'s Modern Rock chart, fans were coming to the shows now for them and left after they played, which wasn't optimal as the opener.

"These were guys [ahead of them on the bill] who were in their late twenties and early thirties, and we were barely in our twenties!" Klopfenstein said. "We felt so bad but I still don't comprehend how it happened. Like we did this dumb thing, I mean the song makes very little constructive sense, which is how we worked back then. There's no rhyme or reason why it worked and it still baffles me to this day."

With so many members in the band at one time, inevitably, the number of internal fights outnumbered the number of hits. Over the years, members would cycle in and out.

Yet the band always played with urgency, knowing that as a ska band, their popularity could vanish in an instant. Reel Big Fish would play major radio events like HFStival in Washington, DC, in 1997. There, Klopfenstein remembers hanging out with Debbie Harry of Blondie and Duran Duran singer Simon Le Bon. Reel Big Fish toured with Blondie and appeared on a Duran Duran tribute album, so hanging out wasn't *too* out of the norm, but when he saw a photo of the three of them in *Rolling Stone*, he was shocked.

"The fact that we got invited to the party at all was unbelievable," Klopfenstein said. "I'm like, 'What am I doing here?' I do not understand.'"

What worked for Reel Big Fish was that they never saw themselves as anything other than just a bunch of misfits who should not have been invited to the dance. But when they were there, they had the best time they could. And in the process, they helped further the third wave of ska.

✕✕✕✕✕✕

Monique Powell started getting into bands like Long Beach's Suburban Rhythm, and her taste expanded into ska. Not too long after, Powell's friends were putting a band together called Larry and wanted her to join.

That band would split, as would her next band, the Shanties. Then in 1995, Powell started singing in Save Ferris. The band was composed of Powell and members of various other groups.

The group's humble beginnings saw them play house parties and local venues, powered by Powell's high-octane vocals. Save Ferris's live show instantly became a hit. As the word spread, the band got a much-needed boost. KROQ's Rodney Bingenheimer got ahold of the band's self-released album. He played "Come On Eileen" on his *Rodney on the ROQ* program, and the response was overwhelming. Soon thereafter, it was added to the legendary taste-making rock station's rotation. All of this happened independently without a record label and with Powell serving as the singer and band manager, with her phone number listed on Save Ferris's demo tape.

Having been on her own since she was seventeen, Save Ferris became Powell's family.

"I loved this band and I loved everyone in it so much," she said. "They were my family. They were my friends. They were my everything. And I really wanted to be that person because I felt like I cared immensely about every single one of them. They didn't feel the same; I didn't know that at the time. I found that out later on."

In 1996, Save Ferris released their debut EP, *Introducing Save Ferris*, which they sold mostly out of the back of their cars. In less than a year, the collection sold in the low five figures on the strength of KROQ's endorsement.

"I had to pull my car over and have a cry because I thought, 'I can't believe that we're on this station that I've been listening to since I was little,'" said Powell.

Major labels started noticing the buzz that was emanating from Orange County. In 1996, the band won a Grammy Showcase award for the best unsigned band, and with Epic Records' David Massey as one of the judges, Save Ferris signed with the label. Epic would rerelease the *Introducing Save Ferris* EP as a full-length titled *It Means Everything* in 1997. Songs from that record were on TV shows, films, and trailers. The band also appeared in HBO's music series *Reverb* and the 1999 film *10 Things I Hate About You*.

The band's rapid success put eyes on them, and for the singer, it was also unwanted attention as the in-your-face front woman.

"I stood out like a sore fucking thumb when it came down to being able to understand where they were coming from," Powell said of the scene. "These people go to church every Sunday. Women play a certain role in life. It's just that it was the environment that we came from. I look back on it and see how fucked it was. I made a lot of enemies being in the band. I've always just kind of been outspoken. I was a little raunchy and had a sexual sense of humor. But it just wasn't culturally acceptable at that time."

No Doubt was a little bit older and although they played shows with them, Save Ferris couldn't escape their shadow. Even when they played big shows, like LA's Palace Theatre in December 1997, they couldn't escape the No Doubt comparisons.

"At that time, girl bands weren't encouraged to play with each other," Powell said. "So neither promoters, agents, nor management would want us ever to play with another female onstage. And I remember if I would see two women like two female-fronted bands on the same bill, I would be like, 'Wow, I haven't seen that before.' We were not encouraged to be friends with other women, like it was a competition against each other."

Not to mention that once the third wave of ska started landing on the airwaves, the Orange County bands had to go to LA to showcase for the labels and music business folks up there. The irony for the ska bands was that they wanted to be successful without the support of the LA music machine.

"We were just lucky to have this weird sound of a bunch of weirdos from these beach towns that didn't feel like we fit in anywhere," Klopfenstein said.

✖✖✖✖✖✖

Following *Tragic Kingdom*'s initial success, No Doubt was enlisted to open for Bush on their spring 1996 tour in support of their breakthrough album, *Sixteen Stone*. The tour, which also featured the Goo Goo Dolls opening, crisscrossed the US as the bands played college campuses and small arenas. No Doubt brought their explosive live show that saw them win over skeptical punks in Long Beach and Anaheim to the world.

What was also notable amid the synergy tied to the band's concurrent rise was that Stefani and Bush singer Gavin Rossdale fell for each other. The pair first met at the annual KROQ Almost Acoustic Christmas concert show in 1995.

As No Doubt became headliners, the band returned the favor to those they used to open for in their nascent days. They had the Vandals and even Face to Face open on the *Tragic Kingdom* tour. The tour continued for two and a half years, with the band playing in arenas all over the world.

Just like the Offspring experienced a year and a half earlier, No Doubt's members' lives were upended.

"It was awesome and awkward at the same time," Young said. "It was awkward to have that drastic lifestyle change. Not just some things—everything changed."

Suddenly, after being perceived by outsiders as a cultural wasteland, Orange County was at the forefront of popular culture. The Offspring were on tour for two-plus years, and No Doubt did the same, circling the globe three times before wrapping in 1997. By the end of the cycle, No Doubt sold over fifteen million records worldwide and landed cover stories in *SPIN* and *Rolling Stone* ("The only shows in town," Young quipped). Stefani's unique sense of style, which included designing her own clothes, turned her into a fashion innovator, something that wasn't in the cards three years earlier.

"We were one of those bands that was always trying to be realistic," Young said. "Even if you do have a great song that could be a hit, the chances of that thing getting pushed by a label or getting a label to sign you or getting radio stations to play it . . . there's so many hurdles and that bottleneck of people. We were aware of that and with basic math, we never expected to have a hit song, nevertheless what we had."

In 1997, No Doubt and *Tragic Kingdom* were nominated for Grammys in the Best New Artist and Best Rock Album categories. They didn't take home any awards, but the Recording Academy was put on notice.

That same year, No Doubt released a cover of the Vandals' "Oi to the World" as part of the Special Olympics benefit album *A Very Special Christmas 3*. Produced by Warren Fitzgerald, the song was accompanied by a music video and was another hit.

"Seeing Gwen sing your song, and then it goes on to sell millions," Joe Escalante said of the song he wrote off the Vandals' Christmas album of the same name, which was released in 1996.

No Doubt closed out the *Tragic Kingdom* tour just down the street from where it all started. Instead of a dingy club, they sold out the Arrowhead Pond, where the NHL's Anaheim Ducks played.

"At the end of the day, it's still that Orange County connection," Kanal said. "It was really important to play shows at the Pond when we were finishing our *Tragic Kingdom* tour. It was pretty epic."

After a break following twenty-eight months on the road, in 1998 No Doubt got to work again with a new manager: Jim Guerinot. "We liked that he got where we came from," Young said. "It was easy to have a conversation with him."

"He came in at a really important time for us," Kanal said. "He was well known in the Orange County circles, and obviously, well known everywhere. But there was that real OC connection and he managed bands that we respected. He was a pivotal part of the next few years of the band."

Now, with debatably the most recognizable young female pop-rock star on the planet, expectations were high for the band's fourth studio album. For the first time, the band wrote and recorded as a quartet.

Influenced by bands such as the Cure, No Doubt's sound evolved, and they had collaboratively written forty songs. Following *Tragic Kingdom*, the safe move would have been for the band to recreate that album. But when they sat down to start writing, the songs weren't flowing so easily. The band decamped to Kanal's newly rented house in the Hollywood Hills to write. Initially, No Doubt planned on working with Matthew Wilder again, but creative differences stopped things before they started. The band eventually enlisted Glen Ballard to produce the album.

"We had something to prove to ourselves on that album," Kanal said. "We wanted to dig a little deeper as musicians and songwriters and do something different than *Tragic Kingdom*, something not expected."

Instead of being just a girl, Stefani's perspective shifted. As she wrote, Stefani tackled topics such as relationships (specifically her long-distance one with Rossdale), family, resentment, loneliness, and indecision.

"Anyone who knows me knows having a family has always been the most important thing to me," Stefani said at the time. "I wanted to be a mother—which is an unconditional giving of love—and a supportive wife, and suddenly, I can't even be a good girlfriend, because I can't seem to find the right time to call. I want to do it all, but I can only do one thing good, and right now I've chosen to do this. Being in a band is a bit of a selfish choice."

Released on April 11, 2000, *Return of Saturn* left *Tragic Kingdom* in the past. In just over an hour with fourteen songs, No Doubt reinvented themselves.

"I actually liked *Return of Saturn* even more," Young said.

"I'm so proud of that record," Kanal said. "That one has become like a real fan favorite."

The album's first single, "Ex-Girlfriend," an uptempo number where Stefani rapped and featured a flamenco lick combined with elements of new wave, was vastly different from *Tragic Kingdom*'s biggest singles.

The reviews for *Return to Saturn* were mostly positive. *Rolling Stone* said the album was "a superstar follow-up that not only betters its predecessor but also radically departs from it." Stephen Thomas Erlewine of *AllMusic* agreed, writing that the album was "a terrific, layered record that exceeds any expectations set by *Tragic Kingdom*."

Despite not exceeding *Tragic Kingdom*'s sales, *Return to Saturn* set No Doubt up for the rest of their career. The eclectic sound and willingness to experiment would serve them well in the years to come.

"Because of where we went as songwriters and as musicians pushing ourselves to different places, I think those songs really connected," Kanal said.

No Doubt's connection to where they came from is still strong. Despite their fame and in some cases moving up the freeway to LA, the band hasn't forgotten where they've come from.

"My parents still live in Orange County so I'm there every other week, hanging out with them," Kanal said. "I'm always driving through our old stomping grounds, and I take my kids to Disneyland and we'll drive by my parents' old house on Harbor Boulevard, where we rehearsed back in '87, maybe '88. There's always going to be that connection to Orange County."

21

THE END

In 1998 Social Distortion released *Live at the Roxy*, which was recorded over a five-night stand at the famed Sunset Strip venue. Featuring songs from their nearly twenty-year career, Ness wanted the album to have the feel of a classic bootleg recording that properly captured the band's performance.

After returning home from Europe, Danell was excited to spend time with his growing family. But, as he found out, being away from a newborn during his first few months could be taxing.

"When he came home, Duke didn't recognize him. He was terrified of him," Christy Danell-Walker said. "It was heartbreaking. Dennis was super exhausted from being on tour. I wouldn't say depressed, but he was just very sad at the reaction his kid gave him. Finally, things changed and Duke never left his side as he got older."

At that point, Danell mulled over his future as a father and how to balance that with Social Distortion.

"I can't speak for him, but he had to think about how he was going to make a choice [between his family and the band] or how he was going to balance it," she continued. "He couldn't walk away from the people that he loves, meaning the band, Mike, Jim, and their crew. That's been his life since he was sixteen years old. That would have been almost impossible to ask of him. And I wasn't asking it of him."

Following the *White Light* run, Social Distortion went on another hiatus.

For as long as the band was around, Ness was its creative driving force. But he was ready to put out music that reflected the formative records he grew up with and steadily fused into Social Distortion through the previous decade. In addition to producing a few songs with pop-punk group Wank, Ness decided it was time to release new material under his name.

Incorporating classic country, blues, rockabilly, and folk, Ness released his first solo album in April 1999. Titled *Cheating at Solitaire*, the album featured covers of Bob Dylan's "Don't Think Twice, It's All Right," "Long Black Veil," and Hank Williams's "You Win Again," along with two *White Light, White Heat, White Trash* songs written in 1994, "Dope Fiend Blues" and "I'm in Love with My Car."

The album was produced by James Saez, who was an engineer on *Live at the Roxy*.

"I hadn't heard from Mike for a while," Saez said. "But then I got a call and he was going to produce this other artist, an alt-country guy, and I got asked to engineer it."

Saez wound up coproducing the album, and during the sessions, they discussed what would eventually become *Cheating at Solitaire*.

"Doing the solo record allowed him to do like a million things that I think he really wanted to do," Saez said. "Like he really wanted to play some acoustic guitar and have pedal steel."

The album also featured guest spots from Bruce Springsteen, Brian

Setzer, and members of Royal Crown Revue. Ness invited Johnny Cash to sing guest vocals on "Ballad of a Lonely Man," but he was unable to due to illness. Later that year, Ness would release *Under the Influences*, a covers album featuring songs by the likes of Hank Williams, Marty Robbins, and Carl Perkins. There's a reworked, twangy version of "Ball and Chain."

"A lot of it was that I wanted to show people I could do other things," Ness said of his solo endeavors.

Ness's tour would take him all over, including to one of the most notorious festivals in music history.

Along with the Offspring, Ness played at Woodstock '99. The Offspring's set, coming on the heels of *Americana*'s continued rise, was one of the most anticipated of the weekend. Performing on the East Stage, the festival's main stage, the Offspring pulled out all the stops. They were joined by Guy Cohen, the actor in the "Pretty Fly (For a White Guy) video," for this version of the song. However, things were marred when Holland got hit by a water bottle thrown from the crowd. It set the tone for what became a tumultuous weekend.

Unlike the Offspring, Ness had a fairly mundane set. Performing early in the day, Ness ran through a mix of originals and covers before heading out before the mayhem ensued later that night that only got worse as the festival progressed as more aggressive acts took the stage, including Metallica, Korn, Limp Bizkit, Rage Against the Machine, and Red Hot Chili Peppers. By day three, the festival had exploded into a hellscape, full of out-of-control bonfires, looting, bloody violence, and multiple reports of sexual harassment and rape, making it one of the most disastrous events in live music history.

While Ness and the Offspring were spreading the Orange County sound to the world, back home, something was happening in one of the least likely places: South County.

In Dana Point, a group of high school students started jamming together. Punk wasn't on their mind, unlike their predecessors who helped change the culture. Led by Andrew McMahon, a bespectacled piano player and singer, Something Corporate formed in September 1998 after his band, Left Here, which won the Dana Hills Battle of the Bands, broke up. McMahon, drummer Brian Ireland, and bassist Kevin "Clutch" Page teamed with guitarists Josh Partington and Reuben Hernandez (who would later be replaced by William Tell). They were collectively influenced by Ben Folds Five, Bad Religion, the Offspring, Blink-182, Sublime ("They were ubiquitous in our world"), Unwritten Law, Counting Crows, and emerging emo bands like the Get Up Kids, Knapsack, and Jimmy Eat World. Something Corporate may not have been punk in the traditional sense, but they were one of the first bands to meld their influences into the new pop-punk scene.

Something Corporate's piano-driven sound connected with the group's friends first, then their classmates. McMahon's lyrics reflected the issues that directly influenced the daily lives of him and his peers.

"We were just suburban kids with pretty stock suburban sort of problems, like falling in love and driving around with your friends," McMahon said. "We were kids singing to kids and we were talking about things that weren't bullshit. We were writing songs in earnest."

The group got their start playing backyard parties. Why? Because they were too young to play shows at Orange County's notable music establishments. They got their break by playing the nearby Coach House in San Juan Capistrano and the Galaxy Theatre (they would record their debut album at both venues). Something Corporate opened for Better Than Ezra and played with Newport Beach pop-rockers Sugar Ray.

Once the band realized they had gone as far as they could go at those venues, they ultimately started playing at local all-ages music staple Chain Reaction, a club originally owned by Tim Hill, formerly

known as Public Storage. Something Corporate's shows at the Anaheim venue would be what finally got them out of more mainstream
channels to connect with the punk scene. The club's booker, Jon Halp-
erin, knew the band could sell out the House of Blues (they were the
first local band to sell it out), but convinced them to play there in order
to connect with the wider Orange County music scene. Not that it
didn't have its own set of challenges.

Ahead of a show at the Doll Hut, a friend's stepfather, who wanted
to manage the emerging band, loaded them and their gear into the back
of a U-Haul. However, upon arrival, things didn't go according to plan.

"We get there and they weren't going to let us play because we were
seventeen and eighteen," McMahon said. "They were like, 'This is a bar,
you can't play here!' Somehow, he convinced them to let us play to the
three people who were there."

Something Corporate eventually played the Warped Tour in 2002
and drew big crowds. Yet there were days when they'd be pelted with
bottles of urine and were flipped off.

"We were always the odd band out," McMahon said. "Stage managers were beating guys up backstage who tried to do rough things to
us during the sets. I was so grateful for this adversarial role between
my band and the audience. I learned how to work a crowd, how to win
a crowd, how to stand up to hecklers. Things that I would never in a
million years have learned or signed up for.

"We ended up in a scene that we never thought would adopt us."

※※※※

As for Danell, when Ness decided to go solo, his life took a turn—in a
good way. With a toddler at home and time off from Social Distortion,
Danell started working in real estate at the behest of his father-in-law,
who had moved to Newport Beach to open a sandwich shop.

"When I first met Dennis and took him to meet my parents, my dad said, 'So what are you going to do if this music thing doesn't work out?'" Christy Danell-Walker said. "And he said, 'I'll be the oldest blues singer in a bar that you've ever seen but I'll be happy' or something like that. But when he was off tour, my dad said, 'You've got the gift for the gab and you're an entertainer, why don't you just get your real estate license?' I was mortified by the whole idea of it."

Not conforming to the typical real estate agent look, Danell would wear a V-neck sweater over a T-shirt with khakis and rocked blue-lens aviator sunglasses. Naturally, the real estate agents in the area said he'd never make it. Just like the many who doubted Danell, Ness, and Social Distortion, they were wrong.

To the surprise of no one who knew him, the affable guitarist suddenly struck gold.

At his first listing, where he was assisting the listing agent, Danell, sitting on a couch with his feet up on the coffee table reading *Surfer* magazine, sold the house that afternoon.

"He was just very genuine," Danell-Walker said. "I think people read that with him and just knew he wasn't bullshit. He was just being himself."

"He was actually making more money on real estate than he was off the band!" Ness said.

And he was right. In just a few years, Danell sold over eight figures' worth of real estate. He was a natural. Despite his success, he was torn over whether to take on real estate full-time. He loved playing in Social Distortion, but with a growing family, which included a newborn daughter, Danell was seriously considering what his next steps were.

Then tragedy struck.

While his family was out, on Leap Day 2000, Danell was moving a dining room chair to his car when he told his neighbors he didn't feel well. He instantly hit the ground, and by the time paramedics and his family arrived, he was dead at the age of thirty-eight.

Initially, doctors at Hoag Hospital said Danell died of a brain aneurysm, which was the official word in a press release. It was put out a few hours after Danell's death so there would be no speculation as to what happened. Six months later, the true cause of death was revealed.

"I had an extensive forensic autopsy done, because of course everyone wanted to say that it was an accidental overdose or a suicide," Danell-Walker said. "What it was was idiopathic dilated cardiomyopathy. By the look of the muscle in his heart, it appeared as though it was virally infected.

"While he was in Eastern Europe and Asia on tour he had gotten sick about a year and a half before," she continued. "This forensic coroner specialist said instead of the virus settling in his stomach or his intestines, it settled in his heart. So, he literally had a massive cardiac arrest."

"I am saddened beyond any possible form of expression," Ness said at the time. "Dennis and I have been friends since boyhood, starting Social Distortion while we were in high school."

Looking back at Danell's sudden death isn't any easier.

"It was gnarly because even though we had our own separate social lives when he died, I realized that he was my longest friend that was still in my life," Ness said.

Following Danell's death, Ness contemplated ending Social Distortion, unsure of how the band could move forward without his closest friend.

"It's a debate you have with yourself in your own mind," Ness said. "In the middle of that debate, it was like, 'Nah, dude. Like, we started this.' If it was the other way around, and I was the one who died, I'd want him to carry that ball as far as he could take it. It gave me a new purpose. I wanted to carry this on in honor of him and his memory. And then I wrote 'Don't Take Me for Granted' in literally five minutes. I had the music, but all I had to do was just close my eyes, grab a few visuals of his and my life together."

"Mike asked me at some point, 'Do you want us to break up the band?'" Danell-Walker said. "I think he was just asking for my opinion. And I said, 'No, because that would break Dennis's heart. This was his baby. This was his first marriage. And if it can go on, then it should.' But it was hard."

The first order of business was setting up a tribute show in Danell's memory. With Guerinot working his magic ("He pulled that trick out of his hat," Danell-Walker said) and Avalon Attractions producing it, the show took place two and a half months later at Irvine Meadows Amphitheatre on May 8, 2000. The show featured sets from the Offspring, X, Pennywise, T.S.O.L., Agent Orange, Punk Rock Karaoke, Rockstar Barbeque, Strung Gurus, and in their first performance in a few years, Social Distortion. All the proceeds from the event went to Danell's family.

"It felt good from the support angle that so many bands wanted to be a part of it, and so many fans attended it," Ness said of the show. "If he was looking at it, he's like, 'Wow, these people came here for me.'"

The six-hour show kicked off somberly and was celebratory and emotional.

"I think it was cathartic for a lot of those people to participate," Danell-Walker said. "They came from different tours just to work on that show."

Naturally, the show was befitting of both Danell's legacy and Orange County itself. Jack Grisham sold his box on eBay ("I had no fucking money!" he insists, explaining his decision to do so) while during Pennywise's set, permanent seats were ripped out and thrown all over the lower area after guitarist Fletcher Dragge barked at security guards for attempting to keep fans in their assigned ticketed seats. Normally, each row would have cost $10,000, with the show promoter having to write a check. On this day, Pennywise covered the cost.

"I was standing on the side of the stage with Exene and she's like, there goes ten grand," Danell-Walker said. "I could hardly say anything because they're putting on this benefit concert for us. But, the guys in Pennywise stepped up, which I thought was cool."

During X's set, Exene Cervenka summed up the feeling of the bands. "I'm happy and sad to be here."

The Offspring went deep into their catalog to play early rippers like "Beheaded" along with their big hits from *Americana*.

The reunited Grisham-era T.S.O.L. stampeded through one of their first shows without Todd Barnes, who died in 1999 at the age of thirty-four from a brain aneurysm, something that Grisham noted onstage. "While we're remembering Dennis today, let's also remember all the punks that died who didn't get a benefit concert," he said.

Having substituted for Danell when he was on paternity leave, Jonny Wickersham was named as his replacement. It was a position he took seriously, and he understood the pressure he was under to replace the band's longtime rhythm guitar player.

Emotions were high when Ness, Maurer, Biscuits, and Wickersham closed out the day. Before the band took the stage, a nervous Wickersham was sitting on the back steps by the stage by himself. There, he was spotted and consoled by Christy.

"She looked at me and said, 'I bet you have the weight of the world on your shoulders today,' or something like that," Wickersham said. "It just cut right through everything because that was her basically saying, 'Fuck, I know how you must feel.' She's grieving her husband and she's able to take one look at me and realize that I was probably tripping. That was so nice and so fucking cool."

"That poor guy has never been put into easy situations, that's for sure," Danell-Walker said. "He's also one of those guys that is super genuine and super kind."

Ness opened Social Distortion's headlining set by performing "When the Angels Sing" acoustically before tearing into Social Distortion classics.

It wouldn't have been an Orange County punk rock show if everything worked perfectly. In fitting fashion, Wickersham had trouble with his gear, and emotions ran high.

"I was just trying to keep it together," Wickersham said of the show.

By the time Social Distortion closed out the show with a raucous version of "Ring of Fire," it capped off a day that was a fitting tribute to one of the scene's most beloved figures.

"This show ain't about the money," Ness said during the set. "It's dedicated to the memory of someone who set out twenty years ago with me to change things. I'm gonna miss him."

EPILOGUE

It's going to be a high school reunion out there," Mike Ness said of the No Values festival. Taking place on June 8, 2024, at the Fairplex in Pomona and promoted by Goldenvoice, Ness was right. The mega show featured not just Social Distortion in a headlining slot with the original Misfits, but many of his Orange County punk coconspirators.

The Adolescents, Agent Orange, T.S.O.L., the Vandals, and the Aquabats were just some of the bands featured on the bill that also included Iggy Pop, Turnstile, and Bad Religion. It was the perfect festival-sized coda in a year that saw so many of the bands on this bill reuniting or taking the stage with their classic lineups.

"Dennis would have loved to have been a part of this . . . same with Brent [Liles, who died in January 2007 after he was hit by a truck while riding his bike]," Ness said of his late bandmates.

First things first. Before Ness could get to Pomona, something implausible happened in the city where he and Danell grew up roaming the streets and raising hell. On April 3, 2024, on Ness's sixty-second birthday, he was presented with the key to the city of Fullerton. Yes,

EPILOGUE

Mike Ness, the former Punk of the Month at the Fullerton Police Department who'd spend just as much time there as he would rehearsing, was honored as a city dignitary. The Mike Ness who was lucky to make it to twenty-three. This day in Fullerton was declared Mike Ness Day.

"I found the whole thing to be ludicrous," Guerinot joked. "I said to him that there wasn't a day that went by in Fullerton where he did not commit an illegal activity."

"If you would have said that in 1983 he was getting the key to the city, Mike would have been like that's way too corporate like no," Christy Danell-Walker said. "I don't think he would have taken it."

For Ness, the honor came at a time when he was getting back on his feet. While Social Distortion was recording the band's first album since 2011 at Sunset Sound in Los Angeles in 2023, he felt discomfort in his throat. In June of that year, Ness revealed that he was diagnosed with tonsil cancer.

"In the midst of pre-production, I was diagnosed with stage one tonsil cancer," Ness said in a statement. "I was feeling well enough to continue with recording in the studio up until the very day before surgery. The band and I were so inspired and excited to lay down these tracks."

Over the next year, he had surgery, received radiation, and underwent a six-week chemotherapy treatment. By March 2024, he was all clear. Receiving the key to the city on his birthday had extra meaning with the battles of the previous year behind him.

The ceremony, which took place in downtown Fullerton, saw Ness praised by Mayor Nick Dunlap, who told the assembled crowd that he grew up listening to Social Distortion (imagine telling Ness the mayor of Fullerton listened to his music forty years ago?), and Ness had "the classic 'rags to riches' tale, only it's not fiction."

"Beyond our love for music is our love for our community," Mayor

Dunlap said. "That's what brings us here today because we are able to celebrate a living legend who is among our greatest exports to the world, right there with the Fender Stratocaster."

In speaking with the Social Distortion front man several weeks before he was honored, Mayor Dunlop said Ness said "how great it was to grow up in Fullerton and how our city helped shaped him, his outlook, and the band."

The honor wasn't lost on Ness. When he accepted the key to the city and spoke on a warm Wednesday afternoon to the raucous crowd of old-school punks, friends, and families, with most wearing Social Distortion shirts or Mike Ness Day merch sold by the city, he couldn't help but look back at his formative years with a sly grin.

The assembled guests included Ness's family, current Social Distortion members, and Guerinot.

No Values wasn't the only Goldenvoice-produced festival to bring back classic bands from the scene. Sublime played their first proper shows as a unit (Wilson and Gaugh briefly used the name with Rome Ramirez in 2009 before changing to Sublime with Rome following a settlement with the Nowell estate) at Coachella with Nowell's son, Jakob, on guitar and vocals and Eric Wilson and Bud Gaugh back as the rhythm section. Although there were big plans in store for Sublime ahead of the release of their self-titled album, Bradley Nowell never got to experience them and the success of the album following his death.

In the summer of 2023, Wilson was recording with old friend Paul Leary when the *Sublime* producer suggested they ring up Gaugh to play drums on the track they were working on. After speaking with Greg "Mudd" Lowther, Gaugh found out that Wilson was ready to leave Sublime with Rome behind and was working with their old friend Escalante.

"I was done with that chapter of my life," Wilson said of leaving Sublime with Rome. "So I reached out to Joe."

Later that year, Wilson received a call about playing a benefit for Bad Brains front man H.R., and he suggested to Gaugh that Jakob should join them for the show.

"He [Wilson] said H.R. wasn't doing so well and we're gonna do this benefit show for him," Gaugh said. "'I think it would be really cool if you, me, and Jake do it.' So Eric's transitioning from Sublime with Rome at this point. So, we all got together and jammed it out to see if it could work.

"I closed my eyes and it was like going back to the late '80s and early '90s in Brad's dad's garage," the drummer continued. "Relearning all these songs all over again was great, and it had a little edge on it because Eric and I already know him. It was eerily familiar to that point and time in my life. After the first couple of songs, it was surreal: a lot of emotions, a lot of anticipation and anxiety. With Eric, it was like riding a bike. His father trained us how to play so it was like, alright, let's do this. Pop open a beer and here we go. It was reminiscent of the early days."

"People had been talking about it for a while," Wilson said of the reunion. "It was the best timing in the world."

After those jam sessions, the trio knew they had chemistry and it could be special. Beyond the public debut of the younger Nowell in his father's position, their December performance at the benefit was the first time Wilson and Gaugh played together live since 2011.

Now, what was intended as a one-off has grown into something much bigger. The group reunited with Nowell and announced a slate of festival dates, beginning at Coachella in Indio, California.

"If Eric wants to do Sublime with Bud, and they want me to sing in the band, I felt like I had this custodial duty to pay my respect and homage," Nowell said.

EPILOGUE

"The way that everything is just falling together . . . it's just our brother up there working some miracles," Gaugh said.

Nowell's son fronting the band is something all three take seriously, and they can't help but point out that they're getting extra help from the great beyond.

"He is definitely up there pulling strings because you can feel him talking about rehearsals. It's like he's right there with us. There's not a day that goes by where I don't think about him. How can I? Everywhere I go, there's a song on the radio or at the store or somebody's house and a car when you're driving."

"Brad would be very proud of his son, that's for sure," Wilson said.

Sitting in their artist trailer at Coachella, Wilson and Gaugh beamed at the thought of playing in front of ninety thousand attendees. Nodding to Brad, the pair reflected on their legacy.

"We always thought we were the best band in the world," Gaugh said. "It was just a matter of convincing everybody else."

Now, they had the opportunity to finally prove it.

Their performance at dusk was eagerly anticipated, and like all things Sublime, the set could have gone either way.

Anticipation was in the air the day before the band's Saturday set. Longtime Sublime fan Lana Del Rey performed her cover of "Doin' Time" (which originally featured Wilson on bass) for the first time in four years. There were a number of people wearing Sublime T-shirts in the crowd too.

As for the set itself, it wasn't a mess or transcendent. Following a video montage that attempted to reintroduce a band that needed little introduction, the trio launched into "April 29, 1992 (Miami)" in front of a supportive crowd of sixty thousand with Wilson and Gaugh in lockstep. It allowed Nowell to find his way while channeling his father's spirit. After a bit of a slow start, things kicked into another gear during "Wrong Way," which also introduced the day's first mosh pit. As the trio rolled through Sublime hits (wailing with a cover of Bob Marley and the Wailers' "Jailhouse" and playing "Romeo" for the first time since 1988), old feelings were evoked along with a warm sense of nostalgia.

By the time the set closed with "Santeria," the most streamed song by far in their catalog, there was a strong sense of satisfaction. The band was relieved that their first major show went smoothly ("I love you, Dad," Nowell said before looking above), while the audience was pleased to see this version of Sublime.

"We owe this all to the fans," Gaugh said. "It's the fans that kept it alive. We put in the hard work, we did it and then got our magic carpet yanked out from underneath at 10,000 feet."

But now, with a group of friends and family from Long Beach working with them, like Trey Pangborn of the Falling Idols playing on guitar ("We used to go and see him play in junior high school in high school," Gaugh said), Sublime is excited about the next chapter and what it has in store.

In addition to Sublime being unearthed (in Joe Escalante's words), No Doubt reunited for their first show since 2015 at America's most influential festival.

It had been years since the estranged band had been together, but according to *Billboard*, the band was offered $10 million to put their differences aside. Coachella has loads of its own production, but No Doubt brought in their own bells and whistles.

"It's like preparing for a full-production tour for just two shows," Young said. "But everyone is a little older and the muscles are a little more sore. I've had wrist surgery and rotator cuff problems. I'm kind of a broken down middle-aged man [*laughs*]."

Even so, No Doubt's future is very much up in the air. Stefani and her bandmates had been estranged for years before the surprise reunion. She performed solo and has been a host on the NBC program *The Voice*. Kanal, Dumont, and Young stuck together. They occasionally played No Doubt music together at one-off shows and formed Dreamcar with AFI singer Davey Havok in 2017.

"[Coachella is] going to be a really nice bow to tie on the relationship, because we were kids [when we met]," Stefani told *Nylon* in 2024.

As recently as the end of 2023, No Doubt seemed dead like it would never reform. Stefani didn't speak with her bandmates; they played charity shows under the moniker Tom, Tony, and Adrian.

After Coachella, No Doubt's future is unclear. Stefani released a solo album in November 2024 and Dreamcar reunited for a show at Goldenvoice's Cruel World goth festival, and both parties are noncommittal.

"Well, I don't have a crystal ball," she said. "Most things have surprised me in life. One of the things I've learned is to be present in the moment and try to absorb what's happening around me instead of looking ahead."

According to Stefani, the group never fully worked through the issues that plagued them and insinuated that they should have gone to band therapy.

"No, no, we need to, probably," Stefani told *Nylon* ahead of the reunion. "But we have a lot of water under the bridge."

It didn't affect the band's spirits ahead of their Coachella sets. In the buildup, the rehearsals went smoothly, and things were back as they were.

"The vibes and rehearsals have been awesome," Kanal said. "When I get up there, I think there's some part of me that thinks I'm still sixteen. The energy has been incredible at rehearsals and I can't wait for people to see the show we put together."

Once it was showtime, all of the hard feelings that built up in recent years appeared to go away.

The eighty-minute set was drenched in nostalgia. Many of the backing visuals related to Orange County, and videos from the band's younger days were shown during the set. The set also featured an appearance by Gen Z superstar Olivia Rodrigo. She traded vocals with Stefani during "Bathwater" off *Return to Saturn* while wearing an "I Love ND" tank top.

"I remember hearing bathwater for the first time when I had just started writing songs," Rodrigo wrote on Instagram the next day. "It totally turned my world on its head and inspires me to this day. was the coolest honor to sing it with @nodoubt and @gwenstefani this weekend at @coachella !!!! they're out of this world!!!!"

And it helped present why No Doubt is one of the most popular bands. The set touched on nearly every big single across the band's six studio albums. Even the rarities portion—which included "Different People," performed for the first time since 2009, and "Total Hate '95," which hadn't been played since 2012, left the crowd beaming.

"There was such a real excitement from all four of us that we were open to going back and doing some of those older songs," Kanal said of the setlists. "Doing the album versions and the original versions, which was rad!"

Yet, it was the band's powerhouse trio of singles from *Tragic Kingdom* that elicited the biggest reaction and closed out the set. Dumont's riffs still power it, but "Just a Girl" is now a major female empowerment anthem, which Stefani said feels "more relevant now than it's ever been," alluding to the ongoing fight for women's rights in today's America.

"I have no words," Kanal said of the shows. "What a surreal couple of weeks for us. It was just incredible."

Of the two Coachella shows, Kanal said that there was an underlying reason for the group to reform without any commitment to future shows: to celebrate the band's time together with their respective families.

"One of the big motivating factors was that we wanted our kids to see us play," Kanal said. "And that was important to see all the kids hanging out together.

"I was sixteen when the band started," he continued. "And I feel like I'm sixteen when I get onstage again. And I think that's a beautiful way to approach it. In a way, that same energy is palpable. When you watch those videos [of the band's earlier years], I think it has stayed with us in spirit throughout our thirty-seven years."

The crowd size and subsequent media and social media reaction overwhelmed the band.

"It became apparent this is so much bigger than the sum of its parts, like the way the music has affected people," Kanal said. "It's so multigenerational now—they're bringing their kids, or their kids are coming, and it's just so rewarding and beyond our wildest dreams."

The same goes for the Offspring. The band continued to soldier on after the peak of *Americana* and its follow-up, 2000's *Conspiracy of One*, which spawned a hit with "Want You Bad." Though it isn't as acclaimed as its predecessors, *Conspiracy of One* is an album that has endured. So much so that during their May 2024 appearance at the BottleRock festival in Napa, the Offspring invited a surprise guest and longtime fan to join them onstage for "Million Miles Away": British pop singer Ed Sheeran. Following the set, Sheeran showed the band that he had a tattoo of the *Conspiracy of One* logo.

The following week, on June 1, 2024, the Offspring played *Smash* to honor the album's thirtieth anniversary at a packed Honda Center in Anaheim with Save Ferris opening. Monique Powell led the latest incarnation of Save Ferris through a high-energy set that fired up the crowd before Dexter Holland, Noodles, and company went onstage.

When the Offspring took the stage, with a giant skeleton behind the drum riser that replicated their landmark 1994 album, they ripped through *Smash*, playing the album nearly in full.

"They reminded us a few months ago that we put out this record called *Smash* like, thirty years ago," Holland said to the crowd.

"It seems like just yesterday, right?" Noodles said in response.

"And they told us we should put on a show to celebrate it," Holland said.

"And we said fuck yeah we should!" Noodles said as the crowd erupted.

"This is the only show we're doing, we gotta do it for Orange County," Holland said.

"Southern California's our fucking home! . . . We want tonight to be a family night, we know you brought your families . . . and if there's one thing we know about kids, it's that they love their curse words, am I right?" Noodles said before his famous swearing part in "Bad Habit."

Before bringing Blackball up for his line in "Come Out and Play," Holland marveled at the band's longevity.

"It's crazy that after thirty years we're still playing punk rock music," he said before saying that he knew some people there who were born after the album was released. Then Noodles turned to the group's current drummer, Brandon Pertzborn, and said, "I know Brandon our drummer wasn't born yet, he actually was born in the same year *Smash* came out just a couple months later—he was born learning how to play these songs!"

Ending the evening's first set with "Self Esteem," Holland and Noodles took a moment to admire the crowd and take in what they've accomplished since their unlikely breakthrough.

"I don't want this night to end, we're having too much fun," Noodles said.

"Thank you for coming out to watch us play, this has really been very special for us," Holland said to the crowd. "It really means a lot for you guys to join us here to play this record thirty years later. Thank you guys!"

EPILOGUE

As Ness said, No Values was a punk rock high school reunion, and at the same time, a tip of the cap to Goldenvoice's storied history . . . in more ways than one.

Taking place at the Fairplex in Pomona, the punk rock mega event was marred by dysfunction. Fans waited hours in their cars to make the 1.9-mile trek from the 10 freeway to the Fairplex's parking lot. *OC Music News* host and former KROQ DJ Jimmy Alvarez said it took him nearly five and a half hours to get into the festival grounds. Basically, it felt like a Goldenvoice show from 1983.

Once inside, the five-stage festival was a fitting tribute to what Goldenvoice built in its forty-three years. Backstage, Jim Guerinot and Paul Tollett were hanging out. As were members of the Falling Idols and Sublime, with No Doubt's Adrian Young chatting with the Vandals' Warren Fitzgerald in the artist lounge and Brett Gurewitz rubbing elbows with Joe Escalante (who on June 23, 2024, was inducted into Los Alamitos's Hall of Fame). Christian Jacobs of the Aquabats was hopping between stages to take in the action after his band's early afternoon set. As was Gary Tovar, in his trademark white T-shirt during the day and hooded sweatshirt at night, a presence on the side of every single stage.

"I normally don't really like festivals, but this was fun," Ness said.

The Adolescents and Aquabats dazzled with early sets.

For the Adolescents, the ongoing success of and appreciation without one of their founding members Steve Soto has been bittersweet. On July 27, 2018, the OC punk pioneer and one of its greatest ambassadors around the world died at home in his sleep at the age of fifty-four. Soto's death appeared to be the result of his decades-long struggle with poor health, a battle with his weight, and congestive heart failure. His passing sent shockwaves through the music world, inspiring major bands like Blink 182, Green Day, and his OC comrades the Offspring to pour out their sorrow on social media. It made headlines in *Rolling Stone, Billboard,* the *New York Post,* and publications around the world—even FOX News covered it. After his death, Brad Logan of Leftover Crack and F-Minus, has dutifully filled in on bass.

As a player and songwriter, Soto was unmatched and to this day his legacy remains larger than life. "He only lived fifty-four years, which in the big picture isn't a ton," Agnew says. "But those fifty-four years were packed to the hilt, and he lived them exactly the way he wanted to. Someone could live to ninety years old and only live a third of what he lived."

As this timely celebration of SoCal punk raged on, the many spirits of OC legends line Dennis Danell who presided over the fest smiled down on it from beyond, having left this mortal coil far too soon. OC legends like Gabby Gaborno of the Cadillac Tramps who passed a year earlier than Soto in 2017, Mike Atta who died in 2014 (followed a decade later by his brother and bandmate Jeff who passed in 2024), Frank Ruffino of China White who died in 2013, T.S.O.L. drummer Todd Barnes who passed in 1999 and so many others whose sparks of innovation and hell-raising artistry left a mark on the music they loved.

During Agent Orange's afternoon set, they were joined by Jello Biafra, who was DJing earlier in the day, to perform Dead Kennedys' "Police Truck."

"Now this is what it's like when worlds collide: I went to watch Agent Orange (one of the first punk bands I gravitated towards) at No Values Fest and they brought out a surprise guest to perform a Dead Kennedys classic: Jello Biafra sang Police Truck. Never thought I'd see JB sing another DK song, especially one from THPS. Unreal festival, and a moment I'll never forget. Let's ride!" Tony Hawk wrote after witnessing the moment.

During their midafternoon set, the Vandals stampeded through songs across their catalog, mixing "Urban Struggle" and "Anarchy Burger" with "Pizza Tran" and "My Girlfriend's Dead." For fans, seeing Josh Freese behind the kit was a welcome surprise. Thirty-three years after Freese joined the Vandals, Escalante's assessment of the drummer was correct. Today, Freese is the drummer with Foo Fighters as his primary job. However, days before the Foos were set to conquer Europe yet again, Freese made sure to step back behind the kit for the band that unleashed his talents.

"This is the best," the Vandals' Warren Fitzgerald said of the festival. "I've run into people I haven't seen in ten years. It has a very timeless element to it."

Quickly after putting his bass down, Escalante had to shift into his new role: comanaging Sublime. There, Gaugh previewed the band's set, which was vastly different from their Coachella triumph. Proving that no Sublime show was ever the same, the band plowed through mostly deep cuts from their punk and hardcore background. In fact, the only radio songs that they played were set opener "Date Rape," "Wrong Way," and the last-minute addition, "Santeria."

Though the punk rock star power at No Values was immense, the lineup assembled by live music juggernaut Goldenvoice could never have come together without bands like T.S.O.L. that laid the foundation for its founder, Gary Tovar, who was beaming on the side of the stage watching Jack Grisham and company coming out swinging, whipping up a mosh pit in the late afternoon sun to "Sounds of Laughter." Decked out in suits and shades, the band of veteran punkers including original guitarist Ron Emory and keyboardist Greg Kuehn definitely meant business, just as they did back in 1980—albeit with more polish these days and less chance that one of them would commit a crime after the show.

In January, Grisham and T.S.O.L. were back onstage for a sold-out crowd at the Observatory. Also introduced by Tovar, the band plowed through a career-spanning set that included an emotional cameo from bassist Mike Roche, who hadn't been seen performing with the band in quite some time due to Parkinson's disease.

Sitting back in his trailer after the sweltering thirteen-song set that ended with their eternal necrophilic anthem, "Code Blue," Emory reminisced about the early days of the SoCal punk scene that gave life to Goldenvoice and this festival that drew tens of thousands to the fairgrounds more than forty years after the first pissed-off chords were played in their native Huntington Beach. After joking about Grisham—who was caught in the festival's unforgiving traffic, necessitating a ride to the backstage area and leaving immediately after the band's set—Emory took stock of the band's legacy.

"That time period in the late '70s in Orange County, you could go out every night of the week and see some great bands," Emory said. "Later on in 1981–82, thanks to Gary Tovar laundering his drug money, he brought all these phenomenal bands on one show. And Jerry Roach from the Cuckoo's Nest was bringing in a lot of great bands also. I remember back then we were just stoked to play there, sold out the Nest at least twenty times and every time we made twenty-five dollars—and we were stoked, we couldn't believe we got paid to do this!"

Ahead of Social Distortion taking the stage to perform in their headlining slot on the Mission Boulevard stage, Ness was warming up on the side, hopping up and down like a boxer ready to make his way into the ring for a heavyweight bout. As excited as he was in the months building up to the era-defining show, Ness and Social Distortion were ready to roll. The band's spring coheadlining tour with Bad Religion had sharpened the band into form, and Social Distortion only needed to run through one practice to nail down their current set ahead of the show.

With the lineup of drummer Dave Hidalgo Jr., bassist Brent Harding, Jonny Wickersham (who coincidentally performed less than sixteen hours later with his fellow surviving members of Cadillac Tramps), and Ness, they couldn't help but be moved by what they saw: forty-thousand-plus people cheering and paying tribute to what was built over the past forty-five years.

Sprinkling in early songs like "1945," "The Creeps," and "Mommy's Little Monster" (ahead of which Ness reminded the crowd the song was written when he and his fellow punks roamed the streets of OC and LA doing things their way), as well as hits like "Ball and Chain," "I Was Wrong," and "Story of My Life" and a couple of new tracks, Social Distortion showed not only are they still going strong, but somehow, some way, they're continuing to resonate with audiences across all generations.

During the middle of "Reach for the Sky," a song off 2004's *Sex, Love and Rock 'n' Roll* where Ness sang about living for the moment and making it last, Ness paused, lifted his guitar up, and took a long look into the crowd. There, he saw it all, from the sixteen-year-old grappler to the sixty-three-year-old grizzled punk lifer, all in one moment. It was the manifestation of a journey that will live long in the annals of punk and rock history.

Not bad for a kid from the wrong side of the Fullerton tracks.

ACKNOWLEDGMENTS

David Dunton, our agent, and Ben Schafer, our editor, for having faith in this project and our vision. Lauren Mele and Shane Trulin for believing in this when it was just a hopeful idea.

Everyone we spoke with who offered insight, shared stories, and made the scene what it was, and those admired from afar, we couldn't have done it without you.

Jim Guerinot for being ready, able, and willing to speak on a moment's notice, and being the Google of all things OC music.

Bud Gaugh for the Reno hangs, seeing the big picture, and being so generous with your time.

Christy Danell-Walker for being so open about something that's still impossible to comprehend all these years later.

Frank Agnew for being the early punk documentarian with a steel trap memory and a heart of gold.

Mike Ness for summarizing the scene and Orange County in a way only you can, and for being the living embodiment of Orange County punk through the peaks and valleys while continuing to be its avatar.

The Rock and Roll Hall of Fame for being so helpful as a resource for research.

To Randy Lewis and the late Mike Boehm, two intrepid reporters who covered punk rock music for the *Los Angeles Times* and gave it the coverage and voice it deserved when everyone else had written it off.

To *OC Weekly*, its legacy of *desmadre* lives on and will never go away. Viva la Weekly!

DANIEL KOHN

To my family: Mom and Dad, Arlan and Barbara, Jon and Jackie, Alex and Brandon, Sean and Katy, and Seth and Casey.

Nate: Somehow, some way, we did it. The *years* of plotting and scheming, the ups and the middle and disappointments, we got through it without our drive ever faltering. 350, 500, 750, 1200. We're there. Amazing as it is. The bond and spirit are unbreakable. There's no one else I would have wanted to take this journey with.

Richard Bienstock: the intros and words of wisdom are greatly and forever appreciated.

Dylan: someday this will all resonate, but you are wise beyond your years. Your understanding that the weekends away for years were necessary and your faith in your father will never be forgotten.

Carly: Our family's rock. You'd been pushing Nate and me and cheering us on in the background for years. Now we have something to show for it. The sacrifices you made as a de facto single parent while we pursued this, and the grace with which you handled the past five years, humble and amaze me. Your support and love mean everything. I couldn't have done it without you. I love you.

NATE JACKSON

To my wife, Diana, for always seeing the vision and being the best partner in life I could ever ask for. You gave every ounce of support I needed to make this book a reality. I love you forever.

ACKNOWLEDGMENTS

To my parents, Elena and Carl, and sisters, Jill, Jordan, and Taylor—thank you for all your love and support even when times were hard. I love you all very much. Dad, even though you left the Earth just before I got to finish the book, I know you're up in heaven cheering me on.

To all my chosen family—life-long friends and bandmates who've been with me at various times in my journey as both a musician and a writer and introduced me to great music and inspired me to keep pushing no matter what, I couldn't have done without you or the OC music scene that raised me. Special thanks to Richard Johnson, aka "Dick Slaughter," the wildest punk rock cabbie/photographer OC has ever known for the wisdom, ball-busting and killer photos documenting the making of with this book.

To Sunny, there's literally no better dog on the planet. Thanks for keeping Diana company while I was barricading myself in my office to bang this thing out.

To Dan, holy shit, my man. We actually did it! Thanks for being the absolute best partner on this amazing journey. The story of making this thing is one for the books. Still feeling like this is only the beginning . . .

BIBLIOGRAPHY

955KLOS. "The Vandals In-Studio with Jonesy." YouTube, May 20, 2019. https://www.youtube.com/watch?v=V6s59bwbpDk.

Abraham, Damian. "Bill Stevenson Is Back." Apple Podcasts, *Turned Out a Punk*, April 12, 2024. https://podcasts.apple.com/gr/podcast/bill-stevenson-is-back/id940288964?i=1000652285078.

Berlyant, Matthew. "Social Distortion Mommy's Little Monster (40th Anniversary Reissue)." *Under the Radar*, December 22, 2023. https://www.undertheradarmag.com/reviews/mommys_little_monster_40th_anniversary_reissue_social_distortion.

Bienstock, Richard. "The Offspring's 'Smash': The Little Punk LP That Defeated the Majors." *Rolling Stone*, April 8, 2014. https://www.rollingstone.com/music/music-news/the-offsprings-smash-the-little-punk-lp-that-defeated-the-majors-189742/.

Blabbermouth. "The Offspring's Noodles on 30th Anniversary of 'Smash' Album: 'The Songs, to Me, Are Timeless.'" BLABBERMOUTH.NET, March 14, 2024. https://blabbermouth.net/news/the-offsprings-noodles-on-30th-anniversary-of-smash-album-the-songs-to-me-are-timeless.

Blairing Out Show. "T.S.O.L.'s Jack Grisham Talks W Eric Blair. May, 2001." YouTube, July 30, 2016. https://www.youtube.com/watch?v=SCX-8Fjk6ns.

Boehm, Mike. "Banding Together: Rockers Plan Benefit to Pay Legal Bills of Gary Tovar, the Man Who Helped Build Them Up and Bail Them Out." *Los Angeles Times*, June 25, 1992. https://www.latimes.com/archives/la-xpm-1992-06-25-ca-1477-story.html.

———. "Cadillac Tramps Picking Up Speed: Homespun Rock Band, No Stranger to the Gritty Side of Life, Develops Avid Following." *Los Angeles Times*, June 8, 1991. https://www.latimes.com/archives/la-xpm-1991-06-08-ca-335-story.html.

———. "Essential Albums, '78–98." *Los Angeles Times*, December 31, 1998. http://articles.latimes.com/1998/dec/31/entertainment/ca-59113.

———. "Following the Same, Reliable Tracks." *Los Angeles Times*, February 14, 1992. https://www.latimes.com/archives/la-xpm-1992-02-14-ca-2023-story.html.

———. "Looking Back on the Darkest Days." *Los Angeles Times*, April 8, 1990. https://latimes.com/archives/la-xpm-1990-04-08-ca-1648-story.html.

———. "O.C. Record Producer Dies at 39: Obituary: At His Fullerton Studio, Charles (Chaz) Ramirez Had Engineered Much of the Local Sound of the '80s." *Los Angeles Times*, December 5, 1992. https://www.latimes.com/archives/la-xpm-1992-12-05-ca-1198-story.html.

———. "Offspring Lifted Key Guitar Riff, Publisher Says: Pop Music: Manager Denies 'Come Out and Play' Arabian Hook Is Agent Orange Creation." *Los Angeles Times*, April 4, 1995. https://www.latimes.com/archives/la-xpm-1995-04-04-ca-50818-story.html.

Bose, Lilledeshan. "Bradley Nowell: Feb. 22, 1968–May 25, 1996." *OC Weekly*, May 19, 2011. https://www.ocweekly.com/bradley-nowell-feb-22-1968-may-25-1996-6417432/.

———. "Sublime vs. No Doubt? Manager/Producer Miguel Happoldt Says 'No Doubt Was Like Richie Cunningham and Sublime Was Like Fonzie.'" *OC Weekly*, September 14, 2012. https://www.ocweekly.com/sublime-vs-no-doubt-manager-producer-miguel-happoldt-says-no-doubt-was-like-richie-cunningham-and-sublime-was-like-fonzie-6594687/.

Boucher, Geoff. "'L.A. Girl' The Adolescents | 1981." *Los Angeles Times*, June 24, 2007. https://www.latimes.com/entertainment/la-ca-socalsongs24jun24-story.html.

Brow, Jason. "The Offspring's Dexter Holland and Noodles Reflect on 'Smash' 30 Years Later: 'Still Fresh as Ever' (Exclusive)." *Us Weekly*, March 5, 2024. https://www.usmagazine.com/entertainment/news/the-offspring-say-smash-album-still-sounds-real-30-years-later/.

Brunner, Rob. "You Gotta Keep 'Em Alienated." *SPIN*, November 1998. https://www.spin.com/2024/05/the-offspring-1998-feature/.

Carnes, Aaron. "Reel Big Fish: The Story Behind 'Sell Out.'" Substack.com. *In Defense of Ska*, March 15, 2021. https://aaroncarnes.substack.com/p/reel-big-fish -the-story-behind-sell.

Carreon, Mary. "Reliving Classic OC Punk Folklore with the Vandals." *OC Weekly*, April 8, 2016. https://www.ocweekly.com/reliving-classic-oc-punk-folklore-with -the-vandals-7103729/.

Chang, Vickie. "Gary Tovar Has His Goldenvoice." *OC Weekly*, December 15, 2011. https://www.ocweekly.com/gary-tovar-has-his-goldenvoice-6420192/.

———. "Jack Grisham of T.S.O.L.: Bedeviled." *OC Weekly*, April 28, 2011. https://www.ocweekly.com/jack-grisham-of-tsol-bedeviled-6417084/.

Chavez, Marina. "The Offspring: Shot by Both Sides." *Alternative Press*, April 1997.

Ching, Albert. "(Tragic) Kingdom Come Again, Leaving No Doubt Who Rules OC." *OC Weekly*, August 13, 2009. https://ocweekly.com/music-tragic-kingdom -come-again-leaving-no-doubt-who-rules-oc-6399539/.

Chonin, Neva. "An All-'Americana' Punk Band / the Offspring Keep Social Criticism at the Fore of New CD." *SFGATE*, November 22, 1998. https://www .sfgate.com/entertainment/article/An-All-Americana-Punk-Band-The-Offspring -keep-2977356.php.

Christgau, Robert. "Robert Christgau: Consumer Guide." *Village Voice*, March 23, 1999. https://www.robertchristgau.com/xg/cg/cgv399-99.php.

Coker, Matt. "Suddenly in Vogue." *OC Weekly*, December 5, 2002. https://web .archive.org/web/20151004125404/http://www.ocweekly.com/2002-12-12/music /suddenly-in-vogue/.

Curtin, Kevin. "25 Years Ago, Sublime Arrived in Austin and Cut One of the Decade's Biggest Albums." *Austin Chronicle*, May 7, 2021. https://www .austinchronicle.com/music/2021-05-07/25-years-ago-sublime-arrived-in-austin -and-cut-one-of-the-decades-biggest-albums/.

DeMakes, Chris. "Throwback Thursday: Joe Escalante Discusses the Vandals 'Oi to the World!'" Apple Podcasts, *Chris DeMakes a Podcast*, December 7, 2023. https:// podcasts.apple.com/us/podcast/throwback-thursday-joe-escalante-discusses-the /id1515022631?i=1000637770297.

Doe, John, and Tom DeSavia. *Under the Big Black Sun: A Personal History of LA Punk*. Boston: Da Capo Press, 2016.

BIBLIOGRAPHY

Eddy, Chuck. "Revenge of the Nerds." *SPIN*, March 1995. https://www.spin.com/2019/04/the-offspring-interview-cover-story-1995/.

Erlewine, Stephen Thomas. "Return of Saturn: No Doubt | Songs, Reviews, Credits." AllMusic.com, n.d. https://www.allmusic.com/album/return-of-saturn-mw0000057560.

Feeney, Nolan. "Gwen Stefani Is Still B-A-N-A-N-A-S." *Nylon*, April 9, 2024. https://www.nylon.com/entertainment/gwen-stefani-no-doubt-coachella-cover.

Foege, Alec. "Children of the Damned, Never Mind the Sex Pistols. Here's Their Offspring." *Rolling Stone*, February 9, 1995. https://www.rollingstone.com/music/music-news/children-of-the-damned-never-mind-the-sex-pistols-heres-their-offspring-76276/.

Fricke, David. "Tragic Kingdom." *Rolling Stone*, December 9, 1996. https://www.rollingstone.com/music/music-album-reviews/tragic-kingdom-201637.

FullAutoNoise. "Sublime—Behind the Music DOCUMENTARY." YouTube, March 14, 2017. https://www.youtube.com/watch?v=UoR_Q8JZcz0.

Gilbreath, Aaron. "Sublime Played Their Most Powerful Song at Their Last Show." *Medium*, April 3, 2020. https://aarongilbreath.medium.com/sublime-played-their-most-powerful-song-at-their-final-performance-30eb4afff8bb.

Gilhooley, John. "The Punk Rock World Mourns the Passing of Monk Rock." OCMusicNews, May 6, 2020. https://ocmusicnews.com/monk/.

Grogan, Siobhan. "The Offspring Americana (Columbia)." NME.com, November 5, 1998. https://web.archive.org/web/20000817190538/http://www.nme.com/reviews/reviews/19981005121256reviews.html.

Grow, Kory. "Story of My Life: Mike Ness Talks 25 Years of 'Social Distortion.'" *Rolling Stone*, July 22, 2015. https://www.rollingstone.com/music/music-news/story-of-my-life-mike-ness-talks-25-years-of-social-distortion-225517/.

Hansen, Candace. "Maidens of the Moshpit: A Feminist History of Orange County Punk." *OC Weekly*, September 16, 2015. https://www.ocweekly.com/maidens-of-the-moshpit-a-feminist-history-of-orange-county-punk-6589405/.

Henke, James. "Bruce Springsteen Leaves E Street: The Rolling Stone Interview." *Rolling Stone*, August 6, 1992. https://www.rollingstone.com/music/music-news/bruce-springsteen-leaves-e-street-the-rolling-stone-interview-172718/.

Hopkins, Brent. "Punks Pay Tribute at Farewell Concert," *Daily Bruin*, May 8, 2000. https://dailybruin.com/2000/05/08/punks-pay-tribute-at-farewell.

Jackson, Nate. "Hokey Forever: Steve Soto Was OC's Punk Hero from Adolescent to the Afterlife." *OC Weekly*, August 23, 2018. https://www.ocweekly.com/hokey -forever-steve-soto-was-ocs-punk-hero-from-adolescent-to-the-afterlife/.

———. "On What Would Be His 50th Birthday, Bradley Nowell's Spirit Finds Sublime Reincarnation." *OC Weekly*, February 22, 2018. https://www.ocweekly .com/50th-birthday-bradley-nowell-sublime/.

———. "Rikk Agnew: Adolescent No More." *OC Weekly*, June 19, 2014. https:// www.ocweekly.com/rikk-agnew-adolescent-no-more-6430781/.

Jeffries, Vincent. "Prison Bound: Social Distortion | Songs, Reviews, Credits." AllMusic.com, n.d. https://www.allmusic.com/album/prison-bound-mw 0000196195.

Jenkins, Mark. "Social Distortion: Loud and Clear," *Washington Post*, February 6, 1997. https://www.washingtonpost.com/archive/lifestyle/1997/02/07/social -distortion-loud-and-clear/a2c0b8e3-cc04-4232-bda4-249c899d70d3/.

Kam, Nadine. "No Doubt About It." *Star-Bulletin*, April 30, 1998. https://web .archive.org/web/20081118105640/http://starbulletin.com/98/04/30/features /story3.html.

Kaufman, Spencer. "Mike Ness Reflects on Social Distortion's Legacy." *Loudwire*, February 21, 2014. https://loudwire.com/mike-ness-reflects-social-distortion-legacy/.

Kemp, Mark. "Bradley Nowell: Life After Death." *Rolling Stone*, December 25, 1997. https://www.rollingstone.com/music/music-news/bradley-nowell-life-after -death-250120/.

Kohn, Daniel. "Mike Ness Looks Back, Focusing on the Past of Social Distortion." *OC Weekly*, September 9, 2015. https://www.ocweekly.com/mike-ness-looks-back -focusing-on-the-past-of-social-distortion-6592339/.

———. "The Offspring Reflects on 30 Years of 'Smash' with Plenty of Self-Esteem." *Los Angeles Times*, April 8, 2024. https://www.latimes.com/entertainment -arts/music/story/2024-04-08/the-offspring-30th-anniversary-smash-self-esteem -dexter-holland-noodles-wasserman.

———. "The SPIN Interview: Sublime." *SPIN*, February 16, 2024. https://www .spin.com/2024/02/sublime-interview/.

————. "Why Ixnay on the Hombre Was the Album That Helped the Offspring Grow Up." *OC Weekly*, October 26, 2017. https://www.ocweekly.com/why-ixnay -on-the-hombre-was-the-album-that-helped-the-offspring-grow-up-8529520/.

LA Times Archives. "Influence of Mechanics Runs Deep in Punk World." *Los Angeles Times*, May 17, 1996. https://www.latimes.com/archives/la-xpm-1996-05 -17-ca-5426-story.html.

Levy, Joe. "Gwen Stefani Talks Fame, Family, No Doubt, and Receiving Her Star on Hollywood's Walk of Fame." *Variety*, October 19, 2023. https://variety.com/2023 /music/news/gwen-stefani-no-doubt-hollywood-walk-of-fame-1235761584/.

Lewis, Randy. "Punk Peers Give Danell Full-Throttle Farewell." *Los Angeles Times*, May 8, 2000. https://www.latimes.com/archives/la-xpm-2000-may-08-ca-27734-story.html.

————. "Punkers to Play for GOP Group." *Los Angeles Times*, March 8, 1985. https://www.latimes.com/archives/la-xpm-1985-03-08-ca-32582-story.html.

Manic Media. "Sleaze Punk Naughty Women 77–84." YouTube, June 27, 2017. https://www.youtube.com/watch?v=iCenwkywosQ.

Masuo, Sandy. "Offspring Grows Musically but Its Themes Remain the Same." *Los Angeles Times*, November 14, 1998. https://web.archive.org/web/20160822081744 /http://articles.latimes.com/1998/nov/14/entertainment/ca-42522.

Mc, Brian. "'Cause Casey Royer OD'd Himself." Brokenheadphones.com, March 14, 2011. http://www.brokenheadphones.com/cause-casey-royer-odd-himself/.

Meline, Gabe. "Sublime's Last Show: The Oral History | KQED." Kqed.org, May 24, 2016. https://www.kqed.org/arts/11610342/sublimes-last-show-20-years-later -the-oral-history.

Mendez, Stephanie. "'Dear John': The Legacy of No Doubt's Original Frontman John Spence." *SPIN*, February 3, 2024. https://www.spin.com/2024/02/john -spence-no-doubt-legacy/.

Miller, Andrew. "Channeling Social D." *The Pitch*, March 18, 2004. https://www .thepitchkc.com/channeling-social-d/.

Mills, Jonathan W. C., dir. *Clockwork Orange County*, Endurance Pictures, 2012.

Mizoguchi, Karen. "Gwen Stefani Talks How No Doubt's Hit 'Just A Girl' Came to Be," *People*, March 3, 2017. https://people.com/music/gwen-stefani-no-doubt-just -a-girl-the-voice/.

Morden, Taylor, dir. *Pick It Up!: Ska in the '90s*. Popmotion Pictures, 2019.

Norris, Chris. "White Punks on Dope." *SPIN*, March 1999. https://www.spin .com/2022/09/white-punks-on-dope-our-1999-the-offspring-cover-story/.

Offspring, The. "'An Act of God' W/ Adrian Young (No Doubt) | Time to Relax with the Offspring Episode 8." Apple Podcasts, *Time to Relax with the Offspring*, March 7, 2024. https://podcasts.apple.com/us/podcast/an-act-of-god-w-adrian -young-no-doubt-time-to/id1693330502?i=1000648368285.

———. "Collective Effervescence w/ Warren Fitzgerald (the Vandals) | Time to Relax with the Offspring Episode 10." Apple Podcasts, *Time to Relax with the Offspring*, April 11, 2024. https://podcasts.apple.com/us/podcast/collective -effervescence-w-warren-fitzgerald-the/id1693330502?i=1000652150863.

———. "Our Producer, Bob Rock | Time to Relax with the Offspring Episode 9." Apple Podcasts, *Time to Relax with the Offspring*, March 29, 2024. https:// podcasts.apple.com/us/podcast/our-producer-bob-rock-time-to-relax-with-the /id1693330502?i=1000650855791.

———. "The Doctor Is In! W/ James Lilja, MD (Original Offspring Drummer) | Time to Relax with the Offspring Episode 7." Apple Podcasts, *Time to Relax with the Offspring*, February 1, 2024. https://podcasts.apple.com/us/podcast/the-doctor -is-in-w-james-lilja-md-original-offspring/id1693330502?i=1000643821479.

Prato, Greg. "Social Distortion Gears Up for Tour, Talks New Album." *Rolling Stone*, April 1, 2011. https://www.rollingstone.com/music/music-news/social -distortion-gears-up-for-tour-talks-new-album-251097/amp/.

Rabid, Jack. "Adolescents: The Adolescents | Songs, Reviews, Credits." AllMusic .com, 2016. https://www.allmusic.com/album/the-adolescents-mw0000314471.

Reardon, Tom. "The 10 Best Skate Punk Records of All Time." *Phoenix New Times*, October 21, 2015. https://www.phoenixnewtimes.com/music/the-10-best-skate -punk-records-of-all-time-7759704.

San Román, Gabriel. "Inside Out: Early Zack de La Rocha Band and Hardcore OC Pioneers Still Have Bestselling EP." *OC Weekly*, September 16, 2010. https://www .ocweekly.com/inside-out-early-zack-de-la-rocha-band-and-hardcore-oc-pioneers -still-have-bestselling-ep-6592504/.

Schou, Nick. "Don't Start a Riot." *OC Weekly*, July 29, 2010. https://www .ocweekly.com/dont-start-a-riot-6403403/.

Schwartz, Ruth. "D.I." Kill from the Heart, September 1983. https://web.archive
.org/web/20110723171433/http://www.killfromtheheart.com/albums
.php?id=8271&band_id=279.

Smith, RJ. "Drug Bust." *SPIN*, January 1997. https://www.spin.com/2021/05
/sublime-drug-bust-1997-feature/.

Snierson, Dan. "Offspring, Americana." *Entertainment Weekly*, November 20, 1998.
https://ew.com/article/1998/11/20/americana/.

Spencer, Lauren. "Sick Boys." *SPIN*, March 1991. https://www.spin.com/2021/10
/social-distortion-sick-boys-1991-feature/.

Staff. "It's All a Blur." *OC Weekly*, August 31, 2000. https://www.ocweekly.com/its
-all-a-blur-6388700/.

————. "When the Angels Sing." *OC Weekly*, May 11, 2000. https://www
.ocweekly.com/when-the-angels-sing-6392686/.

Stuart, Peter, and Adam Small. *Another State of Mind*. Time Bomb, 1984. https://
www.youtube.com/watch?v=sSk7ANlcFaM.

Sublime. "Sublime KROQ Weenie Roast Interview 1995." YouTube, April 14,
2011. https://www.youtube.com/watch?v=v2VXe0QM0m0.

Swancey, Jason. "Interview with Sublime in Orlando." *Axis Magazine*, July 23,
1995. https://web.archive.org/web/20190721221525/https://agaric40.tripod.com
/info/axis.html.

Thompson, Stephen. "The Offspring: Conspiracy of One." *AV Club*, November 14,
2000. https://www.avclub.com/the-offspring-conspiracy-of-one-1798192537.

Valdiva, Victor W. "The Vandals: Fear of a Punk Planet | Songs, Reviews, Credits."
AllMusic.com, n.d. https://www.allmusic.com/album/fear-of-a-punk-planet
-mw0000114697.

Webb, Robery, "Story of the song: 'Don't Speak,' No Doubt, 1996," *The
Independent*, August 6, 2010. https://www.independent.co.uk/arts-entertainment
/music/features/story-of-the-song-don-t-speak-no-doubt-1996-2044589.html.

Winwood, Ian. *Smash!* New York: Da Capo Press, 2018.

Wood, Mikael. "It Took Bradley Nowell's Son Years to Embrace Sublime. Now
He'll Lead the Band at Coachella." *Los Angeles Times*, April 4, 2024. https://www

.latimes.com/entertainment-arts/music/story/2024-04-04/sublime-bradley-nowell -jakob-nowell-coachella-rome-ramirez.

Yohannan, Tim. "Social Distortion—Mommy's Little Monster LP." *Maximum Rocknroll*, September 1983. https://www.maximumrocknroll.com/band/social-distortion/.

Zelig, Evan. "Interview With Tom Dumont." *Backstage Online*, October 31, 1996. https://web.archive.org/web/20081206023103/http://www.nodoubt.com/press /articles/10BackStage.aspx.

INDEX

INDEX

INDEX

INDEX

INDEX

INDEX